Chillie

Mita Kapur is the founder and CEO of Siyahi, India's leading literary consultancy. She also conceptualizes and produces literary festivals and events. Her first book, *The F-Word*, is a food book, memoir and travelogue. As a freelance journalist, she writes regularly for different newspapers and magazines on social and development issues along with travel, food and lifestyle.

Chillies and Porridge

Writing Food

Edited by Mita Kapur

HarperCollins *Publishers* India

No, this book is not dedicated to you, Bunny, or the kids will have me for dinner. No, this book is not dedicated to Sakshi, Resham, Rehan, because ... well, just like that. But, in a way, all of you do become a part of it since I'd like to dedicate this book to each one of you who lives by the four-letter word: food.

Contents

Introduction

MITA KAPUR

I am obsessed with flavours. And textures. And the smells of food. Even today, if I am somewhere within the narrow alleys of the old city area of Jaipur to run an errand, I find myself drawn to the old lady who sits crouched at the corner of Churoko ka rasta leading to Umrao Jewels selling dal, roti and mirchi ka achaar. The thick rotis smell of just-roasted wheat, and one bite fills your mouth with textures that take you right back to a mitti ka chulha.

I find excuses to go back to Gopal ji ka rasta in search of nan khatais baked in an old iron contraption that serves as an oven. To watch them change colour, turning amber to match the just-switched-on street lights, and wait for the chap to gingerly pick them up from the griddled rows of the oven before placing them in a brown paper bag. To reach into the bag, feel the warm, fuzzy, buttery biscuits which collapse into cottony balls once on your tongue—heaven! Simple joys, simple food, and the treasure of memories that leads to a search for more.

Over the years I've been a steadfast observer of how people talk about food even when they are not eating. However intense the mood may be, however varied the intellectual capabilities of a group of people in a room, food is the ground we level on. Our facial lines relax, the corners of our eyes crinkle, we gasp, we exclaim and breathe deep over our discoveries. I have tortured friends with pictures of eleven-course meals, made them exclaim over photographs of black ale alongside hearty marrow on toast and fried langos in Budapest. Or over pictures of jungle maas being cooked in a dekchi over wood fire in my garden.

Food brings us together as a family, as friends, even as strangers who chance to share a table at a hole-in-the-corner-joint; it opens up silences and creates shared moments, some laughter, and then you move on. But you carry the memory within the recesses of your mind, because you bonded over a food-laden table.

In my first book, *The F Word*, I explored relationships via food and shared some of my favourite recipes with my readers. Several of them responded by saying it felt like 'their story'. That made me hungry: I wanted to know their stories. I wanted to know how they ate, what they ate, what they held dear in terms of taste, form, colour, texture, smell and flavour. Simple home-cooked food, varied food traditions, specialities of regional cuisine, unexpected discoveries made while travelling the world—there is an endless spiral of foody experiences waiting for us just round the corner.

It's a Proustian remembrance—the familiarity of food. An addiction not just to flavours and a routine, but an emotional connect which we carry within ourselves. I remember being persuaded of this as I read through a food writing anthology I had picked up: *Eat, Memory: Great Writers at the Table* edited by Amanda Hesser. After that, I read everything I could find in the genre: *Secret Ingredients: The New Yorker Book of Food and Drink* edited by David Remnick, *The Table Is Laid: The Oxford Anthology of South Asian Food Writing* edited by John Thieme and Ira Raja, *A Matter of Taste: The Penguin Book of Indian Writing on Food* edited by Nilanjana Roy, *Drinking, Smoking and Screwing: Great Writers on Good Times* edited by Sara Nickles, just to name a few.

Somewhere between devouring one book of food writing after another and lying collapsed in bed after a hectic day, taking in the visual feast offered by food shows on television, the urge to put together this anthology became stronger. It would be a collection of stories, reminiscences and essays by some of my favourite writers. The dusty playground of a Delhi colony, a makeshift cricket pitch, a bowl of porridge made for breakfast, friendships over food experiences, slow cooking, the collective hypochondria of a community over food, walking through vegetable markets, the slurring over swigs of mahua, changing landscapes of street food, food iconography, food as a celebration of a life passed by, chefs preferring to cook over studying calculus, the poetry of 'fresh, warm stories'—*Chillies and Porridge* took shape without any conscious geographical mapping or, to be honest, any deliberately imposed parameters at all, except that of taste, subjective as it is. I must thank all the writers, many of them friends, who rallied around and came up with their best at fairly short notice, and I can only hope that you, my reader, will find enough to savour and linger over, and perhaps take away too.

Porridge

JANICE PARIAT

I can still hear the scrape of it. The thin, long sound. Metal on
metal. Shrill as a banshee, piercing the morning chill, and my
dreams. Its sharp persistence disallowing silence and sleep.
My grandmother emptying the porridge pot in the kitchen,
cleaning it carefully, edge to curved edge, with a spoon. At
the time, admittedly, it elicited sullen complaint—my elder
sister burrowing her head under the pillow and I pulling the
covers over mine, in vain. Later, when we were dressed, all
convent-schooled up in demure skirts and clean white socks,
it would be waiting on the table, steaming gently, a grey,
gloopy mess.

It is impossible to be eloquent about porridge. As everyday as
rice, yet not as elegant as that fragrant grain. In our house, it was
prepared daily, a humble morning paean—just enough, no less,
no more—as steady as us saying the rosary, rhyme for rhyme, in
the evening. The kind of life the Scottish poet James McGonigal
alluded to in *First Things*:

My granny made porridge first thing
with the same untroubled movements
of hand and eye, the same patience
that she gave to her night prayers.

It is a holy and wholesome thought
to eat porridge and pray for the dead
every day of your life, I now think,
reaching down a white bowl from its shelf.

In the poem, porridge is not incidental. It cannot be replaced by something else. Sausages and eggs, toast and jam, cereal and muesli. The point of it is in the routine, and having cooked it often, I know it takes time and attention. In the poem, I like the way the lines run to the end of the verses, how the general moral—the 'you'—changes to 'I now think', a movement from the past to the present, re-enacting the poetic movement to, and the coming about of, this understanding. How, at the end, the lines sit neatly, firmly, as though contained, cradled, in a bowl.

For the uninitiated, porridge is a dish of ground, crushed or chopped cereal, boiled in milk or water, usually served hot. Admittedly, not quite the stuff fine-dining dreams are made of. Porridge is as unexotic as, well, porridge. Yet as trends come and go, this humble one-bowl meal trudges on, quietly filling bellies around the world first thing in the morning. One might even imagine it quite abashed by the claims of Alistair Moffat, writer, journalist and founder of the DNA Project in the UK that the greatest invention in human history wasn't the wheel, the Internet, the iPad or even sliced bread. It was porridge. (Moffat, whose most recent book is titled *The British: A Genetic Journey*, claimed that feeding children porridge left women free to have more children, who then went on to populate the earth.)

While porridge could refer to any grain (rice, wheat, barley, corn, buckwheat, polenta, grits, kasha) cooked in this manner, the term usually implies oats—in many forms including rolled, crushed, ground or steel-cut. Porridge can be added to the list of things whose exact origins have been 'lost in the mists of time', but suffice to say, it's been a traditional food in much of northern Europe and Russia—understandably the cold countries. And famously in Scotland.

Since the late medieval times, oats were grown in Scotland as a staple diet of the crofters (small-scale food producers unique to the Highlands and islands of the region), and have been described as 'the backbone of many a sturdy Scotsman.' Initially, with no method of preserving the oats, they were boiled into a thick paste, then cooled and stored in a wooden porridge drawer. When cold, the mixture turned thick and solid and could be conveniently cut into slices and eaten over several days.

Traditionally, porridge was cooked in a heavy saucepan and stirred with a spurtle, a wooden stick, less a ladle and more an over-sized chopstick. Superstition would have you believe that the porridge should be stirred using only the right hand and in a clockwise direction to ward off evil spirits. It's hard to tell what the evil spirits would make of instant or microwave porridge today—briskly ready in under two minutes—but purists will tell you that porridge takes time. That, in fact, is part of the pleasure of cooking it. One has to keep stirring. For how long, you ask? Well, that depends on the type of oats you use. Fine-rolled oats can be cooked in three minutes, but they don't absorb much water. Whole flakes, or jumbo oats, call for six, but are even more delicious after thirty. Pinhead oats need to be soaked for at least half an hour before boiling. The recommended ingredient is good-quality medium-ground oats—two tablespoons of this in half a litre of water (or half water and milk), and a pinch of salt. Bring the water to a good rolling boil, slowly pour in the oatmeal, stirring vigorously the whole time, until it has returned to the boil. Reduce the heat. Cover the pan. Simmer gently for twenty minutes. Add salt, and simmer for another quarter of an hour. It should be of thick but pourable consistency. Serve hot in wooden bowls, and eat, as some people say, standing up, out of respect for the noble dish. (This probably arose from busy farmers doing other things while eating their morning porridge, or as an aid to digestion.) Swirl on the double cream. Or not. Herein lies its flexibility. While some may frown at the idea of sugar in porridge, others not only approve but suggest a tot of whiskey. To each, as they say, their own. If you opt out of an alcohol-drenched breakfast, choose cinnamon instead, or sunflower seeds, mixed nuts, jam, honey, bananas, mixed berries or chocolate. As a child, I'd tear thick slices of white bread into my bowl of porridge, allowing it to soak up the milk and sugar, using my spoon to whip it into a gooey, lumpy mess. It was an odd, simple pleasure. When I cook porridge now, and scrape the bottom of the pan (as quietly as I can), I cannot help but be glutted by recollection.

Like McGonigal, I too learnt more than a few things from my grandmother. I recognize now, as he did, the kind of life she represented. She was born in Shillong in 1926, the second youngest of five siblings. Their reduced circumstances were worsened by the fact that her father, a tailor, was often ill and unable to work. She too was a sickly child, suffering from various illnesses of the lungs. Oddly enough, it was the Second World War that strengthened her. At fifteen, after 'tweaking' her age (recruits were only sixteen and above), she joined the war effort, and was posted to Silchar and then Guwahati, where she worked as a telephone switchboard operator. This was when she flourished. Stacks of sepia-tinted photographs show her surrounded by friends, mostly American men and women soldiers, neatly attired in uniform, her face filled out, her hair bright and curly, smiling into the camera. They tell of friendships and camaraderie, but also of something else. During her time there, she was eating better than she had her entire life. Bread and tinned meat, condensed milk and tea-time treats, and every morning, milky, wholesome porridge. She earned enough money to send home to help the family. She visited them laden with gifts of food. She was courted, or so the story goes, by one of Henry Ford's grandsons. But she declined him for William Arthur Feegrade, a young Anglo-Portuguese gentleman in government service, who'd been secretary to Sir Robert Reed and Sir Andrew Clow, the then governors of Assam. When she returned to Shillong, my grandmother's 'war years' were stashed away, her uniform and photographic memories relegated to a tin trunk under the bed, but they lingered on in other less tangible ways. Her disciplined lifestyle, her loving yet strict upbringing of their four children, her attitude towards waste and excess, especially when it concerned food. ('Waste not, want not,' she'd tell us, or 'Your eyes shouldn't be bigger than your stomach.')

And, of course, her love for porridge.

What my mother and her siblings still eat for breakfast today. In turn, my sister, and I, and our first cousins. My sister's daughter's first solid food meal at six months was oats. A habit running through time like a thread. While my mother remains a staunch oats enthusiast—often turning it into a dinnertime meal—I have, admittedly, strayed on occasion. What else can one do when confronted with limitless shelves of morning cereals? Do I want Froot Loops or Curiously Cinnamon Swirls? Dorset Honey Granola or Wheatabix? Luxury Triple Chocolate or Red Berry

Treats? Cheerios, Shreddies, Coco Pops, Wholegrain Apricot Wheats, Alpen Strawberry bars, Kellogg's Frosties, Rude Health Just Nuts, Crunchy Nut Chocolate Hazelnut or Toasted Rice and Wheat Flakes? It seems the world has exploded, caught in a frenzy of morning cereal worship. I can spend hours before the supermarket shelves having an existential crisis about breakfast. Then the other concerns. Should I go organic? Gluten free? Let's not even start with the kind of milk. Oat, soya, almond, rice, hazelnut.

Yet, on the top of my kitchen shelf, tucked away in a glass jar, is a stock of plain, unfussy oats. Waiting like an old, loyal friend. One morning, I will tire of choices, of fancy flavours and sunflower seeds, of Belgian chocolate swirls and toasted almonds, and bring it down. I always, inevitably, do. A spoon or two of the flat white grains, a little oat milk, and the pot on to the flame, and stir, stir, stir. My topping of choice now is a sliced banana, a swirl of treacle or honey, a sprinkling of cinnamon. But the thing is to eat it plain, untarnished. Smelling of earth, and comfort, the kitchen of my childhood home. No wonder then that porridge often features in Neil Gaiman's *The Ocean at the End of the Lane*—as solace and familiarity, warmth and safety. Porridge, though, is also an odd thing, neither solid nor liquid. The same smoothness, stickiness and solidity that make it so filling and wholesome can, to some, be peculiar.

E.M. Forster, in *Howard's End*, uses the consistency of porridge to convey the disorientation Margaret feels in her first trip in a motor car:

'The motor's come to stay,' he answered. 'One must get about. There's a pretty church—oh, you aren't sharp enough. Well, look out, if the road worries you—right outward at the scenery.'

She looked at the scenery. It heaved and merged like porridge. Presently it congealed. They had arrived.

Who knew the rather un-poetic texture of porridge would serve as a simile for landscape, for the world losing its solidity. The passage also gives a sense of what porridge is like as it cooks and cools, liquid turning to solid, neither one thing nor the other, until finally one stops and eats it.

Perhaps literary porridge is always a metaphor for something else. Little did I know that this humble meal would interweave too with my life as a reader and writer.

Growing up in 'pre-liberalized' India in the 1990s meant escapism came mostly in the form of books. I devoured Enid Blyton's prolific offerings as eagerly as her fictional characters gobbled scones, potted meat sandwiches and macaroons. (All served with lashings of ginger beer, of course.) Her descriptions filled my culinary imagination: where could we find treacle tart? Or clotted cream? What on earth was bacon? To me, these were as fantastical as the food she actually concocted— google buns (sherbet-filled currents), pop biscuits (honey-filled cakes), and toffee shocks (sweets that swelled in your mouth and then exploded). In an interview with the BBC in 1963, Blyton explained that children look for reassurance in stories, for the familiar. If this is true, the one thing I found recognizable in her books, amidst the alien landscape and diet, was porridge. Many of her young characters, in preparation for a day full of adventure and mystery solving, tuck into huge breakfasts that more often than not include a steaming tureen of porridge topped with golden syrup and thick cream.

In *Magic Faraway Tree*, Blyton infuses the ordinary with the magical:

> They all had breakfast. Moon-Face cooked some porridge. 'What do you want on your porridge?' he asked Jo. 'Treacle-sugar-cream?'
>
> Jo couldn't see any treacle, sugar or cream on the table. 'Treacle,' he said, 'please, Moon-Face.' Moon-Face handed him a small jug that seemed to be quite empty. 'Treacle!' he said to the jug in a firm voice. And treacle came pouring out as soon as Jo tipped up the jug. Silky wanted cream—and cream came out when Moon-Face said 'Cream!' to the jug. It was great fun.

Porridge also features in 'Goldilocks and the Three Bears', possibly my least beloved fairy tale (although there does exist a variation where the intrusive little girl is eaten by the bears)—but an even older tale is 'Sweet Porridge', narrated by the Brothers Grimm. This is the story of a little girl and her mother who were poor and had nothing to eat. One day, the girl walked into a forest and met an old woman who gave her a magic pot. When she said 'Little pot, cook,' the pot would cook sweet porridge. It would stop only when she uttered 'Little pot, stop.' The girl took it home to her mother and now they were free to eat sweet porridge as often as they chose. Once, when the girl was out, her mother ordered 'Little pot, cook.' She ate until she was satisfied but didn't know the words to make it stop. It kept cooking until it spilt out into the kitchen, into the whole house. The porridge overflowed onto the street and into the other houses. The little girl finally came home and said 'Little pot, stop' but whoever wished to return to town had to eat their way back.

I like that this is a cautionary tale for grown-ups rather than children. And it has the most marvellous last line—'whoever wished to return to town had to eat their way back.'

If porridge inhabits both the realms of the ordinary and the magical, in the UK (which has been my home for several years) it has also long been associated with the poor. The Scots. Invalids. Prison food (which is why 'doing porridge' became slang for a jail sentence). Children with little or no choice in the matter. Often, characters in literature do not just happen to eat porridge; the fact that they do says something about them and their circumstances. The worst thing is when it isn't enough.

In one of my favourite Charles Dickens' novels, *Oliver Twist*, the gruel, thin and tasteless, was a permanent want, a thing meted out in such feeble quantity that it evoked rebellion even in the most wretched Victorian workhouse. The novel's most memorable, and heart-wrenching, scene takes place in a large stone dining hall:

> The evening arrived; the boys took their places. The master, in his cook's uniform, stationed himself at the copper; his pauper assistants ranged themselves behind him; the gruel was served out; and a long grace was said over the short commons. The gruel disappeared; the boys whispered each other, and winked at Oliver; while his next neighbours nudged him. Child as he was, he was desperate with hunger, and reckless with misery. He rose from the table; and advancing to the master, basin and spoon in hand, said: somewhat alarmed at his own temerity: 'Please, sir, I want some more.'

It's a line that has echoed through the ages: on stage, screen and animation, powerful as it is on the page.

I remember reading Charlotte Brontë's *Jane Eyre* in college, and empathizing with the character for many reasons—one being the food served at Lowood school. Our women's paying guest accommodation in Delhi meted out similarly badly cooked fare at every meal time. At the school for girls, Jane's first meal is memorable for all the wrong reasons:

> Ravenous, and now very faint, I devoured a spoonful or two of my portion without thinking of its taste; but the first edge of hunger blunted, I perceived I had got in hand a nauseous mess; burnt porridge is almost as bad as rotten potatoes; famine itself soon sickens over it. The spoons were moved slowly: I saw each girl taste her food and try to swallow it; but in most cases the effort was soon relinquished. Breakfast was over, and none had breakfasted.

This description so disturbed Brontë's first biographer, Elizabeth Gaskell, that she tracked down witnesses at the school at Cowan Bridge (model for Lowood), who admitted that though the founder provided decent ingredients, the cook often used water that had run off the roof. So not only was the porridge sometimes burnt, but often, as described in Gaskell's biography of Brontë, 'offensive fragments of other substances [were] discoverable in it.' (Incidentally, porridge features frequently in Gaskell's own social novel, *North and South*.)

While the abridged version I read as a child was robbed, apart from adventure, of all intricate detail, Robert Louis Stevenson's *Kidnapped* remains a literary paean to porridge. Unsurprising, since the central character, David Balfour, is fleeing across Scotland in the eighteenth century, and he joins for repast all sorts of porridge eaters: his Uncle Ebenezer, Mr Henderland in the Highlands, and the crew on the ship in which he's been abducted.

Yet, if literary porridge is always a metaphor for something else, then it's a marker for a way of life, a social class, an upbringing, a deficient cruelty, an indication of character, or the lack of one. In British poet Elizabeth Burns's poem 'Breakfast', porridge stands for, among other things, transformation. It begins, 'They knew about terrible porridge, the Brontës', and moves from a mention of *Jane Eyre* to Emily Brontë's *Wuthering Heights*–that most darkly passionate tale of doomed, desperate love. Through a complex play of imagery, an interweaving of time, Burns focuses not on Heathcliff and Catherine, but on her daughter Cathy and Hareton and their young, life-giving affection. We pass from a vision of death—Edgar Linton laying golden crocuses on his sick wife's pillow—to one of hope and wholesomeness:

> What Cathy does echoes the gesture her father made—a
> gift of yellow flowers for the beloved. She does it lightly
> and playfully, making Hareton's breakfast into something
> beautiful, *sticking primroses in his plate of porridge.*

At the end, when Heathcliff is close to dying, Cathy and Hareton sit outdoors, 'escaping at last from the gloom of the house and the weight of their past.' There is a lightness, a relief, a sense that hardship and suffering could lead, inevitably, to the earth coming alive, to the blossoming of creativity. It is what writers must learn, and what writers have always, instinctively, done: 'They wrote about terrible things, the Brontës, but look how their stories transmute them, lace them with honey and cream.'

In not a dissimilar way, American poet Galway Kinnell, in his poem 'Oatmeal', also links porridge with writing.

> I eat oatmeal for breakfast.
> I make it on the hot plate and put skimmed milk on it.

I eat it alone.
I am aware it is not good to eat oatmeal alone.
Its consistency is such that it is better for your mental
health
if somebody eats it with you.
That is why I often think up an imaginary companion
to have
breakfast with.
Possibly it is even worse to eat oatmeal with an imaginary
companion.
Nevertheless, yesterday morning, I ate my oatmeal with
John Keats.

The poem includes one of the most unappealing descriptions
of all literary porridge, which, as you can imagine, is saying
a lot: 'due to its glutinous texture, gluey lumpishness, hint
of slime, and unusual willingness to disintegrate, oatmeal
should not be eaten alone'—and then goes on to describe the
'conversation' between the two poets. Keats tells Galway he's
enjoyed memorable porridges with Edmund Spenser and John
Milton, and speaks of how he wrote 'Ode to a Nightingale'
quickly, on scraps of paper, which he and a friend rearranged
on a table, and then recites 'To Autumn' slowly, 'with much
feeling, his odd accent sound[ing] sweet.' That two of the lines,
'For summer has o'er-brimm'd their clammy cells' and 'Thou
watchest the last oozings, hours by hours' came to him while
eating oatmeal alone. In the poem, Kinnell conjures a startling
image: 'I can see him drawing a spoon through the stuff, gazing
into the glimmering furrows, muttering' and it occurs to me:
"Maybe there is no sublime; only the shining of the amnion's
tatters."' Here, he links porridge to writing—in this particular
case, the tradition of poetry—and offers it up as a practical,

everyday craft. Writing as the mundane placing down of word after word, a constant, patient stirring. A long wait. Stripped to its barest, most naked, simplicity. Wash away the frills and the glamour— marketing, publicity, launch parties, networking—and you are left with something less outwardly attractive perhaps, but utterly wholesome.

What porridge was for my grandmother—a ritual, a prayer, life-giver, life-preserver, habit, sustainer, routine—writing is for me. Every day a scraping, a scouring, a preparation, a serving, an offering. Food not for the eyes but for the soul.

Memory's Savour

AVTAR SINGH

Eggs.

Not just any eggs, but telor balado. A dish of hard-boiled eggs served in chilli paste. Served with chicken satay and peanut sauce, a pork dish we called babi kong, a salad of fresh greens and perhaps cucumbers and onions in a sweet-ish vinegar relish.

But always the eggs.

That's how I remember lunch at home when I was growing up.

ೞ

Sure, there were other things. There were cold cuts from Steak House in their distinctive blue-grey paper wrappers. There was an anonymous khichdi when my mother was feeling out of sorts, and proper daal subzi if my dad was present. Rajma chawal, naturally, kadhi on the weekends, paranthas when the weather cooled. But if there were people over, if Ma was feeling homesick, if I was back from school, there'd be the telor balado.

CB

They weren't to everyone's taste. In the 1970s and '80s, even into the 1990s, not many north Indians got fish or shrimp paste. The tang of the distant sea wasn't entirely welcome, and you had to gauge your clientele's reception before you offered up the precious, hoarded ikan teri, or dried anchovies. Some polite people gagged it down. The others turned up their noses. Literally. But for me, it's the smell of my childhood.

Rich, pungent, occasionally sick-making—but always home.

CB

Telor balado is the smell of wherever my mother was. Mostly, it was in Delhi, in the home I grew up in. But it's also the home I remember only in flashes, the home my maternal grandparents lived in. In Menteng in Jakarta, the capital of Indonesia.

Jakarta is where my mother is buried. But it isn't where she's from.

CB

Was Jakarta ever home for me? It must have been. I remember it well enough. I was there long enough as a preschooler to actually be enrolled in a preschool, if only for a few months. I went back for my grandfather's eightieth birthday, a celebration that has stayed with me, even though I wasn't yet ten.

I remember the house, the street it was on. The ice-cream man who came by in the afternoon. I remember eating noodle soup in an informal restaurant that has, I believe, since closed. We ate on a veranda you had to climb up a wooden staircase to get to. The noodles came in china bowls and there was a local version of grape Fanta to wash it down with. I'm not sure restaurants like that exist in Jakarta any more, except as tourist traps and for the local fetishists of nostalgia. Noodles now come pre-packaged from China and Japan. The usual visitor desirous of a noodle soup gets his fix in a mall, sharing formica tables in a food court with other victims of anodyne global branding, eyes glazed with consumerism and MSG.

☙

The food in Jakarta is still breathtaking, however. If you make the effort to find them, the spaces available to eat in are just gorgeous. In India, the ruinous cost of real estate hampers restaurateurs from putting their ideas to work in authentically beautiful spaces. In Jakarta, either land isn't as dear, or the owners aren't as greedy. Now you find new restaurants in old bungalows and in gardens set about with wooden pavilions. These cater to a different clientele than my old noodle spot. Expat bankers, local yuppies, well-heeled families—they all inhale the haute Indonesian food on offer, the beautifully presented gurami, the 'new' take on 'authentic' Peranakan cuisine, the whatever it is of the moment, along with the carefully curated art, furniture and other memory sponges that such places come preloaded with.

In the malls, there are also fancy restaurants. Like anywhere else, there will be dim sum and prosecco with your pasta and 'handcrafted' sushi. Out on the streets is a cornucopia of flavour and texture, catering to the working man and woman who also demand their share of tasties. Mixed drinks made of nameless ingredients, roasted meats that will make you dream of Delhi kebabiyas, fish and rice and noodles served in a hundred different ways topped with carbon monoxide, and the other goodies a true Asian metropolis offers.

In 1998, as Indonesia's economy crumbled and people's livelihoods imploded, these streets ran with anger. I was there. My grandmother had just died. With the devaluation, the little money I had was suddenly a lot of money. I took off after the funeral to learn more about my mother's homeland. I went to Sulawesi, making my way to its northern tip, to Manado. The food there is famously spicy. I gagged on plates of fish so rich with chillies that I forgot to breathe. Delicious, but in a dirty, taxing way. Luckily the water was close at hand and translucent and there isn't a chilli in the world hot enough to compete with the cooling power of a swim in the deep blue sea. Close to Manado is the famous reef of Bunaken, where I dove off the edge and swam with some fishermen hunting game. Barracuda, I was told, after a nudge in the water secured my attention towards the still, shimmering silver spear a few feet to my side. And other hunting fish, prized for their meat.

Manado is predominantly Christian and so consumes quantities of pork, which is haraam in the more Muslim parts of the country. Up in the hills are the spice plantations that the Dutch planted here, and the churches that converted the bellicose Minahasa confederacy of headhunting animists to Bible-thumping Christianity. There are Dutch-inspired cakes and pastries in the villages, next to mats on which spices dry, right on the road itself. These hills are where my grandfather was born and grew up.

These hills are where my mother said she was from.

ભ

'Jakarta,' she'd said dismissively as I left on my own little journey. 'This isn't where we're from.'

Having said which, she headed off home to India.

Home? She'd moved to India when she was a teenager, married a man she met in college, followed him to the tea gardens in the shadow of the Himalayas, without waiting to consider whether she liked the food, the spices in it, its texture.

She liked the music, she admitted. She always had. Not the women, though: Chinese opera, she'd say, her nose wrinkling. But the men had lovely warm voices, singing tunes she'd hum to herself as she worked on a quilt, poured coffee, listened to me. Music was part of her patrimony as well. Her own father played any string instrument by ear, according to her. I think I remember him playing a guitar and singing me a song. But it may be a trick of memory, a function of the rememberings of other people that have been transmitted to me and have become mine. As I walked, cycled and drove around the hills of Minahasa, I saw young boys and old men playing their guitars and women singing along softly. In the air was the smell of cloves and other spices that colonialism brought to these hills.

My mother spent her youth among hills like these perhaps, in the Indian Dooars, among bushes imported from China almost two hundred years ago to seed another colonial trade. Did she know the tastes she was supposedly acquiring—the chillies in every dish, the kaju in the barfi, the chikoo in the fruit bowl—had only become Indian because of the arrival of the Europeans and their pit-stops in lands they had misrepresented to themselves as 'India'?

The Americas. The West Indies. The Dutch East Indies.

These hills were where she said she was from. But she never went there. The longest she ever stayed in Indonesia, the country whose passport she carried at the time of her death, was in Jakarta. The city she dismissed.

So where did the telor balado come from?

☙

Tea—and opium—underpinned the British colonial economy in India. Similarly, spice brought the Dutch to Indonesia. My grandfather's family prospered in the Dutch colonial dispensation. An expensive education prepared him for further studies in Holland, where he met my grandmother.

My mother was born in Amsterdam and grew up speaking Dutch, the language she always said she dreamt in. She lived there through the German occupation during World War II. My Dutch grandmother never ate rabbit after that particular experience. She'd merely say she'd had her fill. My mother would later learn that the 'rabbit' she'd been fed as a treat when she was a little girl in wartime Europe was actually cat.

In Manado, there's a tradition of eating 'bush' meat. Dogs are consumed on certain occasions. Whenever my Indian family would bring this up, my mother would just laugh. Why turn up your nose at a dog at a feast, she could have said, when I've eaten a cat because I had to?

The avarice and ambitions of competing nationalisms brought her family to that strait. But she remembered other tastes from her Dutch childhood as well, things we grew to love. The pickled herrings my sisters still crave, the poffertjes (Dutch pancakes) she introduced me to when we visited Amsterdam, the spread she lovingly made for me from melted chocolate and condensed milk. How did they ever afford condensed milk during the war? Or was that a memory her own mother carried from a time of relative plenty before the world went insane?

My grandmother put that time behind her before her cousins could. While they were picking up the pieces in the ravaged decades that followed the war in a shattered Europe, my oma was the pampered wife of an Indonesian diplomat, travelling the world to represent a newly sovereign state. Perhaps it was on those postings with her parents that my mother learnt the secret of chocolate. In Westchester County in New York, my Ma learnt to make American pancakes instead of poffertjes, the very ones she would feed me as a treat on Sunday mornings, piled high with syrup or honey on top. A Delhi morning doesn't have to be about paranthas. But I love those too.

 CB

While still a boy, I would ask my mother, post a feast: where is home?

Wherever you are, she'd always say.

But I knew better, of course. I was a young Punjabi kid in Delhi. We'd got the world figured out. I'd quiz her about how she claimed to be Manadonese even though she'd never been there. I'd ask her why she didn't claim to be Dutch though she looked pretty European. I couldn't understand then the fierce pride she took in that distant country her father, my grandfather, had fought for, that he so desperately wanted to be free. I'm Indonesian, she'd say simply. And oma, I'd point out? She has an Indonesian passport too, my mother would reply. As if it was the easiest thing in the world to imagine: a European woman not only marrying an Asian man, but taking on his nationality as well. To marry a man's country—now that's love.

Of course, it happens all the time. But in reverse. Asians marry Westerners *and* their passports, we're told. Colonialism left its imbalances, and ordinary people are still seeking to correct them in any way they can. Let some brown children be educated at the expense of those surpluses the tea and spice and opium trades left behind.

And now we drink more tea than the British. In Amsterdam, telor balado is presumably as ubiquitous as tikka masala across the North Sea.

But it wasn't when my mother left, as Holland was still trying to pick itself up after the war.

୦ଃ

My mother spent less than a year in Jakarta between graduating from high school in the US and starting college in India. That was the sum total of her time in Indonesia without me. In that period, she apparently put together a fund of memories, including culinary ones, that would fuel her nostalgia for home when she was sick of us, our food, the land we lived in.

It wasn't Manado, the 'motherland' she'd never seen. It wasn't Amsterdam, the city of her birth, or the village she was shipped off to in the Dutch countryside when the wartime city couldn't feed a child any more. It was Jakarta, a city she dismissed.

Of course, Jakarta was just the medium, the place it happened. My mother was Indonesian. My grandparents really cared about that, so she did too. In the same way that my father really cared I grow up a Sikh. So she made that happen as well.

I don't know where all the recipes came from. My grandmother had a well-known antipathy towards the stove. Perhaps the food came from books. Or friends, or her sister, once she was married and settled in Indonesia. Perhaps she'd actually been eating this food in Amsterdam, in the homes of her mother's friends, as the number of women who'd married Asian students mounted in the years before the war. Her memory was malleable at the best of times.

Towards the end of her life, my mother began to miss her home more. What home, Ma, I'd ask. By then her mind was unravelling, and she'd struggle to voice her thought. I'd remind her of her old formula. Wherever we were, wherever I was, that was home. And I, we, were with her.

Sometimes her mind would be stilled and she'd smile and be quiet. At other times, she'd shake her head angrily and say no, that's not what she meant. She wanted to be with her family, with the sights and sounds she knew around her.

But what were these sights and sounds? Which family did she mean? She'd lived nowhere else but India since she was twenty years old.

෮

Jakarta is where my mother is buried. A little bit of her, in the same grave plot as her parents. The rest I scattered into the Sutlej, there to make its way to the deep blue sea.

I love Jakarta. Now, with all I know, I can say that it is, in a little way, where I'm from as well. Because I understand now that my mother didn't miss Jakarta, or Amsterdam, or being in high school in the US in the early 1950s.

When she moved to India, she was little more than a girl. She was, to a degree, swallowed by India, by us, the family she married into and produced. Perhaps she didn't ever articulate it to herself as such. It isn't so strange, after all. It happens to us all: those of us who grow up and leave younger selves behind and have lives with other people.

To know that happiness, you sacrifice something as well. But it doesn't mean that you don't, occasionally, rebel against being so owned. It doesn't mean you don't miss what you leave behind. That other self, those other people, the bits a smell, a sound, a taste bring back to you. Perhaps you don't even do it just for yourself. For your family, a special other—you do it for them as well. You remember, and you recast that world you inhabited. And then, if they care, your family, your special other—they inhabit it with you. For the duration of that song, that smell, that taste on your tongue.

When I see telor balado, I hear the rustle of a long-haired dog's fur against the silk of my mother's sari. I hear her voice whisper in my ear as I bend to kiss her. I can tell the seasons by where we're sitting in the house. I remember family lunches and meals alone with my Ma as she spoke to me about what happened that day in school. I remember the burgeoning of my own imagination as I sought to understand where it was my mother was from, because all I knew was that she wasn't like everyone else around me.

I don't know if she did it for me. But I know that my curiosity about the world was ignited by my curiosity about hers. My mother missed her older selves enough to try and capture them in the flavours and smells and textures she claimed she grew up with. That they made her happy is enough for me, and when I eat telor balado, she is with me.

I love telor balado. That's how I remember lunch at home when I was growing up.

Tia Rosa

WENDELL RODRICKS

It was almost at the end of morning mass that a chapel bell begins to peal. The priest looks up at the high-vaulted ceiling of the Saint Francis of the Wounds Church in the remote Goan village of Colvale. The blue ceiling of the apse is covered in gilted stars that reside in the church by day and escape to sparkle in the sky by night. The walls of the church are pimpled like a youth in acne bloom, interspersed with peeling paint, some pieces hanging mid-air on invisible cobwebs. Too much salt in the water when they plastered the church has caused this sprouting and peeling. The salty water has risen brick by laterite brick, seeping through the laterite holes. Defying gravity, the saline liquid has risen towards the vault leaving behind a uniform curtain of peeling and spluttering. If you listen closely, you can hear the walls move and the paint splutter like bubbles rising to the surface. Quite like the sound of water that bubbles in the large copper cauldron over the log fire in blackened, soot-covered Goan kitchens.

The statue of Saint Francis on his knees below the crucified Christ is perched high on the altar platform. The face of Christ, resplendent with a pure silver halo, is bent towards the kneeling saint whose outstretched arms glow with pomegranate drops of stigmata.

A second gong!

At this peal, the eyes of the sparse congregation turn from the altar and it's dim interiors to the glowing light in the east where the sun is beginning it's ascent over the hills of Tivim. Through the pale morning light outside the main entrance of the church, a startled white owl flutters past into the dark recesses of the high roof.

Then a low mournful gong again!

Aunt Emilia whispers, 'Someone has passed away. It sounds like it is someone near your house.' She makes the sign of the cross and murmurs a prayer for the departed soul.

On the fourth gong, the owl flies out of the church and swallows the sun.

On my way home, I feel the darkness of that moment when the owl darkened the sun, solar eclipse style. With each step, I approach the mourning chapel bells. Opposite my house, I can hear the plaintive voices of ladies in black dresses and long mantilla veils. Along with a few men in mothball-perfumed jackets, they are chanting a *ladainha*—the rosary, sung in Latin.

In the darkened salon, Rosa lies in a purple felt coffin. Her face radiates in peaceful repose. Am I imagining it, or has someone put a lit diya in her mouth? I have never seen her glow so.

Her alabaster hands riddled with pale blue-green veins clutch a sparkling crystal rosary. Those are the fingers that clutched my baby hands when we walked on the hills plucking orange-coloured cashew fruit, golden mangoes, purple jambools, ivory yellow chunnas, black curvandahs with blood-red flesh within. In her soothing voice, she would point out the otters in the river, a rare crocodile, dancing peacocks, an elusive wolf and singing bulbuls.

When we returned home at sunset, after the Angelus bells had pealed and we had said our evening prayers, Tia Rosa would arrive home with her cornucopia of goodies. *Bolinhas* coconut cookies made with village eggs, a green chutney sandwich made crunchy with grated green apples, a slice of *bibinca* flambéed in Cointreau. There was always some innovation with every preparation. She was an excellent cook. But she preferred to dine with her sister, my mother, since she was a lone spinster. Her husband was the kitchen, the apron her bridal dress.

Living across the road had many advantages. The biggest was that Tia Rosa taught me to love the colours, the aromas, the textures that resided in her kitchen, in her hands and in her wondrous mind. What was impressive is how she created fusion food long before the word was made fashionable by chefs around the world. Her favourite word was 'blend'. Followed by 'with imagination'. Long before I applied those words of wisdom to clothes, I learnt the basics from humble kitchen ingredients.

'Today I am going to teach you an easy tender coconut jelly,' Tia Rosa told me one hot summer morning. Damudor had plucked the matured coconuts the day before and was requested by Tia Rosa to bring down three tender coconuts as well. Now they lay gleaming like polished, waxed footballs larger than my face. With expert flicks of her wrist, Carmeline the maid exposed the Calangute white, sand-coloured flesh, scooping the top off in a sabre stroke to reveal the clear juice within. Drained into a glass bowl, chopped scrapings of the tender coconut flesh was added to the coconut juice. Goan molasses coloured the coconut water a golden Muscatel wine hue. Melting a few strands of china grass gelatin, Tia Rosa expertly blended the gelatinous liquid with the tender coconut water.

'Now, my child, this is the regular recipe. What do you want to add to it?'

I scratched my mop of hair, chin resting at the level of the pink-veined marble kitchen top.

'Why don't we add you to the recipe?' I replied, winking at her.

'Excellent idea! Go to the garden and bring two pink roses from near the hibiscus shrub.'

In went the pale pink, perfumed rose petals.

That night, Tia Rosa said a special 'Grace before Meals', extolling the virtues of my creativity with the dessert. I was in rapture at the end of the meal when everyone commented that the rose petals perfumed the golden jelly, but did not overpower the taste of the coconut. Subtlety was a key ingredient I had learnt from my aunt. Each day there was something to learn and marvel at. A chicken mayonnaise salad was infused with the delicious taste of diced, ripe Mankurada mango, crisped up with chilled lettuce and drizzled with crushed black pepper harvested from the garden.

At the barbecue, shellfish was splashed with Pernod, beef steak with malt whiskey and local mullet wrapped in bacon. The heavenly aromas, colours and flavour mixes became a game of sorts between us. Can we try throwing some pine seeds and dried black currants into the mutton kebabs? Shall we add marmalade to the bread-butter pudding? How about dusting the raw papaya salad with ginger juice, roasted peanuts and sesame seeds? For the olive oil and lime dressing, shall we try olive oil and tamarind juice? Instead of the standard pork belly with masala, let's place the pork on fat onion rings drenched in beer, cover in sea salt and slow bake it for three hours till the meat shines like leather and almost falls off the bones. Squeezing a lime over these steamed asparagus will add to the nutty flavour. Tonight when we serve a bitter chocolate soufflé, can we add grated orange rind, a little salt and black pepper to heighten the cocoa taste ... and then serve with chilled red wine?

The possibilities were endless, creative, breathtaking in their imaginative potential.

And now, as she lay in her coffin, I began to think up what I could do to make her look special. In the garden I fashioned blood red roses into a small heart and placed the wreath on her chest. In that dim salon, the red glowed and seemed to have a heartbeat of its own each time the candles flickered around the coffin.

One day Tia Rosa told me with a twinkle in her eye, 'Tia Maria Fernanda taught me this recipe. We are going to elevate the humble drumstick vegetable to cuisine standards. I will teach you to make a drumstick mousse. Looking at my surprised expression, she added, 'Now close your open mouth and wide eyes, and help Damudor collect two dozen drumsticks from the garden.'

The drumsticks were cut into four-inch long pieces and boiled, two cups of the boiled drumstick flesh was blended with half a cup each of milk and drumstick stock, three heaped tablespoons of grated cheese, a tablespoon each of butter and breadcrumbs, and two pinches of baking powder. Into this batter went five local village eggs whisked to a froth, salt and pepper. An oven proof casserole dish was greased and dusted with breadcrumbs. Into the casserole went the heavenly mousse mixture and baked in a medium oven for fifteen minutes.

'Uncle Joao is allergic to eggs,' Carmeline pointed out.

Pat came Tia Rosa's retort. 'What are eggs? Protein, right? Use five tablespoons of yoghurt instead.'

The mousse is delicious when served warm or cold. Guests would ask in disbelief, 'Is this drumstick or asparagus?'

'Drumstick!' I grin, till today, and the shower of compliments follow.

The fat black caterpillar of the funeral cortege wound its way to church. Now I am no more the little boy who clutched Tia Rosa's hand on the Colvale hillsides. I am a grown-up hiding my tears behind memories of a favourite aunt and her incredible culinary art.

A group of two dozen langurs come to shriek a fond farewell from the rooftops. The same langurs she had cursed when they broke the terracotta tiles as they danced on the roof while being allowed to feast on the mangoes, guavas and papayas. 'I shout at them, but never mind. We took their jungle with our houses and buildings. Let them enjoy what God gives us each season.' With that Tia Rosa firmly forbade my gun-trotting Uncle Jose from ever using his rifle on the langurs on her roof.

I slip out of my thoughts when the stones and mud begin to fly on the coffin in its six-feet-deep cave. They look like the raisins, currants, orange peels flying into the Christmas cake Tia Rosa made each year. I recall how she slit and chopped 225 g each of dried black raisins, white currants, orange peel and ground almonds and soaked them in a cup of Cognac three months before Christmas. Two weeks before baking day, Tia Rosa would ensure there were twenty-four local 'gaunti' eggs collected. Later, the entire household would be put to work. 'You blend 550 g butter with 350 g sugar till creamy. Carmeline, beat twenty-four egg yokes with ten egg whites till frothy as lace.'

She would insist I stand by and watch as she blended the beaten eggs into the creamed butter and sugar, a trickle at a time. Flour and semolina, 225 g each, were mixed with one-and-a-half teaspoons of baking powder. This was folded expertly in a 'cut and fold' technique into the egg, sugar and butter mixture. In went the long-soaking, now plump with liquor, fruits with 100 g of sliced almonds. Even now, at this final stage, Tia Rosa would use her 'blend with imagination' motto. To enhance the nutty flavour of the slivered almonds, a teaspoon of carom seeds was folded into the batter. Poured into two greased and dusted cake tins, the cakes were baked in a medium oven for half-an-hour. During baking time, we were counselled to say a rosary for Tia Rosa or the cakes would be a disaster.

The aroma floated across the entire street and sent Aunt Emilia into a green rage. 'There she is again. Year after year she makes that damn cake which the parish priest raves and raves about, ignoring my coconut cake. Just because she is a spinster, dresses well and cooks better than anyone, all the men are at her feet. I am sure when she dies, Padre will say extra-long prayers at her grave.'

Which is exactly what happened!

At the end of the lengthy prayers for Tia Rosa's soul, lightening and thunder blister and crackle in the sky; the heavens open and huge drops of rain herald the Goan monsoon. Our tears mix with those from heaven.

As I leave the graveyard, I swear I can smell the aroma of Tia Rosa's Christmas cake wafting up from the earth.

It has stayed with me ever since.

Bongs, Bawas and Bigotry

BACHI KARKARIA

Growing up a Parsi in Kolkata is a bit like khichdi au gratin. A combination that's difficult to manage, or imagine. But we got by and there were life lessons to be learnt from the experiences which I will try to serve up here. Reheated, admittedly; edible, certainly; palatable, hopefully.

Our family didn't burst into Rabindra Sangeet at odd hours of the day or night, though we were quite willing to display our own ethnic-authentic eccentricities at the drop of a topi. Our traditional Parsi Sunday dhansak did not arrive at the lunch table bristling with the fish that the predominant Bengalis cannot survive without in their cuisine. It came with the mutton that Parsis must dig into to be able to function cogently. Nor did we lace our akuri with maastaard oil, and we never indulged in such 'fusion' atrocities as piling it atop a luchi instead of on propah blighty Bawa toast.

But I am happy to report that the hybrid upbringing sullied my allegedly pure genetic mindset. Especially because it made me aware of, first, the fraudulent nature of the uniqueness that all communities lay claim to, and secondly, the subtle way in which food exposes our hypocrisy in that grand delusion known as Unity in Diversity.

Let me start with the first specific reference to the two communities I was most exposed to in my formative years, and beyond. The Parsis and the Bengalis are equally proud of their exalted place in the scheme of things. Both believe they are a class not only apart, but unquestionably, in a class of one.

Several decades ago, the Mumbai-based *Parsiana* magazine published a telling cartoon by the multi-talented Manjula Padmanabhan. It featured two stooped, scrawny, beak-nosed bawas in their sadra-vest and legha-pyjamas, with one asking the other in bemusement, 'Best community? Which others are there?' It struck a double chord because Bengalis, whom I have known (and loved) over the years, too might express lofty surprise at being told that they aren't the only ethnic entity on the planet, or at least the only one worth the reckoning.

Parsis and Bengalis are unique in their own way, of course, but they also share a common uniqueness as the following points of pride and prejudice bear out. Amartya Sen may have had his fellow Bongs in mind when he wrote *The Argumentative Indian*, but excuse me sir, we are right up there with you. Parsis may not presume to compare their literature and poetry with that of the Bengali, but we can match him as indefatigably in any argumentative sphere.

Since I'm not scoring debate points here, let me make an honest confession. Our cuisine simply doesn't have the same variety, nuance or refinement as that of the Bengali (or, for that matter, of the other communities who speak of their kitchens in reverential tones—and tomes). After all, we fled our Persian homeland over 1000 years ago to preserve our faith, not our food preferences, and our foremothers had little time to pack their recipe books for which there was no room anyway, in the little boats on which they sailed to shores unknown.

Moreover, till we got a taste of the good life on the British table, we had eked out a living in the fields and forests of Gujarat where the boats were tossed up. So while today we may turn as soggy as a failed souffle yearning nostalgically over our lost rustic recipes, not too many bragging rights can be stirred into buried pots of lamb cooked under burning hay, dried Bombay duck stewed in vinegar or sweet tea-time snacks leavened with toddy which had stoked our migrant ancestors.

Unlike the landed Bengali gentry of yore, we didn't have the luxury of lifting nothing heavier than a pen for generations. Unlike in Gujarat, in Shonar Bangla, rice rose, if not unbidden, then certainly in abundance from the green-gold fields, and fish leapt out of ponds straight into minion-filled kitchens, where Mashima could create dishes as florid as the poetry Babu Moshay was coaxing out in his study, or languidly perusing in his personal library.

Of course, as with the rest of India, and indeed the world over, historical facts have never been hindrances to bigotry. Parsis love their food with the same unbridled passion as Bengalis. And will defend to the death their right to have it—and insist on its superiority over the competition. More often, they will leave the eloquence to the Bengali and simply get down to business. Each community can match the other in packing a punch. Or paunch.

Proof of this commonality between their boasted uniqueness can be seen in the wedding halls of both. While other communities have succumbed to the siren song of mish-mash buffet tables, where the roast loin lies down with the rara lamb and foreign salads chill out with the ice sculpture, the

Parsi and Bengali wedding feasts remain in all their glorious,
cornucopious purity. In the former, replacing the dried-apricot-
laden, potato-straw-topped chicken with murg makhani is as
much an act of high treason as the latter daring to dish out
bekti meuniere instead of doi machh, teler koi, muri ghonto
and every other variety in curried, fried, stewed or other
sanctified form. Pretentious fathers of the bride try, but the
bulwark of the community holds up the fort, battens down the
hatches, and any which way stops barbarian food from belching
at the gates.

And here's an extension of that fraudulent uniqueness. The
natural corollary of this obsession with food is the obsession of
both communities with the digestive tract. It's alimentary, my
dear Bomsi Bannerjee. Only the Parsi can match the Bengali,
groan for groan, in hypochondria, and in both, nothing is as
common and dire as any ailment related to the passage of food.
Or, more correctly, it's non-passage.

All Indians make a fetish of the otherwise unobjectionable
habit of regular bowel movement; morning turns to moaning,
even mourning, if a healthy plonk (or plop) isn't achieved first
thing—after, of course, the persuasive glass of chai. But among
Bawas and Bongs, this mundane, and elsewhere unmentionable,
routine is literally a rite of passage. Like all such rituals, it is
accompanied by drama, and made all the more 'melo' in the
presence of an audience.

My Bengali homeopath had one explanation for every ailment,
from an aching head to a painful toe. After the usual catechism
of questions, he would throw down his pen, and with a matching
flourish pronounce: 'Gash!' Forget the Krishna-Godavari Basin
or even the North Sea, there's a fortune awaiting the company
that can commercially extract and exploit the vast gasfields lying
not-so-dormant within the Bawa and Bong anatomy.

The aforementioned Dr Mukherjee was a small-timer sitting in his musty Ballygunge-lane clinic with dusty bottles of Nux Vomica crammed into glass cases opaque with age. He was also a homeopath, but in another league altogether, operating out of the appropriately grand address of Palace Court. You applied for an appointment, and got it by postcard—three months later. But such was his reputation that patients were prepared to wait—or die in blissful anticipation.

His sole diagnosis was not gas. He was called upon to deal with the whole Materia Medica of illnesses that his patients could imagine, and he gave them full play—the illnesses and the patients. The waiting room was a long wait, packed to the teak beams of the vast hall. A factotum would pompously call out seven names at a time; the chosen would solemnly troop into the doctor's sanctum sanctorum and, with due reverence to the imminent ritual, arrange themselves in the semi-circle of chairs around the imposing altar aka desk.

Then, one by one, and to the awe and envy of the rest, each would recount their disorder at loving length and dramatized detail. No surprises here: most of these centred on problematic digestion. And with such a captive audience, each one delivered a stellar performance. For example: a bout of vomiting would be described with a rolling of eyes (and a virtual roll of drums): '*Atto bomi, atto bomi, bhaba jaye na*, you cannot imagine!'

Unfortunately, my family also subscribed to the 'move or die' morning mantra. Fortunately, its discussion was limited to pre-breakfast, and the prophylactic/remedy was restricted to a weekly dose of Milk of Magnesia. The thought of it quite ruined the Saturday Chinese dinner we were treated to, I suspect, as a softener. My little sister was coaxed into swallowing a tablespoon of it not with the Mary Poppins formula of 'a teaspoon of sugar makes the medicine go down', but with a couplet which was as revoltingly gooey: '*Baby piye julab, ne chhat par ugey gulab.*' The prompt sequence of the effect of downing the laxative and the lush manuring of roses on the terrace was graphic, and quite plausible to our gullible minds. We soon stopped believing this nonsense, but for my father, till his dying day, the clockwork morning 'go' was Heaven and the weekly purgative was Purgatory. Needless to say, constipation was Hell. That bit at least was true as I was to discover painfully.

This essay is essentially about eating, specifically about my double whammy upbringing as a Bawi in Bongland. I cannot be accused of diversionary tactics if in the preceding paragraphs I have lingered, like last night's masoor ma gosht, on the alimentary end of the digestive tract. But I will now return to my culinary combo, congenital and environmental.

As I mentioned earlier, we did not have rui machher dhansak, our jinga no patiyo wasn't cooked in sharp shorshey-bata style instead of the traditional paste of red chilli, garlic and zeera, and then finished off with vinegar and gur. It's not just the fusion which would have created confusion. The main ingredient would be the culprit. Jinga is shrimp in Parsi-Gujarati thanks to the Marathi influence of Mumbai, the mother-ship of the community, but in Bengali it refers to the less-exalted ridge gourd.

When I had excitedly informed my school chum, Shipra Das, that we would be serving her our festive dish of dhan-daar and jinga no patiyo, she turned up her pert nose. Humble dal chawal accompanied by a dish whose main ingredient was a vegetable also called toorai was certainly not her idea of a celebratory lunch, dhonnobad.

Shipra would not have wrecked our friendship had we instead lain on our festive fish—fried in a patiyo, simmered in saas, or steamed. The last-mentioned patra ni machhi resembles the Bengali paturi machh since that too is spiced and wrapped in banana leaves before cooking. But both parties will sniff and tell you that they are cousins more hissing than kissing. We coat our pomfret with coconut chutney and steam the parcel; the Bengalis slather their ubiquitous mustard paste on a bhetki and griddle-fry it till the leaf envelope turns brown. Both communities claim the superiority of even the everyday fried brinjal, our tarela vengna, or their equally oil-soaked begun bhaja.

We concede victory to the Bengalis in their vast net of fish dishes, but we get our flourish of trumpets when it comes to eggs. No Indian community is as yoked to this oval-shaped square meal. Being incorrigibly carnivorous, we cannot swallow any vegetable dish unless it is studded with chunks of meat. On lean days, we have it topped with an egg. Vimla Patil, who used to be the editor of *Femina* when I joined the Times group as a trainee, loved to recount her reverse Shipra moment. She thought she would get something Spanishly exotic when she ordered the poetic bheeda par eeda; instead she got two eggs staring insolently back at her from a bed of over-fried okra.

Perhaps because I wasn't hatched among the majority of Parsis, my life doesn't get scrambled if I don't get an egg a day, or even for weeks. But when I came to live in Delhi as the *TOI's* resident editor, I developed an insatiable craving for egg; this may or may not have had anything to do with my temporary residence being Jain House. It was as hospitable as it was palatial, and Shankar Maharaj pampered me with delicacies that left nothing to desire except the pleasures of flesh. Strangely, I was quite happy to croon *'Love me tinda, love me true'*. Except for that oeuf-ish longing.

So when I went over to friends' homes, I'd clamour to cook up our makeshift dish of eggs on sliced potatoes. Not having grown up in Mumbai, I did not call it by the Parsi name of 'papeta par eeda', but in the manner of our Calcutta Muslim cook, 'aloo par anda'. My hosts would inevitably misinterpret this as aloo parantha, and immediately fob me off with a 'No, no, we eat enough of that! We'll just stick to the lovely kali daal we've made for you.'

The Parsi dominance in the egg domain had never been challenged in Calcutta. Or in any of the cities across the country where I have spent significant amounts of time. That's because no one eats egg with the same addiction, and usually restricts the form to boiled and plonked in a curry, whipped into an omelette or scrambled into a bhurji—which, if I may say so, is a sad, dry imitation of our rich and creamy akuri.

Bengalis are finicky about the way a vegetable is sliced for different dishes; they will buy the gleaming katla only if it is 'smiling' as it lies on the fishmonger's slab. But they are surprisingly unfussy about their eggs. They are quite content to chomp on the 'boiled deem' (pronounced 'boildim', as one word, like 'bakedish') that cohabits with a sandesh in their tiffin boxes. Or as it used to be sold to government babus from blotchy glass cases on the lunch-time pavement outside the Raj-time Writers' Building.

If we retained our culinary purity as a minuscularity in Calcutta, happily gorging on Bengali fare without bastardizing our own, it was of a piece with the rest of India. In the matter of gastronomic integration, the international has always been more successful than the national. Think about it. A dosa stuffed with keema is as far as it goes, and most Indians would consider it too far. The Tam Brahms are arguably the most straitjacketed in food, and for them, such an abomination is unmentionable, unspeakable, unforgivable and, of course, untouchable.

Led by Gujarat's intrepid 'pasta-bens', Indian yummy mummies (and even those with un-gymmed tummies) experiment daily with the taco-bhel school of cooking. We stuff samosas with exotic ricotta, and tortillas with homely matar-aloo. We have created that great staple of Chinese eating-out, gobi manchurian. Bred on local 'peeza' smothered in Amul cheese, we spurn the one we encounter in Naples as a pathetic impostor. Every evening a Shivani, Simran or Seema is outsmarting Sainsbury's in the matter of the chicken tikka sandwich. They feed their children on the classics and innovations of Masterchef—but as only mummy can reinvent them. Kothmir in the casserole and basil in the baingan bharta is par for the course.

Indians dish up global desi with a vengeance; we are willing and able to wok on the wild side when it comes to creating Indo-Other Country Cuisine. But we draw the line at Indo-Other Indian creations. It's a lakshmana rekha we do not cross. Not because we don't dare to, but because we don't care to.

The unspoken truth, our dirty, murky secret, is that despite all our global gastronomics, we are clannish, parochial and unrepentantly bigoted when it comes to sullying our own culinary purity by impregnating it with the flavours of other regions. In this Indian caste system, there's an 'untouchable' strata: OPC, Other People's Cooking. We may talk glibly about pan-Indianism, but please excuse me, we don't want other Indian food getting familiar with our own in our pans. Sure, we will go out to gorge on Punjabi chhole-bhature, Kolhapuri mutton, Maharashtrian masale bhaat, Hyderabadi biryani, Goan xacuti, the whole Gujarati thali, all the food from Kashmir to Kanyakumari. On occasion, we may try out the recipes from magazines and cookery shows, but that's where the cookchie-coo ends. We won't let it sully our own fare. Not just our regional fare, but drilled down to our narrowest sub-community segment. The NIMBY factor applies to the fusion of Indian foods as much as to the hazardous waste of nuclear fission. Not In My Back Yard, Not In My Clan Food.

Only the very brave or the very foolish will cross this line. The Punjabi matron who has no problem replacing her tandoori paste with chipotle grill marinade would never dream of adding a smear or two of Kolhapuri kombdi masala to give that unique kick to her chicken. And my favourite Bengali belle would give up Rabindra Sangeet altogether before she deigns to add some rajma zing to her chholar dal or a smidgeon of bottled vindaloo mix to her machher jhol. 'Japanese Bhashabi paste? Now that eez bheri good. *Bhishon bhalo.* Even my shashuri likes it in her chochori.'

So there we are. United we stand, divided we follow only our own clan recipes. And why we should not? They only are the best, no?

Walks with Lyla

NILOUFER ICHAPORIA KING

Few things make me as happy as a market, a real market, not the kind with more t-shirts and mugs than vegetables. Put me in a market anywhere and time both races and stands still. At a market you've got your finger on the pulse of what's going on in a place, the forces that keep it moving, the real life that lies under and perhaps enables the languorous pleasures of the leisured. It's what I want to find out about first thing in any new city. In my present hometown, San Francisco, we never miss the weekly thrill of the big and busy Alemany Farmers' Market unless we're away or too ill to move. On visits to my old hometown, my muluk, or native place, Mumbai, I don't feel properly settled until all my favourite haunts have been checked. Most of these haunts are market areas, and Mumbai with its twelve million people has markets everywhere. You could see the city as one giant market, with markets within markets, nested like Russian dolls. Some of these are official with buildings and licensed permanent vendors; others are

41

informal, springing up wherever they're needed, setting themselves up around the official markets, under trees, in places where office-goers congregate, outside railway stations or in the middle of an intersection. At any time of the year, with monsoon rain drumming down or in enervating heat, these markets are alive and never more so than when there's a festival approaching.

Going around any market, an observant walker is bombarded with impressions, sights, sounds, smells, ideas, emotions. In profound and touching ways, we see countless examples of economy of means, whether it's the display of goods or the negligent artistry with which effects of heart-stopping beauty are achieved using nothing but imagination. We see endlessly inventive responses to logistical problems. Over and over, we see ingenious examples of reuse, recycling and repair, whether it's in the way things are wrapped, or how waste paper, metal and glass are reused, or how vegetable matter gets consumed by goats and cows, or how broken things are painstakingly repaired or put to other use. In a city where cultures and languages keep rubbing together, bizarre juxtapositions pop up everywhere and leave you weak with delight. There's the reassurance of continuity along with the stimulation of change in response to the swift currents of modern life. There's the often ignored art of repeated action, those physical movements performed and perfected over decades or generations. It can be the perfectly calculated flick of the wrist in squeezing spirals of jalebi batter into oil, or judging exactly when to take them out. There's the power of useful, everyday objects, made the same way for centuries, perhaps in new materials or modern colours. There's the beauty of finding repose and joy in the middle of apparent chaos—a fruit seller taking a nap on a mound of watermelons, children playing with an improvised toy made from a rag and a broomstick. Above all, there's the human component, interchanges filled with humour, regard and tenderness. Let's not forget the animal world. Mumbai's avian mascots, our rackety, mischievous crows, find their way into everything; pigeons are given food and lodging; dogs, cats, goats and cows wander at will, loved, tolerated, accommodated. Once or twice, I've even seen an elephant.

I grew up in the immediate pre- and post-Independence period, being sent off to boarding school in Kodaikanal, where every month we would be let loose in the Kodai bazaar with our meagre pocket money. Given a choice, we would rather have spent the money on neon-orange syrupy jalebis or mouthwatering vadas from bazaar stalls than the nun-approved wrapped sweets and biscuits from shops with names. In Mumbai, our mothers who tended to avoid crowds, heat and grime, sighed longingly for the wonderful supermarkets they had seen or heard of. 'In America,' they would exclaim, 'they have places where you wheel a trolley around and put things in it. All so clean! Not like our markets.' No, indeed, not like our markets at all. (Years later, my first exposure to American supermarkets left me feeling, as a Thai friend once put it, as though one were shopping in a morgue.) Once a year, at the end of the school holidays, there would be an expedition to Crawford Market to equip me for the school year ahead: trunks and bedding rolls for the three-day train journey, dark green socks and cardigans for our uniforms, tins of IXL jam from Tasmania, biscuits and tins of Kraft cheese to share at teatime. The areas beyond Crawford Market didn't really come into my life until I was in my twenties when a friend involved in craft exports started taking me with her to the silver market or to the printers and dyers and pearl stringers, and I've never stopped feeling grateful to Silloo Mody for this life-changing and life-giving introduction to Bhuleshwar and the heart of the city. Twenty years or so later, another dimension got added to my solitary walks when my cousin's daughter Lyla came to live in Mumbai. Her sharp yet tender eyes and ears for every aspect of Mumbai life make Lyla the perfect, tireless prowling companion.

Our market world lies in South Mumbai which I know best. For a long time, I did not know there was another market besides Crawford Market, now Mahatma Jyotibai Phule Market, but still known by its old name, Krafit Market, in the Mumbai vernacular. Fascinating for its nineteenth-century building, its cavernous interiors, the spectacular displays of fruit and vegetables, its varied specialized selling areas, Crawford Market can't be set aside, but my favourites are the markets that are less frequented. There are markets that I go to for particular things. I always stop at Fort Market, at the top of Phirozeshah Mehta Road in the central Flora Fountain area, where Keki Umrigar of Umrigar Stores stocks his own blends of Parsi masalas like dhanajiru (a complex blend of far more than the coriander and cumin its name implies), sambhar, distinct from the sambar powder of the South, dhansak masala, plus Navsari-based Kolah's cane vinegar and other Parsi favourites like sweet-sour lagan nu achar made of dried fruits in a grated carrot base, gharab nu achar made from fish roe, and methia nu achar, a love-it-or-hate-it mango pickle redolent of fenugreek. Nowadays, these Kolah products come in triple–thick heavy plastic bags, a boon for travellers. Many friendships have foundered when requested bottles of oily methia or gharab nu achar have leaked all over the contents of a suitcase with disastrous consequences. Mr Umrigar opens the shop only between 11.30 and 1, and from 6 to 8 in the evenings, and even then only if he feels up to it, because in his life outside the market, he's a well cleanser, his true calling.

Another market good for specific errands, Colaba Market, the southernmost, serves a wide range of shoppers: people doing their everyday marketing, those in search of the exotics of Mumbai—radicchio, rocket baby corn, red and yellow capsicums, the iceberg lettuce scorned by American epicures, and people who come from distant fishing villages not for food but to buy their traditional men's loincloths, Koli rumals and zany squares whose patterns and motifs reflect their wearers' lives and interests. On the road leading to the Colaba Market is Kailash Parbat, noted for its bhel and pani puri and its mithai. A small, informal cane stand nearby sells mud-caked lotus root, hard to find anywhere else. Further down the road, before the entrance to Colaba Market is Camy Wafers, a small shop with a huge selection of savoury and sweet things, and wafers, of course. This is where my friend Firoza might buy mithai for my husband and bags of sali, straw potatoes, for me when she comes to the United States.

Then there is the Grant Road Market with its large main building on one side of the railway station, a market I like to walk around in just to check it out. Locals tell me it has excellent fish. I go there for our Parsi chalk-na-dabbas, stencils for our version of rangoli. On the other side of the station, there's Bhaji Galli, a street lined with vendors selling beautifully displayed fruits and vegetables of dazzling freshness and variety. The monsoon season brings in many wild-gathered rarities like young colocasia shoots.

Our big walks around Bhuleshwar and Null Bazaar take us through contiguous yet separate cultural universes, one Hindu, the other Muslim, but neither wholly the one or the other in the Mumbai way. We generally start our Bhuleshwar and Null Bazaar excursions in the Crawford Market area, at the Badshah Cold Drink Depot which is just that. Seasonal fruits line the walls; the tables are decorated with sprays of mango leaves, the

menu is a litany of fruit juices and milk-based drinks. We're
here for just one thing: Badshah's famous falooda, which in
Mumbai is a rose or saffron (choose the rose!) flavoured milk
drink like no other, served in tall glasses with soaked basil
seeds and wheat starch noodles at the bottom, then a band of
dark pink rose syrup, and on top a few inches of milk finished
with a scoop of kulfi. Here in San Francisco, I make falooda
with pale, exquisite organic rose syrup from Lebanon, but I'll
always have a weak spot for our 100 per cent synthetic, luridly
pink Indian product. In my college days at St. Xavier's, we
often came to Badshah, but had to go up a steep flight of stairs
to a stuffy, low-ceilinged room, the 'special accommodation
for ladies and families', but now, everyone sits in the same
space.

If our destination is Bhuleshwar, we move from one specialized
market zone to another, from the generally useful (hardware,
flapping house dresses, clothes pins, hair clips, mattresses and
cushions, rat traps and soap dishes) or entertaining (juicy-
looking wax fruit, plastic parrots on wheels) to cloth, spices,
precious jewellery, street food, a temple, silver jewellery, patwas
(bead-stringing) pots and pans, tie-dyed clothes and strings,
flowers, kitchen tools, vegetables, another temple, religious
paraphernalia, ending up with one of the city's best known
Gujarati farsan makers.

Our usual starting point is opposite Crawford Market on
Abdul Rehman Street which dead ends in a mosque, Jama
Masjid. On either side of us are carts selling clothes, dried
fruits formerly in bee- and fly-covered mounds, now draped
in plastic, vendors of cooked food and people wandering
about with some choice seasonal offering like green-skinned
singoda or Alphonso mangoes. Just before the mosque, we turn
right to Mirchi Galli, lined on both sides with shops selling

masalas and meva. Pranavbhai, one of the owners of Ramanlal Vithaldas Mevawala, fourth generation in the business, spends time discussing the fine points of masalas and meva, such as the particular properties of dried chillies from all over India, walnuts from Kashmir or Afghani raisins and jardalus, calling for sample after sample to be brought out to us on stainless steel plates, without ever making us feel that we've interrupted business. I might come away with jardalus for my husband who loves them and has never had one still soft enough to bite into, and bags of dark red Kashmiri chillies which for a long time were not easy to find in San Francisco. Across the road is the cloth market, but that's a separate excursion. We jog to the left at Jama Masjid, then turn right down Zaveri Bazaar, the street for jewellery made of gold and precious stones. There's an occasional tea stall or a wandering vendor, but the serious street food is in Khao or Nasta Galli almost at the bottom of Zaveri Bazaar. We turn right at Third Agiary Lane and walk to where fruit salad carts signal we've arrived. The whimsical, brilliant arrangements of fruits combined with raw beetroots and cucumbers never fail to delight, but this is where we leave it. If we haven't had falooda, we might eat something from the vendors selling pao bhaji, vada pao, bhel puri, dosa, grilled papad or vegetable sandwich, all so temptingly displayed with unselfconscious artistry, and now with a greater awareness of sanitation, generally well-covered against flies although we won't comment on the bucket of water used for rinsing plates.

I never tire of watching street cooks and keep remembering the words of Kusunoki Tonomura on what are perceived as the lesser arts: we tend to underestimate the beauty of simple movements perfected over time. As ants to sugar, so Lyla is to jalebis, especially when they're warm, crisp and freshly bathed in syrup. Years ago, there was a street stand where one could stand mesmerized, watching the negligent ease of a deft hand depositing perfect small spirals of batter over an expanse of bubbling oil in a vast karai. Alas, the operations of Jagannath Chhaturbhuj Halwai have now moved indoors and out of sight behind a tiled wall, but the jalebis are still served warm, crisp and freshly bathed. Around Khao Galli are stalls selling jewellers' tools and necessities. I buy sturdy handmade tweezers there, the same archaic design now rendered in stainless steel and really useful in the kitchen. We move on now, either by turning left and rejoining Zaveri Bazaar, or right, which gets us to roughly the same place, the area around the temple of Mumbadevi, Mumbai's presiding deity, and Chandi Bazaar, the city's silver market. Our next food-related errand is to replenish my supply of silver and gold leaf at one of two places: the Vitrag Kesar Mart in Mahajan Galli, a warren of small shops and businesses, or the more than 200-year-old Jain temple (Shree Godiji Parshwanath Derasar) at the top of Kika Street opposite Chandi Bazaar. After slipping off your sandals, you go into the temple vestibule and turn to the right into what looks like a post office. A man at a computer terminal asks you what you want, tells you what you need to pay for it and hands you your varak in sealed plastic packets. Not that long ago, you walked up a flight of stairs into a long room with black-capped bookkeepers in white kurtas and dhotis, sitting on white mattresses in front of handsome wooden chest desks, making their entries in red cloth-bound ledgers with bamboo quill pens.

After depositing broken necklaces with the patwa who has been doing my work since he was an apprentice, we walk across the street to the utensil market, Barthan or Tamba Bazaar, where many things once made of brass and copper are now in aluminium or the even more popular stainless steel, but often in the same ancient forms. I come here to buy perforated stainless steel moulds for Parsi panir (panir no vasan), or stainless steel jars with lids, perfect for storing a month's supply of ghee for a small household. Many decades ago, a foreign expert was hired to write a report on Indian domestic metalware, to reimagine it in terms of the export market. The report was buried quickly. It said that things were perfect as they were and to change nothing, except perhaps to make the bottoms of Indian cooking pots a little more stable for Western burners.

At this point, we can do two things: keep walking along the utensil side of the street and turn right past the official Bhuleshwar Market building to Kabutarkhana, or go to the near corner and walk down Kika Street past the arita-washing stall to Third Bhoiwada Lane, full of non-food temptations like bandhni cloth, to get to the same point. In the middle of the Kabutarkhana where there is indeed a pigeon hostel, lively women with kewra leaves in their hair, every one a diva, sell vegetables, flowers and bundles of neem twigs for tooth brushing. On one corner is the A–Z Gruh Vastu Bhandar where we find kitchen tools and implements, perhaps a shallow metal vaghar or tadka ladle with a lacquered wooden grip, or beautifully crafted rolling pins, mixing spoons and batter spreaders. Off to the right, your nose leads you to Phul Galli, where in the cool darkness vendors make headily scented garlands of roses, spider lilies, jasmine and marigolds. For a very short time, a jokey young man had a shop at Kabutarkhana called Ben Percy because, as he explained, he sold purses to the bens (sister) of Bhuleshwar.

We walk on towards Bhaji Galli, the Bhuleshwar one, breathing in a cocktail of limes, green chillies, fresh coriander, curry leaves and fresh turmeric. Gujarati epicures from all over the city come to Bhuleshwar to shop here. Heaps of green mangoes in the hot months mean pickle-making, and vendors obligingly do the heavy work of cutting them up. Dudhi,

tindora, parval, karela, pumpkin, brinjal small and large, val
papdi, guar phalli and regular green bean, sprouted pulses,
drumstick, amaranth, spinach, fenugreek greens, turmeric,
ginger and mango ginger, coriander, dill, mint and lemon
grass, sweet and ordinary potato, elephant's foot yam and plain
old onion, cabbage and carrot, and more and more. This is
where you would look for lotus blossoms for puja, or bijoda,
Kutchi citrons. We move on past Maganlal Dresswala towards
Madhav Bagh, a nineteenth-century residential and commercial
compound with a Krishna temple at its heart. Food-focused or
not, Madhav Bagh is always a joy to walk through, past vendors
of clothes, music and videos, household goods and religious
paraphernalia. I still treasure a kitchen towel showing a large
hamburger with the legend 'American Burger'—and this from
the heart of vegetarian Hindu Mumbai. Once, in the middle of
noonday hubbub, I heard Bach flute and harpsichord sonatas
drifting from an upper-storey window, competing with filmi
songs and the ever-present cawing of our beloved crows. On the
other side, towards the CP Tank Road gate, there's a homeless
shelter for cattle, the Panjrapol, run by a joint Hindu – Parsi
trust, where the gentle-faced animals are tenderly cared for.

We leave the gates of Madhav Bagh and turn to the left,
following its perimeter past the shop with the hard-to-resist,
traditional, two-toned ceramic pickle jars of all sizes, to Hiralal
Kashidas Bhajiawala, a third-generation shop selling farsan,
a category in Gujarati cuisine encompassing things eaten as
snacks, as 'time-pass', to quote a local observer, sometimes part
of a meal, sometimes not. Bakulbhai Shah and his brother
Gaurang now run the business they inherited from their father,
whose sudden death brought them back to India from their
engineering studies in the United States. 'The Mumbai shop
was set up in 1936. Before this, my grandfather, Hiralal Kashilal

Bhajiawala, used to make bhajias in Surat. He was a famous chef and his speciality was kandbhajias. He would be called for community feasts and in those days very few places had halls so people would sit on the roadside and eat. Then, when the main meal would start, my grandfather would be paraded before the people who were seated and they would be told that he was the one who had made the kandbhajias. His salary for this would be one shawl and one guinea (gold, 8 grams, from England). He really prospered. Then there was a split in the family and my grandfather came to Mumbai. By then it was just him and my father because my grandmother had passed away. It was 1936. My grandfather took a loan of 5000 rupees and started the shop. He sent my father to the US to study electrical engineering. He was the first Indian student to become an electrical engineer from Syracuse. I am the third generation in this business. My grandfather was illiterate. He could only sign his name. And he didn't believe in banks. He dealt only in cash. He bought in cash and paid in cash. Once a week the mehtaji (bookkeeper) would come home and all the traders would be paid. All the money was kept in a huge tijori in the house.'

Apart from streamlining procedures, the brothers have changed very little. Though they deliver farsan all over the city, the shop remains the anchor of the business and there are no branches. There are over fifty items, including bhajias, but we're here for the dhokla in its various addictive versions, jalebis or khandvi, one of the glories of Indian cuisine. (My failure to master the khandvi, no matter how many lessons Gujarati cooks including Bakulbhai have given me over the last fifty years, makes me aware that sometimes the simplest things take a lot of practice to be perfect and that perhaps it helps to have Gujarati genes.) There are specific chutneys for morning and evening and both are made from green papaya. The morning chutney is made with papaya 'boiled and cooked with mirchi, besan, jaggery, imli, salt and haldi 'which go well with gantias and jalebis that people tend to eat in the morning. The evening chutney is papaya with dalia, red chilly, jaggery, imli and salt, just mixed together—no cooking—and eaten with bhajias.' Always popular is the Gujarati favourite, undhiyu, a vegetable stew of papdi, brinjal, purple yam, sweet potato, a Surti cucumber, all grown around Surat and sent to Mumbai every day by rail. In the winter months there's ponk, green sorghum and 'heaty' sweet preparations such as salam pak made with spices, herbs, seeds, edible gum and adadiya pak with a Bengal gram base. I haven't been to Mumbai in the winter months, so I've never tasted ponk, a seasonal green wheat preparation. Parsi cuisine, however, has incorporated vasanias, the name for these heating sweets. Chatting with Bakulbhai, so generous with information and tastes, makes the perfect ending to the Bhuleshwar walk. By now it starts getting dark, so we call it a day and look for a taxi. This is the short, edited version of our walk. With digressions, such as visits to the pearl stringer, it can take hours more. We can no longer count on people and shops being there forever. Gone is the animal-trappings stall on Kika Street, gone is Ben Percy, gone is the bird-food shop at the Panjrapol entrance to Madhav Bag, and gone is the Nylon Museum on CP Tank Road with its brown brassieres arranged in a chevron pattern.

Our Null Bazaar excursion is as much cultural as it is a food-related expedition and we usually combine it with a foray to Chor Bazaar, the area's best-known source of junk and antiques. My father used to be sent to Chor Bazaar in his youth by his chemistry teacher at St. Xavier's School, a Father Hoogwerf, to buy second-hand laboratory equipment. Later on, he took me with him to look at furniture and antiques, but we never ventured beyond Mutton Street, the main thoroughfare of Chor Bazaar. My Null

Bazaar wanderings began in the early 1970s when my curiosity about what lay beyond Chor Bazaar needed to be satiated.

Once more, we start at Badshah Cold Drink Depot and take a taxi to Null Bazaar along Mohamedally Road, less crowded now that there's a flyover, turning left at V.P. Road (Vallabhbhai Patel Road) and stopping at the Mumbai Lungi Mart, not a food destination but a fine place to look for presents of cotton lungis. Null Bazaar is often ignored in favour of Chor Bazaar across the main road along Mutton and its cross streets, but it's well worth a circuit, even if we haven't come here to buy mutton, which some say is the best in the city. We start to the left of the Lungi Mart, following the line of vendors selling appealingly displayed fruit, one of the glories of Null Bazaar, until we come to the main market building. You can find vegetables here, and they're fine, but rarely as spectacular as in Bhuleshwar and Matunga, which cater to discerning vegetarian shoppers. Lyla and I like doing a round of Null Bazaar just to keep up with what's the same and what's new. The perimeter of Null Bazaar is even more active than the market building itself. One side has kitchen and tableware, including two fine stalls of unglazed earthenware surahis and pot-bellied matkas with little taps that customers come from all over the city to buy. The other side has handmade scissors and knives, paan-chewing paraphernalia, frankincense, agarbatti and kumkum stalls, supplies for Hindu pujas as well, along with brooms, cordage and stacks of leaf plates big and small, now sadly being elbowed out by more modern paper and plastic.

My food quests in this area are across the street on the edge of Chor Bazaar—the samosa shop on Saifee Jubilee Street where the samosas aren't noteworthy but the samosa pattis are exceptional. These are the skins of Muslim or Mumbai-style samosas, those flat, shatteringly crisp triangles filled with meat, vegetable or egg fillings. The strips are made right in front of you by floury lads rolling out large, flat discs of flour and water dough, baking them on iron tawas and separating the layers, and cutting and stacking them in neat bricks. I bring these back to the US with me when possible because finding them here in San Francisco isn't always easy and making them at home is difficult. I did it once. This type of samosa seems to be fading away in favour of the humpy Punjabi one which holds better. People sigh and reminisce when I ask what's happened to the samosas of yesteryear. Our other destination, past tables laden with cooling sticky red halwa studded with nuts, is near Taj Ice Cream on Saifee Ambulance Lane. The present owners have been in the business of hand-churned ice cream for over 120 years. They use real fruit, not synthetic flavours, and are deeply committed to their craft. My favourite flavours are the ones you don't find in the US—sitaphal and chiku. On a recent rainy afternoon visit, all they had until the evening was strawberry. It was the best strawberry ice cream I've ever had, and from now on, all others will be judged against it and will be found wanting.

If we've combined this excursion with one to Chor Bazaar on a Sunday, we might be ready to leave, but if it's a weekday, it's worth walking a block or two ahead on the main road to Gol Deol, a Shiva temple right in the middle of the road. The area around here is a wholesale spice and grain market where I used to buy cassia leaves and daggad phul (a lichen, *Parmelia perlata*) to use in our Parsi dhanajiru masala, but now you get them both in the US. While we're in this quarter of town, we often end with a side excursion to Gama Rotiwala, also known as the Decent Tandoor Bakery, a short taxi ride away on Dimtimkar Marg in Nagpada, right in the red light district. Here's where you find the most delicious flat bread shaped and slapped into the tandoor to order, while you marvel at the beauty and precision of the young bakers' movements. (Because the shop is almost back to back with a synagogue, the same tandoori roti is sold as Jewish bread, a lovely example of Mumbai's practical-minded ecumenical ways.) Fragrant stacks of these rotis wrapped in newspaper and tied with string make a great present for Mumbai friends who never venture into these parts of town. I've even brought them back with me to the US where they keep beautifully for nearly two weeks. A venerable old man used to go on rounds with them and for years my mother bought a bundle a week and had a crisped triangle for breakfast with one of WIT's jams. I happened to be in Mumbai when he announced that he wasn't going to be able to come any more, that he was too old and it was too hard to haul himself around the city, but he did hand over a card with an address in Nagpada.

It was Lyla who introduced me to Matunga Market. For me this place is a double thrill, the combination of Mumbai and South India, my two muluks. I spent my childhood until the age of fifteen in various parts of South India, and I still yearn for the sights, tastes and smells so deeply embedded in my memory. Matunga is a residential and commercial area inhabited by people from all parts of the South, and by Gujaratis. The newsmagazine Lyla writes for, *Front Line*, is owned by The Hindu group, based in Chennai, so she has a direct line to South Indian connoisseurship in food and drink and knows exactly where to go. It's been twenty years since we had our first excursion there and each one since has been as thrilling as the last. This is a place I want to go to with ten stomachs or ten teenage boys with unappeasable appetites because Matunga is the mecca of South Indian food—whether it's 'meals', which means vegetables, rice and so forth, or 'tiffin', a term as all-embracing as the Gujarati 'farsan'.

We can start our walk at the market itself, but we often take a taxi to King's Circle where tree-lined roads radiate outwards. Several of the best-known Matunga food destinations are right on or just off King's Circle. Mysore Concerns sells coffee beans from Karnataka, ground to order, and also ghee from Coimbatore, which I must get the next time. Anand Bhavan, Mysore Café and Café Madras, all big Matunga magnets, are on King's Circle too, and I can't bear it that we can't have something at every one of them. In keeping with Mumbai's ecumenical culture, this is where you'll find popular Koolar, not South Indian, but one of the few remaining Irani restaurants in Mumbai. Our destination might be the Idli House where we choose the more esoteric of the offerings—idlis bundled in kewra or jackfruit leaves. Idlis come with chutneys, podi, a powdered chutney sometimes called gunpowder, ghee or coconut oil depending on the idli of your preference, and sambar as well. Filter coffee is a must in small stainless steel tumblers resting in bowls. This is the real thing, not the cheating variety that uses instant coffee and makes a big show of pouring back and forth.

We backtrack and get onto Telang Road which takes us past Mani's, where the food is from the Palakkad region of Kerala, near the Tamil Nadu border. Mani's offers both meals and tiffin, and if you're lucky enough to be in Matunga at Onam, the meals are extra special, and some day I hope the timing will be in our favour. Mani's is always filled with happy eaters. Like all the restaurants discussed here, Mani's is a no-nonsense place where the food comes first and the atmosphere is provided by the buoying sight of people enjoying their meal. As you approach the Matunga Post Office, you pass people making birds and flowers out of palm leaves, and then walk past a line of flower shops, some of them festooned with elephant-sized garlands fashioned out of jasmine and roses different in style

and construction from the Bhuleshwar Phul Galli variety. Other
vendors sell strands of scented flowers to be worn in the hair or
around the wrist.

Giri Stores, right at the corner, is a hub of Matunga with all the
paraphernalia of a Hindu South Indian cultural life, whether one
is from Kerala, Karnataka, Andhra Pradesh, Telangana or Tamil
Nadu. I've bought books there on South Indian cooking, and
the chatty and informative owner has kindly procured coconut
ladles for me when I neglected to buy them in Kerala. In the
front, there are perforated stencils for making auspicious chalk
impressions on floors. These are different from our Parsi ones
which don't depict cows, snakes or elephants. Going past stalls
selling household linen, saris, lungis, mundus and angavastrams,
we reach Kanara Stores, the headquarters of Ayurvedic medicines
and other hard-to-find items from the South. A dark, cool place
with handsome wooden bins and cupboards, Kanara Stores is
one of those place-that-time-forgot shops you hope will go on
forever. This is where you might find a dark, medicinal forest
honey, the kind we love, or superior jaggery, or where Lyla will
buy tali powder for her hair. We are tempted to linger and take
up too much of Mr Baliga's time with endless questions. Across
the street are stalls selling snacks like the addictive plantain chips
of Kerala, and interspersed amongst them are the utensil shops.
If you're looking for a coffee filter or an idli steaming vessel, go
no further. I've bought little spouted vessels for drizzling oil and a
puttu (steamed rice and coconut roll) steamer—a metal (formerly
bamboo) cylinder sitting on a vessel to hold the steaming water.
At any utensil shop, here or in Bhuleshwar, the assistants will
happily inscribe your name on the object. We take this for
granted, but my friends in the US beam with pleasure.

The market itself is a building with shops selling food, clothes,
grains and provisions (I'm always hunting for coconut vinegar

from Kerala), but it's the scene outside that's a spectacular carnival
of vegetables. Most of the vegetables you see in Bhuleshwar are
found here, with the addition of many items favoured by people
from the South—tubers like hausa potato and manioc; banana
stems and flowers; many varieties of bananas and, of course,
their leaves for use as plates or wrapping; melon-like golden
cucumbers; leafy greens in season; fresh, green peppercorns;
skinny rat-tailed radishes called mogri; fresh turmeric and
tender young ginger. This is one of the most exciting vegetable
scenes I've ever experienced, and it never disappoints in any
season at all. After the vegetables come a line of fruit sellers with
conventionally elegant displays of seasonal fruit, but nothing to
equal the wild extravaganza of the vegetable section. If enough
time has gone by between the tiffin at Mani's or the Idli House,
we go around the back of the market building to one of my
favourite restaurants in the world: A. Rama Nayak's Udipi, Shri
Krishna Boarding (since 1942), the parent concern of the Idli
House, serving the vegetarian food of Mangalore.

We climb up, look at the queue which might be horrendous
on a Sunday and buy tokens—one price for a 'limited' meal
meaning they don't come around with second helpings, or a
full meal which is the same but with unlimited quantities and
a sweet thrown in. Both categories are served on a banana leaf.
This is not a place for lingering. They want you in, well fed, and
out, so even if the corridor is full, it's rarely a long wait. Not only
the food but the whole experience is well worth a little patience.
The service is elegantly choreographed so that you are served
your meal within minutes—vegetables, perhaps aviyal, sambar,
puris or chapatis plus rice, along with the addictively refreshing
South Indian buttermilk seasoned with ginger, green chillies and
curry leaves. I love this place. Signs and leaflets tell you exactly
how they want you to behave and rather than being offensive,

this gives you a sense of the owners' ferocious commitment
to feeding you well. We need to walk off this delicious lunch
so off we go prowling again. Chheda Stores, a snack and dry
fruit shop across the road, is a great coming together of the
two major population groups of Matunga Gujaratis and South
Indians, though the emphasis is on Gujarat here with a vat of
undhiyu, a papdi stew traditionally made in a buried clay pot. If
the line was too impossibly long at Rama Nayak, we might end
up at Ramashray opposite the market—perhaps more coffee for
me, tea for Lyla and one of their conical plain dosas that are
served Chinese hat fashion. We've been in Matunga several
hours but we've barely scratched the surface. Some day, I want
to find a hotel near Matunga and spend a week exploring and
eating and then colonize a friend's kitchen with a carload of
Matunga produce and City Lights' fish and seafood.

My friend Vikram Doctor, a journalist with *The Economic Times*
who writes about food and food-related issues, told me about
the City Lights Market not far from Matunga, in Dadar. This is
the market I know the least and would like to know much better
having been there just twice: once with Lyla when the monsoon
emptied itself all over us but which didn't dampen the lively
scene in this fish market of all fish markets, and another time,
recently, with Vikram. He is a regular here with his favourites
among the spirited, don't-mess-with-me divas whose repartee is
as sharp as their long curving knives. There's a section off to the
right for freshwater fish so loved by Bengali cooks, and the main
one is an education on what's available in local waters—from
the lowly but delicious bombil or boomla, the Bombay duck, to
the wildly extravagant slippers and spiny lobsters (scyllariadic).
There are some unusual wild greens in the wet season, Vikram
tells me, and also meat, eggs and all the rest of the things you
expect to find, but the main draw is the fish.

Almost fifty years of market prowling and there's still the sense that one lifetime will not be enough to plumb the depths of all of Mumbai's markets, to revisit the familiar and see what's new. Each visit now brings the realization that all the dense richness and texture of street life as we see it now might not go on much longer. In a few years, the area around Null Bazaar will be transformed. Wooden buildings will be replaced with a forest of skyscrapers. There are murmurs that Bhuleshwar, too, might be subjected to what's known as cluster development. Promises are made to accommodate existing businesses, but I wonder what will happen to the vulnerable informal sector. The artist's rendering of the Bhendi Bazaar of the future, encompassing the areas we have wandered through, do not show street vendors or those micro-enterprises selling perhaps just wild berries in a gunny sack, or green chillies and limes threaded together against the evil eye, or wandering sellers with their portable cane stands. It's the informal sector that provides both a living and sustenance for the poor, it's the informal sector that contributes so much life and character to our cities, and it's the informal sector that's most at risk, powerless and victimized by schemes and regulations that equate progress with the sterile anonymity of urban life in the West. One can only hope that the spark and spirit that suffuse the streets of Mumbai will find new and completely unexpected expression in the city's high-rise future.

Chilli High

BULBUL SHARMA

It was a gloomy, wet morning in 1965 when my mother landed
in England. She was nervously clutching in her hand a red
velvet bag. It contained her precious gold jewellery, her tulsi
beads, and six red chillies. Now, almost fifty years later, I am
doing the same thing. In my luggage there are five packets of
dried red chillies along with home-made 'chat masala' and
'panch phoren'. Sniffer dogs eye me suspiciously at the airport
but then go away since they are not sure what this heady, nose-
tickling aroma means.

Things have changed from the days my mother travelled. Now
you can buy red chillies in London quite easily, but they do not
contain the same flavour as our home-grown ones. Deep ruby
red with a hint of orange running along the sides, our chillies
are pungent and can set your tongue on fire with the first bite.
They will bring tears of joy to your eyes and clear your head.

Like most Indians, I am addicted to chillies and cannot do
without them. At home there is no problem since green chillies

come free along with a bunch of fresh coriander when one buys vegetables from the market, but when I have to travel abroad, the scene gets dismal. I can last about three days without tasting a green chilli but after that I am like a demented person searching for anything that will give me a chilli high. At first I thought this was a family trait confined only to our clan, but gradually I found that there are hundreds of fellow Indians who suffer from withdrawal symptoms when they are in a place where red or green chillies are nowhere to be found. Over the years I have made friends with the unlikeliest of people, the only thing connecting us being our relentless search for a chilli fix. 'Have you got any left?' a bank manager hisses in to my ears. I ignore him. 'Only half but I can share it three ways,' replies a professor who is more generous than me, furtively digging into his briefcase.

My adventures with the chilli began when I was a student in Moscow during the bleak Soviet period. The only vegetable you saw there was the symbol of working-class pride—the humble cabbage. Huge football-sized cabbages, pale and translucent as jade, were served to us everyday for lunch and dinner, either boiled, baked in lard or burnt crisp. The burnt dish was the best since we could not taste the cabbage at all in the cinders, especially if you added lots of salt and pepper. A bit of tomato ketchup would have helped, but those were the days when the Russians hated all things American and ketchup was a bad word and you could be fined for uttering it.

As I ate this burnt offering which the fertile land of Mother Russia had produced, I would remember my grandmother's finely shredded green cabbage dish served with hot poories. Tears would roll down my cheeks as I recalled the single green chilli sitting on top of the delicious cabbage like a tiny emerald glittering on a crown. My fellow students thought I was crying because I loved the Soviet cabbage so much and would generously heap more on my plate. Then, one day, I told them the truth.

'Chillies ... you want chillies?' asked my roommate, a lovely dark-eyed girl from Georgia. 'I will get you some. My grandmother grows them in the Kalkhos (a collective farm). She is not allowed to, but she grows them all the same.'

It took Elena quite a while to get through to her grandmother since there was no phone in her village and the postal services were erratic. But one day, just when I had given up all hope, a small parcel arrived. The hostel warden, a giant of a woman with a black moustache and mean eyes, called Elena to her office. She took me along for moral support.

'What is in this packet?' growled our warden staring at Elena and then turned to smile at me ferociously, looking like the famous wolf in grandmother's clothes. They had instructions from high above to be polite to foreign students.

'Chillies, Comrade Galina Petrovna,' said Elena.

'Chillies ... from where? You know food from outside is forbidden?'

'They are from my grandmother's Kalkhos. I want to show my friend from India that we can grow anything we want,' said Elena, thinking on her feet.

There was a brief pause as the warden unwrapped the parcel, tore the brown paper with her huge fingers and then bit the string off with her bare teeth.

There on the white plastic table lay ten chillies—four red and six green. They had travelled all the way from Georgia by train, then by van to our hostel—from one extreme corner of the mighty Soviet Union to another, yet they looked as fresh as newly picked chillies. The warden shrugged her shoulders and let us go. We ran to our room and I sat down at my desk, took out a packet of salted biscuits and ate one whole green chilli as my friend Elena watched me, smiling like a proud mother duck watching her duckling nibble a strand of weed.

My next trip abroad was to France sometime in 2005, and I took a bagful of chillies with me this time. Not a pretty velvet bag like my mother had carried, but a plain plastic one that would keep the chillies fresh. I was going to be there for ten days so twelve chillies would do if I rationed myself strictly. It was not easy, I learnt very soon, to smuggle chillies into a smart restaurant in Paris. The waiters have eyes as sharp as fishing eagles and can spot a tiny speck of unknown substance on your plate from far away.

'Wat iss theeze?' he sniffed and pointed to an innocent green chilli lying by my plate.

Everyone at our table stopped talking and stared at me.

'A chilli ...' I stammered. You are not going to let yourself be intimidated by a French waiter, I said to myself, and thought of my Bengali great-grandmother who had travelled to Shimla in 1920, braving the imperial British Police who were extremely suspicious of native travellers and their assortment of bundles. They threw away the jars of pickles and garam-masala. My grandmother must have carried a bag of red chillies with her.

'Today is Tuesday, the 12th of July. We Indians have to eat one green chilli on this very auspicious day,' I said, thankful that there were no other Indians sitting at our table.

Today I can eat green or red chillies with French food brazenly and nobody raises an eyebrow. In fact, very often my friends ask if they can taste one too and I have to grudgingly offer them one. The French have come a long way and now even offer fresh oysters with chilli and garlic.

Chillies too have come a long way since and now you can easily find them all over Europe. London, of course, is the best place to find chillies and even the smallest supermarket will have them tucked away on a shelf next to garlic and fresh ginger. In England there are annual chilli fairs with thousands of people showing off their home-grown chilli produce. You can buy chilli chocolate which is really delicious, chilli ice cream which tastes foul, and chilli biscuits which is the best laxative you can have besides our very own Pudin Hara.

While one part of England celebrates chillies with style and innovative recipes, there are places where no one has ever tasted a chilli.

In the Outer Hebrides which lies beyond Scotland, a chilli is an exotic and almost mythical thing. It is almost like a Yeti—something everyone has heard about but never seen. I discovered this fact when I travelled to this remote area a few years ago. At our hotel, an old and elegant wooden fishing lodge, they had only ever seen four people from India and they had never tasted a chilli. 'I have seen one growing in my friend's green house. He won a prize for this plant this year in the rare exhibit section,' said the girl behind the bar. She must have seen the greedy look in my eyes because she very kindly offered to take me there.

The town, if you can call it that, had about eleven houses, three pubs and one fire station. 'We have never had a fire as far as I can remember but we like to have the fire brigade. It gives our town something to look at,' the girl said as we drove through the amazingly beautiful landscape of vast blue lakes and rolling golden hills. There was not a building for miles. I felt I was the last Indian left on earth and suddenly began to get a panic attack. I longed desperately to be in Lajpat Nagar eating chat sprinkled lavishly with red chilli powder.

The chilli plant was displayed proudly on a high table in the middle of the green house. The leaves shone as if polished lovingly every day. Four slender green chillies lurked among the leaves. My mouth began to water. The owner said he had managed to get the plant from Mexico and it had survived three harsh winters. He had also grown a few baby chilli plants from the original mother plant. He showed me these little, fragile green stems, fretting over them like an anxious mother over her new-born baby. 'Hope they will be all right in the winter. I have a special lamp for them since we do not get daylight for more than four or five hours in the winter,' he said, frowning with worry.

'Chillies know how to survive. They are tough plants,' I said to him in a soothing voice since he looked really distraught. 'They came to India with the Portuguese who brought them from South America. I have seen them growing happily in flower pots in London pubs.'

'Yes, but what about our cruel winters? They will die. I hope I can get a new plant and start all over again,' said the chilli gardener in a gloomy voice and turned his back to me, probably to hide his tears.

Then I did something I will always be ashamed of all my life. I reached out and plucked one green chilli. I quickly hid it in my bag and left the green house.

As all thieves say, 'I could not control myself. It was a crime of passion.'

As soon as I had swallowed the stolen chilli with a soggy cucumber sandwich, I made a mental note to send six packets of chilli seeds to the unfortunate green-house owner whom I had so shamelessly robbed. A month later, when he replied to thank me for the seeds, he very gallantly did not mention the loss of one precious green chilli from the mother plant.

As I hunt for chillies in remote supermarkets in various cities all over the world, grabbing the packets before anyone else can, I wonder what we ate before the Portuguese brought chillies to

India. There was black pepper I am told by chefs, and that is why most traditional Indian cuisines do not use red chillies, tomatoes and onions, also brought to India by the Portuguese. Kashmiri food is cooked mostly with dry ginger powder called saunth, aniseed powder or saunf, cloves and cinnamon. Bengali food uses panch phoren which is a mixure of fenugreek, aniseed, black cumin, mustard seed and cumin, and Bengali cooks mistrust the delicious rich red Punjabi gravy made with tomatoes, onions and garlic-ginger paste since it contains two ingredients not known to ancient Indians—tomatoes and onions.

To return to the chilli, it arrived in India only sometime in the sixteenth century and stayed confined to in and around Goa for a few years before spreading out far and wide all across the country. Now Assam has the fire-breathing tiny chillies, the strongest of them all—one bite can take the roof off your palate, while Andhra Pradesh is the biggest producer of this plant which belongs to the genus Capsicum. Chillies may have come to us just a few hundred years ago but people have been eating or cooking with chillies since 7500 BC. I can imagine early man looking at the badly burnt meat, the tough root vegetables and asking his woman, 'This food is so bland—do you have any chillies?'

Recent research by botanists show that the chilli plant was widely cultivated in Mexico more that 6000 years ago. Columbus was one of the first Europeans to taste a chilli when he travelled to Central America and he brought some back to Spain. A physician who had also gone to South America with him wrote at great length about the medicinal properties of the chilli and soon it became a plant everyone wanted to grow, taste and trade in. The Spanish claim they told the Portuguese about the chilli plant and introduced them to its virtues, but the Portuguese deny that and say their canny traders knew about this wonderful plant long before the Spanish did.

What is certain is that Goa was the first place in India to grow chillies in abundance—otherwise how could they have made the most delicious vindaloo in the world?

As I write this piece I am sitting in a remote town in Ireland with no chillies to be found anywhere unless I catch a bus and travel three hours to Dublin. I have one dried, sad-looking red chilli left in my suitcase which I have been nibbling on at every meal like a hungry rat gnawing on a piece of old cheese, watched suspiciously by the other people at the table. Soon I will start getting hallucinations and see chillies marching everywhere along with pink elephants.

I suddenly hear a strange sound and look out of the window. There is a large rose-ringed parakeet screeching outside. In its big, clumsy toe it holds a bright red chilli. Like a person in a trance, I get up from my chair and slowly reach out of the window. All is fair in love and war they say, and though this is neither, I snatch the chilli out of the bird's claw and begin chewing it. The wise, old parakeet recognizes a fellow Indian and keeps quiet. Then it ruffles its wings and gives me a look that says, 'If I had another chilli I would have given it to you,' and I know the bird is a friend from my past life and I was a chilli-eating parakeet once.

The Food Wicket

ROCKY SINGH AND MAYUR SHARMA

We stepped out of the house and up to the roof to get some fresh air. This power outage was going to be a long one and we could see the transformer at the corner shooting sparks as a crowd slowly gathered around it. Luckily, the wind was blowing the other way and monsoon evenings in south Delhi weren't too bad then. I lay down on a sheet which I had brought with me and looked up at the stars. Like all children the universe was an exciting place for me, a mysterious place. Bats flew across the bright night sky and somewhere close by an owl screeched. Just another rainy evening in Delhi. 'Don't sleep yet,' my mother called out, 'dinner's almost ready.' 'I won't Ma—I'm hungry,' I said before going back to my ... well, evening dream.

Seems like another world, doesn't it? Fresh air, stars in the sky and owls calling. But south Delhi wasn't so bad not so long ago. The early 1970s were a time of wonder for me. The world was a much simpler place. There was no TV to speak of and the little black-and-white box we had usually showed Krishi Darshan and a range of shows that we could neither understand nor had much interest in. I would stumble into the house covered in sweat and dirt from our taxing games of football or cricket or just chasing other kids round and round our little colony park playing cut the cake or chain. Wonderful games both. As soon as I entered home, I would be handed a big glass of milk usually with a little Rooh Afza or Horlicks in it. This was a special treat I looked forward to while walking back from the park. It would go down fast, then a quick bucket bath and jumping into my pyjamas and it was time for dinner. Like most other households we would eat a little later in the summer due to longer sunlight hours and earlier in the winter due to shorter days. But life was grand and my grandmother made the most amazing food you can imagine. Friday nights were chicken curry nights and those were the big ones. The spices for all the food would come from my uncle who was posted with the Guards in Madras. Except the garam masala, for as my grandma explained, the best garam masala came from Amritsar and that was the one she had grown up eating. I would run into the kitchen as she put the finishing touches to the chicken curry. A kadchee (ladle) full of ghee (good ghee only came from our village Rajpur, in the Hoshiarpur district of Punjab) was heated over a direct flame, sharp tongues of it jumped up as the ghee bubbling up from the kadchee caught fire, a heaped tablespoon of garam masala was sprinkled on the hot ghee and it was immersed sharply into the curry. The aroma—I can still smell it.

The leg pieces were literally the bones of contention between my sister and me (my brother came much later—he is eleven years younger than me) and my mother would settle the debate by saying, 'So what would a gentleman do if a lady wanted the leg piece?' and my sister would get the leg piece. Luckily for me, I have a sister who loves me a lot, not to mention my having mastered a look of misery on being denied food that very few can resist even to this day. So the leg piece, more often than not, found their way back to my plate.

Caramel custard made in a pressure cooker was Friday dessert and still has the power to make a child out of me. I love it. There was always an evening walk after dinner, a gentle stroll when my sister explained important things to my mother while I looked for frogs in the long grass by the side of the road. It was back to bed afterwards and we would listen to *Forces Requests*, an English music show on radio where young lieutenants and captains sent messages to their sweethearts and we snapped our fingers to the catchy beats of rock 'n roll. Ah Fridays ...

I find that when I think back, most of my memories have a food association. My favourite Saturdays were spent in Ambala. Food was always so important to everyone in the old days. Every memory had a food connect. When I think of my paternal uncle's home in Ambala (he lived in the flag staff house and he was the commanding officer there), the memory of a giant kitchen with the aroma of freshly baked cakes for the evening tea comes to mind. I remember my aunt, a diminutive woman, who no one *ever* crossed, walking around directing the staff as they got the tea ready. I was her faithful follower and was rewarded with cake batter, cookies and sponge cakes the likes of which I have never before, or since, eaten. A good sponge cake is a peep into heaven, my friends, and those of you who have eaten one know what I'm talking about. None of that crumbly, dry, light stuff that passes for sponge cake these days for me please. Give me the heavy, butter-laden marvels that I would spend hours watching in the oven, waiting for them to swell. Then a slice of golden spongy goodness with a tall glass of sweet and cold coffee was the highlight of my day. If I had behaved well, it could even be two pieces which were always better than one.

But those Saturday evenings were special. Dinner was a festive occasion and what a feast we would have. I remember my uncle sitting at the head of the table like a giant mountain with eyes that had crow's feet at the edges. He had the look that men of great accomplishment get; luckily he was one of the rare ones who also managed to derive joy from his accomplishments so the conversations at the table would be great fun. Of course, being a lieutenant general, decorum and discipline were to be adhered to at all times and not a single slurp over the soup course or a little burp at the end of the dessert was tolerated. We would all, my two cousin sisters and their younger brother who was quite a bit older than me, be dressed for dinner and the word 'immaculate' comes to mind for the only sort of behaviour that would be acceptable.

The dining room overlooked the garden where giant trees reached for the sky and massive money plant vines wound their way around the trees. The conversation and the laughter and the smell of roast lamb and potatoes are deeply ingrained in my memory. Dessert would usually be ice cream and if we were exceptionally lucky, there would also be hot jalebis from the Ghee ki Jalebi guy near the gun shop in the market. Either way I remember walking the lawns satiated and ready to drop after a long, hectic day of doing what god alone knows little boys do.

The nights were not silent like they are now. There were always the crickets, the frogs and the night birds and because we were in Ambala, the regular shriek of jet engines as fighter planes took off and landed from their evening sorties. Sometimes I would steal a little piece of cake and nibble away at it in bed, taking care not to drop even a crumb for I would get caught.

Sunday was the greatest day ever. Rather than sleep in late I would jump out of bed as soon as my eyes opened. A quick bucket bath and I would be out, walking down the street, to try and get the other boys to play with me. I would stand outside his house and shout 'Mayurrrr' in response to which I would usually get Mayur's dad who would step out into the balcony and say, 'Let him finish his homework and he will join you boys in the park.' A shrug and I would be off, and a shout or three afterwards would yield a small core group of boys who would spread out in all directions like a well-trained army; then more shouts would bring down more boys of all shapes and sizes. The questions were all valid. 'Do you have Samir's bat?', 'Did you get the six wickets from Vikram?', 'Do you have a cork ball or a cricket ball? 'Cause Manoj has a cricket ball, get that and I'll finish breakfast and join you', and a dozen other such gems. In 15-20 minutes, which always seemed like a lifetime, a small army of determined-looking boys would be marching to the colony park. Cows would be cleared out, dogs would be chased, dung would be gathered with any implement at hand and thrown over the railing, little stones would be removed from the 'pitch' and the eldest among us would walk over and dig in the wickets at one end and then, with severe advise from all gathered, measure out the twenty-two yards between stumps. Captains would assert themselves and then the toss to choose teams would take place. This was serious business, mind you, and could mean glory or heartache for the whole day.

Once the teams were decided on, the game would begin in earnest, and about half an hour into the game is when the first breaks would start to get taken. Why were these important? Let me tell you.

Mayur and I grew up, and to this day live, in a small place called Uday Park in Delhi which was a small colony where plots of land were given to the families who had lost a member to the war of 1971. The resulting demographic therefore was a lot of working ladies who were the heads of the family and a lot of kids without fathers who had only each other to really learn from. Ours was a world where every noble cause was real and not just a 'lesson'. Being a 'good friend' was the most critically important thing in the world and letting a friend down was a blasphemy of unspeakable proportions. We told each other the usual stories all kids in India hear and we were the characters in them. We were Ram and Lakshman and the mighty army that marched to Lanka. We looked out for one another and it was us versus everyone else. We taught each other lessons in loyalty, goodness and strength. We stuck together and our support structure was us. The older boys were responsible for the younger ones; the younger ones in turn respected the older ones. The girls who played football and cricket with us were pals and those who played with dolls were to be avoided at all costs. When the chips were down, it was either turn to a father who was not there or a mother who was the sole bread earner and was away. Neither worked for us and so we evolved the greatest bond it had been our honour and good luck to evolve: the bond of friendship that runs deeper than most relationships.

No matter what the problem was, we were always there for each other. If someone broke a window while playing cricket, we all stood in silence with the breaker and got screamed at by the uncle or aunty whose house had suffered the damage. If someone was not well, we all accompanied him or her to the local doctor. If someone was falling behind in studies, one or more of us brought them up to speed; we exchanged comics and books till we were all readers, we discussed ideas with our naive black-and-white wrongs and rights and became the people we admired. To this day we do it: a sort of one for all and all for one. The advantages of having this whole group of people to back you are many but the greatest joy of all was, is and will always be, the food!

We were a little India crammed into one small area. There were 'aunties' from all across the country. War isn't selective— from Kashmir to Kerala, from Gujarat to Arunachal they were all there. Do you begin to see why the breaks were so important?

A quick first break took me to hot Idlis and Dosai. This is when it paid to have friends, and I had many. I would ensure Mayur was on my team as his daadi made the most amazing paranthas; while we waited for our turn to bat, it was a matter of minutes to run down and ask her to make some paranthas for us. Between paranthas we would run back and forth from the park to see the status of the game because batting too, after all, was important. Once into the fielding part it was a little tougher to get away but since we were all solid pals, the batting team provided a substitute fielder as we ran to Joyjit's house for some machher jhol. We would be endlessly hungry due to all the running we did and lunchtime was an important occasion when everyone discussed what was being made in everyone else's homes. My favourite was, and to this day continues to be, Pinku's house where Raj Aunty would make the most amazing Kashmiri Pandit food. Yes, it was all vegetarian as she was a vegetarian but the kathal she made was better than any mutton you will ever eat. Her daughter, who was my classmate in school, has gone on to become world famous and I'm talking about Dr Shikha Sharma of Nutri Health Systems who is the best-known face of nutrition in India. Luckily for me, Shikha always ate small quantities which meant more for me. Once in a while, I still get that much-loved tiffin with a few of my favourite things in it. But that's another story.

It could be mutton made at Puneet's house by Mona Aunty, or Bhopali dishes made at Bobby's place by Baby Aunty or those amazing stuffed karelas that were made by Malti Aunty who is Manoj's mum, which were almost as good as the chicken curry that Rita Aunty made at Biri's place. The list goes on and the foods were magical. Post lunch we would be forced to rest for an hour as siestas were still the order of the day back then. This is when the fruit situation kicked in. Fruits were not things that were bought in ones and twos from the market. Fruits were sent in by the crate from family members who owned orchards, and were brought in by family that would travel to Delhi from ancestral villages. Mango season particularly comes to mind here. Buckets filled with water and topped to the brim with mangoes were left in a corner somewhere. In a couple of hours the mangoes would be cool and we would eat them literally by the bucket. Plums, pears and litchi were my favourites and came from our place in Dehradun. One family could never finish those quantities but help was always close at hand. Now you may begin to see a pattern emerge as to why Mayur and I are such good friends to this day. We would help other people find solutions to their food-storage problems—we were always like that.

Cricket would resume at four in the afternoon, and only mad dogs and us were out playing. Kids who lived close to the park were responsible for cold bottles of water being brought to the park during drink intervals. But this was only till 5 p.m. After five the party would start in earnest. We could hear 'Garaaaaaammmmmmm' from a mile which meant the choley bhature wallah was coming. I kid you not when I say that you will not find such delicious choley bhaturey anywhere else even today. The guys who come now are the sons of the old man who made his rounds when we were kids, and the cholas still taste exactly the same. The game would be suspended and those who had money would buy and those who did not would beg for a loan which was always extended.

Memories are a funny thing since Mayur and I were always friends. Here are his, very similar to mine.

In the midst of home renovations a little while ago, I discovered a memory-laden treasure—my daadi's sil-batta—the traditional Indian kitchen stone grinder comprising a large, heavy slab of stone (sil) and a smaller grinding stone (batta), usually cylindrical. Memories resurrected the faint aromas of coriander, mint, assorted whole spices, ginger, garlic and a host of other ingredients that went into making fresh chutneys, masala mixes and wet seasoning for dishes. All this often done each time for each meal!

Rocky and I had this long post-dinner balcony conversation about our memories, both individual and shared, from the past four decades (well okay, thirty-eight years!) that we have been friends and lived down the road from each other. We talked of the deliciously tart and spicy, reddish purple kanji that was home brewed by Rocky's grandmother every winter from the juice of black carrots. It stood fermenting in beautiful glass jars alongside others containing a colourful pickled mix of sliced carrots, cauliflower and radishes. All these were prepared from family recipes passed down through the generations. Just down the road my grandmother had her winter-favourite preparation panjiri—wholewheat fried in ghee and sugar with generous handfuls of dried fruits and nuts added to the mix. If there was anything that drove the cold of the winter away, it was daadi's recipes. Similarly, for the devilishly hot summer months of Delhi, there were a host of remedies to battle the heat. Ice-cold lassi (yoghurt blended with water and ice into a frothy, chilled, cooling drink spiced with salt, black pepper and certain 'cooling' herbs/ spices, of which every home had their own little mix), chilled lemon juice and aam panna (tart, chilled juice of raw mangoes mixed with a blend of spices) were the favorites and the amazing thing was that these were not on offer just in your own home. We grew up in a small 144-home colony where everyone knew everyone else and we children were always welcome in each other's homes. Landing up unannounced at a friend's place meant you were sure to get some

goodies to eat and drink as a treat. This same group of kids–and
there were more than thirty of us with a gap of about 5-7 years
between the eldest and the youngest–played together every day and
had many a food adventure in-between.

The colony park was the centre of our world. We played many
games of pithoo (seven tiles), football, cricket, even baseball, with great
fervour and passion. Breaks were not planned and they happened
as soon as one of the many street-food vendors went by on a cycle
or a cart, calling out their product in a distinct voice. Most of the
neighbourhood gang, now grown up and with kids of their own, are
living all over the world but, even now, thirty years later, we bet they
can still imitate their favourite vendor's cry. Rocky's favourite was
the 'Bheeeeeeellpuriiiwaaalaaaa' and mine was 'Kaale kale phaalse!'
The range of street food on offer was incredible and in a single day
vendors went by with ice cream, bhelpuri, chole kulche, pink cotton
candy, sliced discs of chilled sugar cane, tart purple jamun and phalse
to name a few. What made it even more fun was that the preparation
of most of these treats took place right in front of you and could be
customized to your liking. Rocky, for example, always wanted extra
spice and chilli in his savoury treats. Each vendor had his style of
preparation and quirks–the kind-hearted bhelpuri vendor for one was
always a sucker for a sad face and a promise to pay the next day. I
still remember my old friend, the ice cream vendor, who was christened
Doodhnath, the Lord of Milk, because he extended the maximum
credit and would just keep gently reminding us to pay up without
ever mentioning a word to our parents. In later years, when I was
all grown up, he would still swing by and I would buy tonnes of ice
cream which I never ate, just so that in some small measure I could
try and repay his generosity. In true style this little man (he seemed
like a giant when I was little but he was all of 5 ft tall) with a giant
heart trumped me when he met my children for the first time. He
smiled a wide, now almost toothless, smile and whipped out my old

favourite—a mango duet—to hand out to my kids and ... he refused to accept any money for it! Such was the caring, kind, generous world we grew up in!

The food thus became not just about the taste but also about the relationships, the triggers and the memories. I have moved on to all sorts of exotic, branded ice creams and gelatos but each bite I take of my favourite treat brings back the yells of laughter, the sweaty hugs of congratulations at a wicket bowled and the memory of a vendor whose large-heartedness allowed us to enjoy his treats. While speaking of relationships, how can I miss out my bua, my father's younger sister who lived with us. Besides being our protector every time we were in trouble with our parents, she was also the greatest sous chef in the world. She learnt from my grandmother but she was a master in her own right. Her pohas (flattened rice flakes stir fried with spices, sliced onions, peanuts, kari leaves and green chillies) for breakfast were always in great demand and even now, three decades later, when she visits us I always beg for at least one such breakfast. She loves that I still remember and with a big smile always obliges. God bless her!

What made all this even more amazing was that back in the day there was no multi-hob cooking ranges with ovens and no fancy one-touch microwaves for quick cooking. Meal after meal comprising dish after dish was churned out from a single hob gas flame and my grandmother preferred it on the ground where she could squat over it and use the whole kitchen floor as an extended counter space. We did have a refrigerator in later years but food was, and still is, cooked fresh for every meal. To this day my father will not eat food that has been in the fridge and needs to be reheated. He doesn't like eating out either while I on the other hand love that. Why you may ask? Well I don't really enjoy cooking and a cook will never be able to add that much-needed flavour of love that I could taste in every bite of home-cooked food. Surprising as it may seem, even today, that ineffable flavour can still be found in many street-food eateries and even in some restaurants offering fine dining because the chefs have become friends and will match our love for eating with their love for cooking. Food always has been about relationships, emotions, memories and about the sheer joy of sharing an experience.

Just recently, I took my young children for football practice and discovered to my delight that there was a mulberry tree (shahtoot) by the side of the field. I was up that tree in a trice, jumping on branches and then hurrying down to pick up the fruit straight off the ground and stuffing it in my mouth uncaring for the purple stains on my fingers, lips and even my t-shirt. That's how we got most of our fruits when we were young and now it seems it's a big deal to 'eat local and only what's in season'. My children were shocked that daddy was eating stuff picked up from the ground but they saw the light when they were boosted up into the lower branches and had a go themselves. I could go on and on and on (you get the picture!), but I can see Rocky jumping up and down waving his hands to get your attention and take you down memory lane back to the day when ...

This is why we are still friends after thirty-eight years. In one word: FOOD.

Let's get back to our game of cricket which would only then be resumed after Doodhnath had gone. Who was this Doodhnath you may ask? He was our legendary ice-cream-trolley-wallah. The man with a cool attitude and a cool solution to all your heat problems. The man with the ice cream. He was also the man with the copy in which he wrote down what we owed him as we had large appetites and very little money. He would be paid on birthdays and other festive occasions when we ran into some money. Sometimes we ran up bills to the tune of a thousand rupees. In today's day and age that would be roughly the equivalent of Rs 10,000 and that, my friends, is a serious amount of money. But Doodhnath never complained, he never said no to anyone and when you finally did clear your bill, he always gave you a mango duet for free.

Cricket was played well past the time when the light faded. Mothers would be out on the streets shouting for the kids to come home before we finally gave in to exhaustion. We would run home, drink cold coffee and quickly bathe for dinner. They would play a movie on TV and it was the biggest thing of all to be able to watch it. We would sit glued to the screen: the ayah and her family would be out front, the neighbours who had no TV would be squeezed in—and the rest of us? We would make place wherever we found it.

The movie would be watched in rapt attention; no one spoke, no cell phone rang, no internet beckoned, there was nothing to do but watch the movie and after a long day it was a relief. Someone would get up to fill water in the cooler now and then when the air got hot.

After the movie finished, everyone would go home. We would eat dinner hurriedly because Sunday desserts were the best. As we finished eating the smell of halwa would fill the air—made with desi ghee this is one of those smells that I associate with the gurudwara on Sunday evenings and my grandmother. Both give me great comfort. We would wolf down the halwa because Sunday was special for being a two-dessert day. We had awesome gulab jamuns and I ate my share quickly because more often than not, a chubby little fellow would walk in at the opportune moment and make an innocent, pleading face. I had nothing to offer him, but my sister loves me a lot and Mayur's 'I'm begging for food' face is almost as good as mine. So he would get his gulab jamuns. We would go for the walk where we would look for frogs. Then we would drop young Mayur home and make our way back. If there was electricity we would sleep in our rooms; if not we would sleep on the roof. We could see a million stars and the fresh air did us good. Sundays were a great day for listening to late-night English music. We heard all the latest hits before hitting the bed...

Game for Food

SALEEM KIDWAI

Looking back half-a-century to the winters of the 1960s, what I remember beyond homework, exams and winter vacations is how the world of food around me changed with the seasons. With the inevitable consequences of the climatic patterns of the southern hemisphere and the migratory pattern of birds, new and exciting food options opened up in rhythmic cycles. And during the early decades of my childhood, visitors from Siberia dictated our main meals through the winter months.

Partisan as I may be to various members of the gourd family, from the month of September I started looking forward to the end of their long, summer reign. The appearance of water chestnuts was an unmistakable sign of more exciting times ahead. On days when a 15-mile drive from Lucknow could take you right into the heart of a village, freshly harvested water chestnuts were available all along the roads, next to the large ponds they had been harvested from, along the route to my grandparents' homes. In those homes there would be fresh sugar cane to chew, fresh green gram to be pinched open off the bush which had been pulled right then out of the soil. In the evening the green gram would be roasted over open wood fires in which, buried deep in the embers, sweet potatoes would be roasting, to be eaten right there, beside the fire.

Back in the city, there were peanuts to be eaten in the warm sun with newspapers spread out to catch the debris. Freshly made translucent red guava jelly, in large transparent jars, is a colourful image in my childhood memories. A snacker's delight, jelly was handy with bread, chapatti, rusk or biscuit, or just by the spoonful. The jelly, supposedly meant to last for the year, ran out in three months. Mealtimes overlapped with picnicking. Lunch was often eaten in the sun, and on very cold nights, plates could be carried closer to the angethi.

Fresh peas were welcome in all their forms. Turnip or beetroot with mutton and sakpaita (dal cooked with the seasonal herb bathwa) were house favourites. Towards the end of winter there woud be the oh-so succulent minced qeema, cooked with rasbharis (crane gooseberries), the bright orange berries adding a sweet and sour touch to the savoury meat. There were also the ever-present halwas—red and purple carrot halwas, pale yellow egg halwa, and fat round pindis made with ghee and sugar and different kinds of flours: golden wheat, besan or green moong. Gifts of these desserts were given and received—no household cooked delicacies only for themselves.

And then there was the omnipotent winter dessert, the rasawal. This was rice cooked overnight in cane juice and often enriched with raisins and other dry fruits. It was a laborious, back-breaking recipe because it required all-night attention—stirring the juice in a large pot over an open fire. Dark foam, which gathered as the dish cooked, had to be constantly removed to obtain the desired light colour in the finished dish. The rasawal was then cooled and filled into round red earthen pots and their covers were sealed with flour dough. The sealed vessel was placed on a straw ring to make it stable and a chord was tied around the neck to make a handle for carrying. The rasawal pots were then ready to be distributed to the households of a large number of deprived relatives now living in urban areas, longing for the taste of home. It would be a brave relative who would agree to carry the pots by train to other relatives in the city. This custom died naturally but after a few comic tragedies. Family lore is full of stories like when a pot of rasawal, while being transported by train, rolled over and cracked open, pouring out its gooey, sticky brown contents all over a crowded three-tier sleeper car.

However, there was one major winter novelty that has left some unusual memories and made the biggest impact on our immediate family: my parents, us four siblings, an aunt, cousins, and sundry other relatives in the extended family.

During the winter months there was the addition of a must-eat protein to our diets—the winged-game, the ducks and birds that my father was shooting every week. These had to be consumed by us, by invited guests, or by those privileged enough to receive gifts of freshly dead birds. For a few months a year, we regressed into the food habits of hunters.

Hunting was a passion for my father. Given the family's feudal background, this wasn't surprising. Yet my father was a city dweller with a city job, but with this one all-consuming indulgence that required feudal means, which he did not always have. As a younger man he had made his fair contribution to depleting the mammalian wildlife, having bagged his share of tigers, panthers, bears and crocodiles. I have memories of only the last big-game hunting trip that took him and his friends away for ten days. Vivid are the details of the preparations that had to be made for the trip, the whole household working overtime. I also remember the clear glass eyes of the large tiger that was the prize from this trip, when it came back from the taxidermist in Kanpur.

Permission to hunt big game had become hard to acquire and the logistics of such an exercise became increasingly difficult, particularly if it was one individual who took upon himself the job of organizing it. The one-day hunting trip was the only option left and my father indulged in this with vengeance for as long as he could. Winter birds from Europe and Central Asia flocked in abundance to the hundreds of jheels then spread across a 50-mile radius of Lucknow. This, rather than the terai of Nepal, became his new hunting ground. In the 1960s he tried to spend every free day that he had on these jheels. After all, how many clay pigeon shooting competitions could one compete in?

He collected around him a group of friends, younger contemporaries and often their relatives, who were happy to join these weekly adventures through the winter months. Some invitees did not own their own guns, and went along for the fun and the picnic. The group varied week to week, for there were many demands for invitations. And beyond this group coalesced a larger group of those who loved to partake of the culinary spoils of this slaughter, in meals that followed these bloody Sundays.

There were two flat-bottomed tub-like boats, large enough to seat at least four people, that were either loaded on to a trailer or tied to the carriers of the vehicles. Jhulli, my father's favoured shikari-guide and boatman, would arrive alone or with an assistant the day before, having scouted around for jheels where there had been a large bird fall. That's where my father would lead his gang of friends the next morning.

Before that, on the night before, the boats were loaded and the guns checked and rechecked. The hard-to-come-by and expensive ammunition was counted, apportioned and arranged in the carry bag. All the hunting and other needs for the next day had to be anticipated. This was routine work for my father's Man Friday, Shabban.

Equally routine was the night of heavy duty for my mother, older sister and cousin in the kitchen because the full-time cook, a man who brooked no-nonsense from anyone, made it clear that these indulgences were not a part of his duties. Fresh food for two-and-a-half meals for about a dozen people had to be ready and packed to go. Tea had to be served to the guests, who turned up before daybreak. The party would gather to leave well before the sun rose so they had the largest possible window of light to get their aim at the birds.

The packed food had to be dry and non-messy, so it was always the same. Breakfast would be roghnitikias (flat, buttered round bread) to be eaten with khaghina (finely scrambled onion omellete), shami kebabs, a potato or vegetable dish, and tea from the thermos. Each delicate roghnitikia took a lot of time to make but was chewed down in a hurry because everyone was eager to get into the boats either to exercise their forefingers or to enjoy the spectacle of a bird being brought down in flight.

My father had a special deck chair made for himself, which fitted firmly in the boat. It even had a foldable sun guard. He settled in there as they set out for the middle of the lake and watched out for birds rising from the water. A close friend of his joked about how, in his later years, he often dozed off and it was only when Jhulli whispered, 'Miyan! Miyan! Birds!' that Miyan would wake up, take aim, bring down two birds from the sky, put his gun down and probably doze off again while Jhulli hurriedly rowed in the direction where the birds had landed.

This operation was crucial and had to be done with speed and accuracy because a lot depended on it. The bird had to be found hopefully with its heart still beating, and fished out for my father to consecrate into halal meat by reciting the words of the kalima while slitting its throat in one swipe, cutting through the carotid artery, jugular vein and windpipe in one motion. The blood thus drained out of the dead bird. However, if the bird was already dead, the exercise was in vain. Such a bird was set aside and the lookout for more birds continued.

By noon, the game bag usually became respectably full, and the hunters took a break for lunch which would be crumbly tikias, or fresh soft paranthas, to go with more of the kebabs and perhaps pasandas or some other dry meat or vegetable preparation.

Some people rested a bit after lunch on durries spread on the banks. Some played cards or just exchanged *shikar* stories. But not for too long because there was the last chance to get some birds against the setting sun. Blood appetites were fairly sated by the time the sun set.

There would be a snack at teatime before the party wound up its innings for the day. Bags were put together. The cars were repacked and the boats were ready to head back to the city—back to the cave with the hunt.

With Father away, the day, almost always a Sunday, was fairly relaxed for the family. It was the day you could do things without the need for his hard-to-get permission, like going to the movies. It was easy to sneak off to a noon movie show without fear and get away with it (unless someone unkindly squealed). But the evening was a show of another kind at home.

My father would sit there in his special low chair with dozens of dead birds lined up in front of him. The birds were counted and the halal and non-halal sections rechecked. This would be the role forced on me even as I stubbornly refused to be a part of it. To my father, masculinity seemed synonymous with the gun, and on one of my forced outings, I had embarrassed him no end in front of his gun-crazy cronies and their progeny when I vividly demonstrated my inability to put a gun together. This public exposure of a family skeleton had so mortified him that from then onwards, much to my relief, he preferred to keep me hidden in the family closet.

I felt like I was being drawn into the dead bird display as revenge. My father knew of, and even encouraged, my love for animals and birds by letting me keep many as household pets. With my interest in birds, according to him, I should relish the opportunity of first-hand intimacy with wild birds. Except that these were dead, stiff, and covered in dried blood. It wasn't easy handling them. Yet I was expected to tell one bird from another and separate them according to their species. There were all sorts of migratory birds in the bag: Pochards, Pintails, Moorhens. There were birds that were rarer, like the Mallard, and these I was urged to take a good look at. When I complained about how difficult it was to really see the plumage under all the caked blood, my father bought me a beautifully illustrated book on birds so I could tell them apart. Pictures of these birds in their prime plumage and full glory only made it worse. The mutilated corpses of such gloriously textured birds looked surreal.

When my chore ended, others took over. The non-halal birds were sent off as gifts to various friends who had no compunction about eating them. Shabban would have to work well into the night to get the remaining birds cleaned without delay, removing innards and de-feathering them.

The rest of the week saw the cooking, serving and consuming of these creatures. Sundays were usually followed by a mid-week dinner for my father's friends. The all-male gatherings naturally centred on food, particularly on the spoils of the last shikar. Cooking standards of the family were well-known, and now there was the added attraction of varied protein.

Not that this new meat was any gourmet's delight. In spite of the rich cooking traditions within the family, there seemed to be a very restricted repertoire for cooking game. The awareness that the meat of every species had to be dealt with differently was fully understood, and that is where the challenge lay. The flesh of these birds was darker and tougher than chicken. Care had to be taken with how dark the onion was to be fried for each bird so as to not make the resultant curry too dark. The fat of different species had different gamey smells which simply had to be countered in different ways. Some needed more yoghurt for tenderizing than others.

Yet, there were only two ways these birds were cooked. First, there was the inevitable qorma, the cut-up bird in a gravy. Second, there was the whole bird in a pot roast, particularly the larger species like Knob Billed Ducks. Inevitably, a variety of different qormas started appearing at the table—the Teal qorma, the Seekh Par (Pintail) qorma or the Murghabi (Waterhen) qorma. The art lay in evolving a perfect recipe for each game bird. Today my elder sister, who was very involved in all consequences of the hunt, still remembers what sort of meat needed what kind of treatment. With so much attention required to perfect the qorma, it wasn't surprising that there was little experimentation with other recipes.

So was the case with the birds that were cooked whole. They were cooked with one basic recipe, with attention given to treating the different birds differently. These meats could never carry off a dinner by themselves. You could not use them in a biryani or make kebabs out of them. You couldn't add seasonal vegetables to them, nor could you do anything more fanciful like a do piyaza. Therefore, there was always a supplement of regular mutton and chicken dishes on the table.

When the party was over, there was still plenty of game for the family and visiting relatives to consume at every meal over the course of the week. Then the next supply of Siberian protein flew in on the coming Sunday. And so it went on from December to February.

Over the years, things began to change slowly. The bags dropped from an easy hundred birds to much smaller numbers. The diminishing supply wasn't unwelcome to us, though it was a source of depression for my father. The composition of the bags too had begun to change. My father had enjoyed downing migratory Siberian ducks and looking at their varied plumage at the end of the day. While he had earlier been snobbish about Moorhens, which he considered local and too easy to hunt, they now began to form a growing percentage of his weekly harvest. He even discovered the culinary delights of the Murghabi qorma.

My father was an impulsively generous man and had been happy to send his non-halal bounty to non-Muslim friends. Soon, this generosity began to pinch as halal meat numbers came increasingly close to single digits. It bothered him enough to consult a maulvi about what constituted halal meat. The maulvi said that since the intention behind the rule was that man should kill only what he wants to eat, the finger on the trigger was just as crucial as the hand on the knife and if the kalima was read when the bird was shot, its meat was halal. Voila! I can't help but speculate what it might have meant if the maulvi had been consulted during the good hunting years—how much more duck meat would we have had to consume? We, with effete Lucknow noses, had never developed a taste for the gamey smell and taste of the fruits of the wild.

I haven't eaten game since my father stopped hunting. I now indulge myself in distant memories, distilled with age and humour, into a flavour of the past, which was as much about food as it was about a way of life.

Floyd's Canteen

FLOYD CARDOZ

I grew up in a middle-class Goan family in Bombay. Dad was educated in England and Mom's family was from Goa. Every day began with breakfast cooked by our full-time cook, Ermine. A day at the Cardoz home would start with Mom and Ermine planning the day's menu; Ermine would then go to the market with a grand shopping list. My entire focus for the day was what was going to be on the menu for my two meals! Early each day, local Kolis would walk our neighbourhood, hawking the day's fresh catch. Every home would bargain and try to get the best price. I was always on the lookout for shrimps, crabs, mackerels and cockles knowing that one of them would be hitting our table that day.

I would complain if my lunch box contained a 'dry lunch': sandwiches made with Britannia sliced bread and local cold-storage cured meats. These were not bad, but were a far cry from the fish curries and fried fish or shellfish I could get at home. Fresh fish was brought in and cleaned and cooked for the day. I would throw a tantrum if there was no fish on the lunch menu. The best days were when it was cooked in Mama's (my great grandmum's) freshly squeezed coconut oil. We ate only what was fresh and local. European vegetables weren't popular and always available in local markets.

In the monsoon, we turned to dried, pickled and preserved fish, as well as salted pork and Goan choris. Dried bangra with fresh coconut were made into a fish curry. Parra, dried mackerel pickled in garlic, chillies, vinegar and fried with diced onions was served like a warm salad with fish pickle. My great grandmother buried pork under salt in large earthen pots for four to five days and this was made into a light curry which we ate with bread. Life was delicious and good.

Our meals at night started evolving into adaptations of continental cuisine. Meat stews, roasts and pastas graced our table every other night. To make the food more suitable to our Indian palates, Ermine would add chillies, ginger and other spices. But the one constant was that our food was always local and seasonal. Ingredients were never flown in from another state, leave alone another country. We ate what was caught or grown locally and was easily available in the market. The vegetables were crisp and bursting with flavour. The norm was to go to the market every day and get what you needed to cook for that day.

This rule has guided our eating habits at home in New York. Living in the United States, I've been introduced to a whole new world of local ingredients. When I first emigrated, I longed for the fruits, vegetables, meat and fish from home. But as I evolved as a chef, I realized that by doing this, I was moving away from the family's philosophy of local and seasonal foods. I slowly started to enjoy the local produce, meat and fish. Farm stands and farmer markets became my stop of choice on my days off.

My family would eat only the fruits and vegetables that were in season. Tomato salads and corn during the summer, pumpkins and squashes during the fall and asparagus throughout the spring. I served grilled corn sprinkled with salt, red chillies and lime juice. A simple preparation like this blew people away in the US and they started doing the same in their own homes.

I have become obsessed with this philosophy of eating only local produce and I have realized how much better everything tastes this way! I even went so far as to grow a vegetable garden at home and took to farming. The simplicity and purity of eating vegetables in season made me realize even more how much better and flavourful they are. Eating freshly picked beets, cucumbers and radishes is like having nectar. Picking coriander leaves for my weekly masala omelettes has created cilantro lovers in my family. I would plant garlic in the fall and see it sprout six months later. I would use every part of it when still young and then let it mature, harvesting it by the end of the summer.

Eating peaches and cherries in the summer brings back memories of when I was young and in Bombay waiting for the peachwallah to roll his cart into our neighbourhood. Picking strawberries late in the evening when the sun has had a chance to work its magic on the sugars makes home-grown strawberries a treat.

I immigrated to the US in June 1988, and with my bags I took my love for food. I gave myself till August to get a job. I landed my first job on 14th August, just a day before I was all packed to return to India. I had no New York City experience and that deterred me from getting a job in most restaurants there. I started work at The Indian Café on 110 Street on Broadway. New York was a great food city but the quality of Indian food ranged from average at best to poor and was not exactly Indian. Most cooks who worked the stoves and tandoors were farmers or truck drivers back in india before they took up cooking as a second job. I never saw a good Goan fish curry, or sahel gosht, or lal maas, or a great homemade dal. I was exposed to a cuisine that I had no relationship or experience with. I never knew that Indian food was a one pot curry cuisine. For me it was a very strange experience to cook at a restaurant where the Indian food that was served was a changed, adapted version of a one pot of sauce meal. Add cream to this curry sauce and it was served as a korma. Add green simla mirch and it became a jalfrezi. Add coconut milk and it became a Goan fish curry. Luckily, the owners were open to my changing the menu to include Goan, Hyderabadi and other Southern flavours. It was what I knew well. The education in Indian food for America and its people was still to begin. The biggest disappointment was that Indian food in the US was nothing like it was back home. Indian food here meant poorly executed, non-seasonal, greasy, murky mughlai food. I did not want anything to do with this sub-standard representation of Indian food. After a year-and-a-half, I joined Raga, an Indian restaurant that was run by the Taj group. But even here guests didn't understand Indian food beyond chicken tikka masala, saag paneer and chicken makhani.

I then got an oppurtinity to work for the St Regis Hotel in New York. I quit my sous chef position to become a line cook, making salads at Lespinasse restaurant simply to get into the American system. I started my dream job of cooking French food with Asian ingredients. I did not realize then how great an impact it would have on my career afterwards. The chef Gray Kunz let me introduce Indian flavours into the food when he began to see my passion and the vast potential of Indian cooking, techniques and flavours. The more I cooked, the more I started to play with Indian ingredients in the kitchen. I was able to put dishes on the menu with an Indian soul. Looking at baingan bharta and reimagining it to make it a smooth, silky dish rather than a thick, clunky, heavy dish opened my eyes to the potential of looking at Indian spiced cooking in a whole new light. Or taking kabarga and using a different cut like shanks and refining the finishing without taking away the flavours made me excited. Till today I have guests mention my milk braised lamb shanks as one of the best dishes they have ever eaten. I was happy to be introducing so many diners to the wonder of Indian flavours.

It gave me and my cooking recognition, and I rose to the post of Chef d' Cuisine at Lespinasse. No Indian had ever done that before—it was twenty-seven years ago.

I experimented, using haleem as a base for lamb chops. I used baingan bharta as a puréed base for another dish of lamb shanks. I added mango pickle to lamb and beef jus and spices rubs and green cardamom to meats in winter. The combination of sweetness with acidic flavours can create magic. American diners had their first exposure to the wonders of flavour and texture of Indian cuisine that we have grown up with in India. I also realized that my love for Indian food and flavours had not diminished with my stay in the US.

The early nineties saw the beginning of farmers' markets in America. The use of local produce started to get recognized and new trends in recipe development were beginning to emerge. New American cuisine, like all great cuisines, was going back to the basics of food and cooking. Chefs stopped using ingredients if they were not in season—they did not use asparagus or peas in the middle of the winter. They started to use meat and fish that were local. People discovered the magic of flavours that came from local meats, black sea bass and monk fish instead of fish coming from France. Great ingredients, great techniques (like simply roasting and lightly seasoning ingredients), tradition, locavorism and seasonality were the focus. Alice Waters, an author and restauratuer from Berkeley, started the Chez Panisse Foundation which encouraged organic and homegrown produce in cooking. This reminded me so much of what good Indian food used to be back in Indian homes. As the art of cooking took centrestage, it led to the birth of TV shows and celebrity chefs. This phenomenon has continued to grow since then.

In India the trend has been different. People slowly started losing home cooks. Both parents started to work, so the need to eat out grew. Every time I returned home, I found new developments in the food world. People in India had begun eating differently. Stand-alone restaurants started mushrooming across the cities. The food available to all had improved by leaps and bounds. This was all so exciting.

I left my position as Chef d' Cuisine at Lespinasse to open Tabla in 1997 which, at that time, was the first and only Indian restaurant to play with Indian food. We opened to a 3 star review in *The New York Times* and I got to play with the way I cooked. No one had served halibut, red snapper or lobster with Indian spices before or even vegetables like asparagus, heirloom tomatoes and brussel sprouts. It is common now, but no one then had served poha or sabudana all dressed up as a part of a salad. The more I experimented, the more I realized how much our guests loved the flavours. The US was made up of two groups of people: those who loved Indian food and those who hated it. I wanted to convert the second group to the first.

As I cooked, I realized that those who disliked Indian cuisine were afraid of all the lesser-known and unrecognizable Indian ingredients like pomfret and karela and the murky, greasy sauces. The menus in Indian restaurants never changed and were never seasonal. This made it a cuisine that was stagnant and one they did not want to eat very often. I wanted to bring about a transformation in this attitude. When I myself enjoyed home-style Indian food everyday, why could I not make adventurous diners enjoy it as much as I do? I started to introduce seasonal American ingredients to Indian food and our guests began to appreciate it. I emphasized on the philosophy of cooking that was ever present in India: cook with what is available in the market that day, no matter what the ingredient is.

Returning to India today I look around at the restaurants and I see the change. In the past four years the restaurants in Bombay have evolved, but not that much. More chefs and restaurants are worshipping the cuisines and ingredients of the West. Some are running the usual masala of pastas, pizzas and burgers. Menus are extremely long and, to me, mixed and confusing. 'Multi cuisine' is becoming a phrase that is being used by more and more restaurants. I wonder (as should every diner) that with such large menus, how do restaurants keep the food fresh? On the other hand, regional Indian restaurants are still keeping to the philosophy of cooking with whatever is the freshest and in season. If an ingredient is not available, it's just too bad, it's just not on the menu as they will proudly tell you. These restaurants are always busy, making guests wait for tables. The question to ask is if these restaurants are successful, why can't all restaurants follow their philosophy?

Which is why I love Highway Gomantak in Mumbai. If a certain fish is over for the day, it is over. Find something else on the menu. This is the spirit of serving food that needs to be celebrated. This is who we are. I love what Indian Accent in Delhi is doing, making food more accessible, reconstructing and sometimes deconstructing, and using Indian spices in a manner that they don't hit you on the head. The chef at Café Lota in Delhi is celebrating the wonders of India through a different modernist lens.

One of the phrases I often hear from young folks in India is 'Indian cuisine is where you take your parents to.' Our love for things 'phoren' has moved to food too. How many people cook at home any more? Why are we letting age-old recipes, traditions and ingredients die? There are chefs and restaurateurs who would rather travel abroad to eat, but would not travel through India to enjoy its heritage in cooking. If you ask them what would be their last meal, more often than not the answer would be a dish they enjoyed abroad. What's wrong with our grandma's cooking? My last dish would be either my mom's xacutti or her sorpatel with gootlies from A1 Bakery in Bandra. In my opinion most countries' cuisines reach their apex when all its cooks celebrate and choose their own cuisine, ingredients and techniques. Restaurants in France and Spain now cook traditional cuisine with spices, something that was not present in their cuisine, to this extent, a hundred or even fifty years ago. The ingredients used are those that were being used for hundreds of years, but with changes that reflect availability.

I believe a cook becomes great when, and only when, he or she understands where his or her taste buds come from. Understanding their native cuisine gives them an understanding of the nuances of all cuisines. Many Indian chefs say, 'I am a continental cook, I don't do Indian.' I went through this same metamorphosis. I believe I only started to achieve success and fame after I embraced and celebrated Indian cuisine like I had never done before.

I believe the next step for Indian food, restaurants and chefs is to celebrate India. Look for ingredients from the far reaches of the country. Celebrate the cooking of all regions. Figuring out a way to use ingredients that our forefathers used in everyday cooking will evoke magic. I visited markets in Mumbai where I saw rat tail radishes, green jowar, water chestnuts, amaranth leaves, khatta saag, varieties of pumpkin and squashes, various types of rice and beans, but yet never saw one of these ingredients in any restaurant. These ingredients have evolved for our climate and way of life. They are best suited for the life here and are sustainable. At the Bombay Canteen which opened in February 2015 we strive to celebrate and showcase our great cuisine. We refuse to use imported meat and fish and only source native Indian ingredients.

I also believe chefs should celebrate and support each other by forming a community that supports them. Competition is healthy but it's best to be allies supporting one another. Share your local growers and farmers: the more they produce the better it will be for the entire food community. If one of my sous chefs leaves me to become a chef, I would consider myself successful. If another restaurant copies one of my recipes, I would feel flattered. I believe the better a restaurant gets, the better the restaurant community gets.

My final philosophy still remains: 'Good food and cooking is not only about how a dish tastes or looks on the plate, but how good it makes the cook cooking it and the guest eating it feel!'

Coming Full Circle

MANU CHANDRA

It was sometime in the year 1996. I was chilling at home with the usual mayhem characteristic of B-24 Malcha Marg. In a house that had four kids, Shankar the eldest, me at number two, Kabir who was four years younger and Mira the youngest at six, but also an endless stream of visitors, my brother's friends, my friends, outstation relatives, grandparents, pets and enough and more to keep one's mind off the one thing I was to keep my mind on. Class ten had just started, and it was the first dreaded board year.

My proclivities towards all things academic were legendary by now, and for all the wrong reasons. The cracks had started to emerge the year earlier when I moved from an experimental educational system, with no exams, to a formal one. Passing class was largely acceptable, and the pressures that came associated with getting high grades didn't really exist in our household. I could pour over the Times Life series on international cuisines for hours, and even read random editions of the Encyclopaedia

101

Britannica, which took up pride of place on the longest glass-enclosed book shelf in the drawing room. But hand me a textbook, and I could stare at a single page endlessly and have absolutely nothing register.

Not surprisingly then, if one of us scored a 45 per cent, we were taken to Nirulas; if by some stroke of luck it was 60 per cent, it would still be Nirulas—our family never discriminated. (I have little to no recollection of anyone's exam scores in the family because they just didn't seem to be the cause celebre that they are now. I must have aced the twelfth grade, else there was no way that I could've managed the cut-offs to Delhi Universities most sought after.) In fact, all birthdays were at Nirulas too. You see, nothing else really existed. And a treat was a treat, for sustenance we all ate at home. How times change.

The school, Mirambika, which I had recently left, had almost no textbooks save math, and social studies if memory serves me right. But even in these departments the approach to teaching was far removed from conventional. Calculations were done on Abacus made by us in carpentry classes. Jasbir Singh Malick, the larger-than-life corporate honcho-turned theatre actor-turned math teacher, would teach us theorems as well as Shakespeare. I remember once asking him what the logic behind the formula that he had just written on the board was. It took the next two classes to understand the fundamentals of seventh-grade math via college-level theories. The idea was to teach, never merely to educate. One could also dress as they pleased, and given that class sizes seldom exceeded ten to twelve students, there was a sense of intimacy in all that we did.

Mirambika didn't go beyond class eight, so one had to move to a 'structured' school, in white uniforms, canvas shoes et all. My entrance exams to the next school were such a disaster that the Mirambika faculty had to collectively pitch on my behalf to just get me through to the other side. We called our teachers Bhaiya and Didi in Mirambika, and the family stuck their necks out for me. So there I was, an experiment from an experimental school, sitting on hard wooden benches, following word to word what was written on the blackboard, unsurprisingly not much different from the textbook. In math class once I asked the same question about a formula to the slightly curt but helpful teacher. The question was met with peals of laughter from the entire classroom before Ma'am had a chance to react. My benchmate nudged me under the desk and said, 'It's a formula, a formula cannot be questioned', and the class resumed. Some of us migrants shut down, the others took to it like fish to water. Everything else—the school bus politics, loads of company, sports and co-curricular activities—were just perfect. The canteen on campus, one I had already familiarized myself with from my days in Mirambika (the larger campus was the same), used to have these eggless atta cakes and fresh plum and rhododendron juice, served ice cold and such a welcome respite from the gruelling Delhi summer, which would invariably be amplified by the four-hundred metre asphalt running track right next to it. The cake used to stick to the tops of our palates because it lacked leavening agents and fat, but wasn't half bad with the plum juice. Kids in a hurry to eat the cake would often be seeing prying off the masticated muck stuck to the roof of their mouths with their fingers. It wasn't a pleasant sight, but neither were the cakes.

I made it from class nine to ten by the skin of my teeth, or so I'd like to imagine. In fact, I think after I had failed the fourth re-exam for the math paper, the then principal of Mother's International School summoned my mum to her office. I sat outside, acutely aware of what was about to transpire, and stared at the big and rather unattractive mural of some form of sun rays in the corridor. The sheer ugliness of this bizarre monstrosity passing off as art kept my mind off the impending doom. This was the magical corridor, where people in mid-sprint and slide across the glossy granite floor would come to a screeching halt before breaking into a slow walk, and then resume their usual antics as soon as they were out of earshot. It was also the quietest corridor in an otherwise noisy school; the architect had probably not factored acoustics into a largely concrete structure filled with age groups eight to sixteen. The office in that corridor made even the teachers nervous, for the lady that sat within could turn the best of us to stone. The only time I felt that the lady inside was human is when I once went in during lunch time to drop off a file as an errand for the class teacher and discovered her eating paranthas, achaar and bhindi ki subzi out of a little pink tiffin which I could swear had some cartoon character on it. Food, you see, can make so much seem human. An extremely trying year in the formal system had attuned me to expect the worst, and Bugs Bunny on tiffin box notwithstanding, nor my excellence in all fields like drama, sports, quiz, debates, was going to stop the eventuality that loomed ahead. I sucked at mathematics, and the way things were then, it was enough to keep one held back a year. Mum walked out after what seemed like an eternity, tapped me awake from my trance and said, 'Let's go.' That's all she said; we drove back home, and not many words were exchanged except that I was through to the next class. No donations had been made, but an undertaking that I would excel was enough in an era when the word of a parent had its own merit and reason still existed in plenty—even in the little office down the dreaded corridor!

My love for cooking had already surfaced by this time, and I was spending long hours experimenting with food in the kitchen at home. Mostly though I'd assist in the classic recipes that my dad's UP Kayasth mother would painstakingly put together each day. It was something I could focus on without feeling distracted or tired. Besides engaging the senses, understanding a recipe took applying both math and science, but the tangibility of it all made learning so much easier.

I could scale up recipes for cakes, but struggle with ratios in the classroom. I understood emulsification of meat and fat and vinegar and oil far better than the juvenile molecular drawings in the physics textbooks. That seizing meat proteins and relaxing them through slower cooking methods were far more gratifying and less damaging than dunking anything that went in the pressure cooker was way beyond anything bio class would've covered. And nowhere do I remember school teaching us how collagen and bone marrow could enrich a broth and add body to the stew. A trip to the butcher was one where each cut and musculature was studied depending upon the application. There was also no better way of understanding how the fins of fish were defence mechanism till you had your finger pierced by one while cleaning it, or how they remained buoyant other than while cleaning out their guts and discovering the bladder. That one should always rub some oil on their hands when cleaning raw jackfruit because the sap will cling onto one's skin and dry and oxidize, making it all black and nasty. If only school would have drawn parallels to what we partake in daily, would the learning have become so much easier? The kitchen, as it were, became my best classroom.

In the midst of the mayhem at home that evening, I was told that I was to pack my bags and be sent to my maternal grandparents home in Asiad Village, a small hamlet-like gated community in south Delhi. Nana, a self-taught ex-colonel from the EME core was, to much of our delight, a whiskey-loving, meat-eating Tamilian Brahmin, with a family in Madras so big that let alone names, I still find it hard to remember how I'm related to whom. Nani, a theth but educated bridge-loving Punjaban, was impeccably dressed for her daily outing to the DSOI (Defence Services Officers' Institute) club and an entrepreneur (she started at fifty and cashed out by fifty-six). The logic was I'd get more time to study, especially under their notoriously disciplined watch, and also be close to a lot of my peers from school and the school itself. What no one anticipated was that they had mellowed with age and pandered to my cooking and experimentation more than anyone would have liked.

The next couple of years (I passed everything with flying colours) I began to build a set of cognitive abilities which gave me a strong intuitive sense with all things food. In a way I was already becoming a chef, without ever having to dabble in professional kitchens. A game I remember with fondness, which I played upon arriving home from post-school sports, famished, was ringing the doorbell to the first-floor apartment and have Bhagvaan Singh the cook open the door. I could tell him exactly what had been made for lunch without stepping in. The smells were, at least for me, a dead giveaway. Bhagvaan Singh would prod me on.

'Is it chole with garam masala or tomato?'

'Is it only gobi or aloo gobi?'

'The chicken curry is with dahi or sukha?'

'Is the sambhar with drumsticks or small onions?'

I'd usually nail these too. I graduated the Bhagvaan Singh exam when he once asked if the chicken was with bone or boneless to which I'd replied that no self-respecting Punjabi would cook boneless chicken at home. Later in life I'd discover how easily I would take to enjoying wine and differentiate between a good and not-so-good one with ease, while most of my peers would struggle with just red and white.

Some of my friends thought that I had become obsessed with food, and it was in some way a sanctuary that would help deflect whatever deficits I had on the academic front. That would not stop them from having me be the chief party organizer and chef and cook at most school parties, usually at my oldest buddy Nitin's house, who was born to be a party animal and still parties with a vengeance almost twenty years on (I'm helping set the menu for his wedding in November 2015 as I write this piece). I would slip away into his mom's kitchen when the conversation got too boring outside, because it is far more gratifying to watch a pan of seekh kebabs sizzle and sputter than listen to the girls giggle over some other student's poor waxing regime. Teenagers! Aunty would fix me her signature elaichi chai with less milk and we would talk for hours discussing recipes.

For most of my friends the seekh kebabs from a popular south Delhi meat shop were the epitome of comfort. They'd pay absolutely no heed when I told them that I was pretty darned sure that there was loads of soya mixed into it, and that the real deal tasted entirely different and in a good way. I suspect a lot of them had started cooking boneless chicken at home—but I wasn't judging. We were already in the throes of a processed-food boom, and somehow drinking coke from a can was far more gratifying than a bottle, and the monoculture that plagued the food industry for over a decade was beginning to take root.

I had also always heard my nani speak about her own cooking skills, but after her three kids were married off, the grandkids had grown up and the husband had settled into his own rhythm between work, cricket, the Lhasa Apsos and whiskey, she took a sabbatical. She wrote poetry and scripts, and I would have to listen to them. I never did learn Urdu in school (even though my paternal grandpa was an Urdu scholar and a celebrated criminologist) and began to enjoy the beautiful word play that this alien yet familiar language wove. I could sit and listen to scripts and poetry, but what I could not bear to sit through was episodes of *Khaana Khazaana* and sermons by Murari Baapu on TV. I thought *Yan Can Cook* was infinitely more entertaining. She followed through on her script and produced a telefilm with some prominent TV actors of the time playing lead roles. Notable among them was an extremely affable young Muslim boy who was really good to all us grandkids and later went on to become King Khan of Bollywood. The movie was never aired! A regret she carried with her till the very end.

It was also a bit of a turbulent time in the Asiad home. The coming of age of a teenager was fraught with tragedy, of which I had little to no grasp, but was expected to play an active part like an adult. The younger Mama was going through a bad divorce and had lost custody of his kids; the elder one, who had already had his second marriage break apart, was involved in a nasty house fire from which he barely escaped. It was too much for the old couple to take, and one evening as we sat around the dinner table, the three of us, eating Nana's favourite paalak gosht with rice, everything changed. I was a slow eater who would have a disproportionate amount of rice to gravy, eating very little of the good stuff and focusing more on the rice (one suspected I also had Bengali genes, but that has never been established). The good Tamilian that he was, he egged me on to take a larger helping of the paalak gosht and also eat with a bigger spoon, or as they did, with their hands. I still eat my food with a teaspoon on most occasions—just one of those things that stays with you. But that night I obliged, and heard what became my grandfather's last words. They were said with a handful of his favourite food in his mouth and with a glass of Peter Scot by his side. I think we were watching *Aandhi* on cable TV, whose haunting song 'Tum aagey ho' he used to sing in a beautiful though heavily accented voice. I attempted CPR and rushed out to grab a school friend's dad who was a senior cardiologist and neighbour. Reacting to the most dire situations and doing so with a cool head became as much part of my profession and persona here on.

Nana came about in the AIIMS ICU for a couple of hours the next day we were told, but none of us met him then; it was downhill from there, and over a couple of weeks later. That night as I sat with my mama and mum outside the crowded and sultry waiting area of the ICU, the mobile phone (which was a novelty and belonged to the elder Mama) rang. It was my dad. My ailing dadi had passed away in her sleep. Two of my culinary champions and heroes, possibly my favourite grandparents, who also happened to be the best of pals, were both gone within a few hours of one another. It was so devastating that one couldn't even figure how to grieve and so, true to form, I took over the responsibility of making sure everyone who started filing into the homes to pay their last respects was fed. Dadi took with her a treasure trove of recipes, which classically had been passed on word of mouth. Some stayed with my many aunts, dad and the maid, but I suspect more was lost. She could cook impeccable food for up to a hundred people at a time, but now most people prefer to have it catered by professionals.

Nani never really recovered from the loss. She gave up going to the club, and with the end of her club forays, I lost one of my favourite treats of nargisi kofta from the DSOI. That mince around the egg was always the right consistency, and spiced with just the right amount of garam masala and pepper. I'm sure all clubs used some pre-packaged meat masalas because they all had a tendency to taste the same, but it was a joy nonetheless. The egg however was always overcooked, but with mince of that quality who really cared. What I didn't miss, however, but Nani quite enjoyed, was the American Chopsuey which was a club staple: sweet, ketchup-and-cornstarch laden, with carrots, beans and cabbage and loads of flat, crispy noodles. I think even people with the finest taste often indulge in terrible food choices, and that's how I ignored the chopsuey. Years later I would discover that A.D. Singh, the restaurateur extraordinaire who I started to work with, also had a soft spot for the Breach Candy Club American Chopsuey. QED.

What also got packed away with Nana's passing was Nani's most incredible collection of exquisite jewellery: the kundan sets in beaten gold, a most regal set of emerald necklaces, many a solitaire and a fine mango-shaped ruby pendant, ornate gold kadas with jaali work so fine it was a marvel that the thing held together. There were many others, but I fail to recollect the details. Even her massive collection of kanjivarams, bandhej, ikats and chanderis, shawls like jamavars, shah tush, pashminas and brocades were neatly packed covered in cloves and locked away in big trunks. I had learned about fabrics, Indian handicrafts and different weaves from her. She always had insights into cultural nuances, historical significances and genesis of the crafts and geographical specializations that still don't exist in any school curricula but really ought to. They called her 'the princess' at the club because no woman before, and I gather after her, arrived dressed as impeccably as she did each evening. Nana had always indulged her, and I guess she couldn't bear to see things that reminded her of him.

She too began a slow, unbearable decline, which she only momentarily came out of when we both hatched a plan to start an Achaar and Kaanji business. The entrepreneurial streak that had made her a wealthy woman from being a housebound officer's wife was back, and possibly the only glint I saw in her eyes save the time I came and told her that I'd fulfilled her dream of getting into the college she always hoped I'd attend.

The older Mama, somewhat recovered, and now effectively homeless, moved in with both of us. Part of the large terrace was converted into a mini-apartment for him with a hall and bedroom, and whatever was salvaged from his home. His razas and artefacts from around the world which he had collected as the Global President of the Round Table found their way into the house. Mama was always a bit of a playboy and possibly a case study in how to be a bon vivant; but what kept us buddies was that his love for food and wine was one of a kind. He was the kind of guy who every hotel general manager and chef worth his salt in Delhi knew and indulged. The man was blessed with the gift of the gab and would smuggle me into Djinns, the most happening nightclub in Delhi at the time (I suspect more because I was the designated driver), and get the chef there to whip up a sublime morel, chicken, pine nut and honey starter. He would spend long hours researching recipes for the perfect roast ham, and together we would attempt a lot of exotic food in the small but well-equipped kitchen of Asiad Village. The younger Mama, who by now had remarried, and his wife would often be our dinner guests. The tables were always impeccably laid out—napkin rings, candelabra, placemats and silverware polished to a shine and placed just so. He's been living in Goa for over a decade now, running a food import and distribution business, and still calls me to discuss the merits of whole Australian lamb carcass with gusto despite the onset of Parkinson's. It's also a veiled sales pitch, but who cares when you know that some people still live and breathe their food with as much passion as that.

The Achaar and Kaanji business was Nani recreating her best recipes, while I sat with Nana's dictaphone (he was a gadget freak well before the tech boom, with walkmans, digital watches, dictaphones and the like) and noted down the proportions. Some of the measures relied on a fistful of ground mustard and half-a-handful of kalonji seeds. The word andaaz would always be recorded as andaaz, because it's just one of those beautiful words in Indian cooking that can never be quantified and remains to date the best metric. The Aloo Ka Achhar with mustard oil and methi seeds was one of my absolute favourites, as was the quintessentially Punjabi Gobhi, Shalgam and Gaajar Achaar. We made huge batches in giant barnis which had been bought from the old city, with masalas only bought from Delhi's famous Roopak stores. Nani would never compromise on the quality of ingredients and Roopak always sourced the best. I also did my first recipe costing around this time and printed labels from a stationary shop in Hauz Khas Village, which the computer genius younger Mama had designed on his Macintosh. The achaars were marketed within Asiad Village and sold out in no time. Some of those recipes continue to be a source of inspiration for me for dishes I've put on my menus over the years. The Kaanji popularity, seasonality and limited batch production kept it out of the commercial loop. Instead it was gifted to Nani's eight brothers and sisters and the direct family with one vat always saved for my mother, who had always been a big fan of it. We lost Nani in my second year of college, and with her, the last pillar of that generation. Something told me that I may need to carry that torch forth—though I'd never have guessed in which way.

College started on a great note when I realized that an entire campus full of folk already considered themselves a cut above all the other colleges around. There's something to be said about being in the company of so many who already thought of themselves as a little bit cooler than everyone else. When you're young, being in a group such as this does wonders to your ego. We referred to the canteen as 'the café', while it remained the canteen for all others. Mince cutlets, or Mince as they were called, and dalda cooked scrambled eggs were all the rage, despite a soiled laminated page which had a bunch of other items listed on it, often with prices crossed out and penned again with a ball pen. Requests for slight tweaks in my food were met with a level of hostility for some time by the two servers who had been there for decades. But they eventually warmed up to me, and let me go help fix my own things in the grimy and always busy kitchen. This probably made me one of the few Stephanians to get full access to the kitchens of the Café. I suspect, however, that I may have been the only one who was ever interested.

But what stood out for me, and for many generations before me and I reckon even after, was the famous Rohtas' ke samose that were sold at a tiny little stall in the courtyard outside the café. It was the only thing he made; and if there was a Jiro Ono of the samosa world, I think Rohtas would find a place in the Samosa Maker hall of fame. The place was always bustling with students from all streams, with many perched on the coveted concrete seats around the big tree in the centre smoking Navy Cuts, which some sucker would buy a packet of and the rest would mooch.

What Rohtas had managed to get absolutely right, and what made his little samosas works of art, was the flakiness of the pastry shell—thin, but just about, rolled evenly with the much desired edges in perfect proportion to the size of the samosa. This was true of Dadi's gujjias made during Holi also, and understandable why she wouldn't let anyone but the experienced make them. Because if it wasn't kneaded, rolled and crimped a certain way, with just the right filling to pastry ratio, the thing would become a mess! Decades later my folks have got it almost in the ballpark, but that's after years of trial and error.

I loathed it when some of the friends used to break the corners away from my Rohtas' samosa and leave me with the rest; hence I always ordered extra. That, combined with the fact that he never over boiled the potatoes, used only ones with high starch and kept them relatively chunky. They were flavoured mildly with just some chilli, zeera and salt with some coriander and peas. The frying temperature of the large kadhai was always moderate, and the cooking slow, allowing the pastry to crisp nicely and evenly. This small attention to details is what made those things practically addictive; and the fact that his rotation of stock was so high that getting something that had been sitting out for a long time was next to impossible. Now Delhi is no stranger to samosas, and one can argue that it easily has some of the country's finest (the Bengalis make a pitch for their shingaras each time this discussion comes up), so for one little college stall guy to have the cult following that he did (Bengalis included) was a resounding endorsement of the quality they stood for. For the amount of scorn that we usually attracted from a bunch of kids from other campuses, Rohtas' ke samose was, above all, that pettiness. Even the Law Faculty students would deign to walk into our gates because while their canteen was really good, the samosas weren't a patch on ours. The Stephanians had something really solid to brag about.

It's little wonder then that some of the strongest food memories of people comes from places like these: small, unassuming, surgically focused on just a couple of basic products that do the same thing, consistently, almost every single day. No chef or QSR will ever match what some of these outfits do. My business partner, for example, still drives me to the vada pav guy outside Mithibhai College in Bombay to have the oversized vada pav, which is distinctly different from almost everything else I've had in Bombay. What helps it along the way is also the generous amount of butter that is applied to slightly less elastic pav. The vendor is apparently a legend and can put some of Bombay's top restaurants to shame with the volume of sales he generates from a small kiosk—and with good reason.

Having said that, I've also had some of the worst vada pavs in Mumbai; with pasty potatoes, poorly fried in burnt oil, layered in dry and even stale pavs and rather inferior ghaati masala and a chutney which is a sorry, watered-down excuse for the real deal. Yet they do brisk business. But that is a fallout of mindless eating, when almost no thought is given to what is being consumed and in no state of mind to appreciate quality or fuss over the nuances when dashing off to catch the 8.20 from Dadar station. But it's folks like Rohtas or the Mithibhai College guy who can stop the rushing sea of humanity dead in their tracks for the attention and affection they bring to their seemingly menial craft. It's hard to ignore it even if one is not a 'foodie' because of all the requisite boxes their product ticks to become truly outstanding. That is also why most people remember their grandmother's or mother's food so fondly.

I headed off to New York to finally pursue a professional chef's degree at what was considered one of the finest culinary schools in the world at the time. It was the Hogwarts of cooking schools in my mind. A campus atop a hill overlooked the incredible Hudson River surrounded by forests that would turn a million shades of autumn during fall and hundreds of aspiring chefs walked around, toques on head and knife rolls by their side. The Culinary Institute of America was truly a dream come true for someone who wanted to make their passion into a career, and their stellar track record proved it.

I had come to campus after spending a couple of weeks with a mad Greek friend of my parents, who lived in the über chic East Village in Manhattan and loved food like few people do. Till date he goes into a rapturous mode whenever he eats something that strikes all the right notes. The now slightly predictable but still-fun-to-watch sequence of events plays out exactly how it always did. He closes his eyes, throws his head back and then rolls it round and round, all the while making appreciative sounds of joy. He then snaps out of his reverie, slowly opens his eyes, kisses his fingers and says, 'Now that is fucking food.'

Paul the Greek, as most of the neighbourhood called him, or Mr Metrakos as I do, knew his way around the little places south of Union Square like few others. He'd stand outside his apartment on most days and have even the likes of Julianne Moore blow a kiss at him, as they walked past, somewhat hurried in typical Manhattan style. At six feet four inches and a demeanour not dissimilar to Yogi Bear, he was one of the most likeable guys in the area. After thirty-five years in the same place, even in a place like Manhattan, one does become a fixture.

I ate my first real burger with him at Knickerbockers in West Village, the same day I arrived there. Paul, an old family friend, had picked me up from JFK airport in his massive pickup truck, and we drove towards Manhattan. As if on cue, the radio started playing Billy Joel's 'New York state of mind' as the car rolled up the steep motorway near Queens and then up to the highest point, where suddenly the entire Manhattan skyline came into view. Something told me that I was going to love this town.

I was underweight and a meagre eater and was so overwhelmed by the quantity of meat in a single burger that I knew I would be sick if I ate anything more than a third of it. It was nothing like I had eaten before: succulent, juicy, grilled, pink in the middle and with only the flavour of meat and cheese. Despite its relative simplicity, it was outstanding! No doubt it was the excellent meat and fantastic bread and real cheese that brought the product together, but for someone who had grown up on

Wimpy's burgers in Hauz Khas and even the dry stuff at Nirulas, this was nothing short of a revelation. This was precisely the approach to the burgers I took when I opened the first Monkey Bar in Bangalore many years later. Good meat and good bread! Bangalore, a city that had a nostalgia-driven love affair with sloppy burgers with copious amounts of mayonnaise and very little meat, suddenly rediscovered the burger again—only this time stripped down, and totally delicious. And like with any food, there were enough who felt that this couldn't be a patch on what they had held as their favourites, but the intention was never to compete, just put out what in my view was definitive.

Grilled Octopus, Arctic Clams, Moulles Frites, Hamachi, Venison, Yellow Fin Tuna and a bunch of other things were experienced by me for the first time on our little lunches and dinners out to the places tucked away in the small streets in SoHo. I had already read about so much of these, but till one doesn't eat a freshly shucked Maine oyster or a light lobster roll it's hard to imagine what it all adds up to. But of all the outings with Paul, the best ones used to be to Mr Metrakos's sister's home in Astoria every Easter. She was a whizz with traditional Greek food. And everything at the table would sing with the simple flavours and the aromas of excellent olive oil from their own farms near Thessaloniki in Greece, with the ingredients fresh and slowly cooked with minimal herbs and additives. One Easter cookie in particular has always stayed with me, and now features on my menus. It was a simple olive oil, almond and flour cookie called Kourambiethes, which are dusted with powdered sugar. For those who always speak volumes about Kayani Bakery's cookies should see what olive oil can do to baked goodies.

Culinary school was mostly what I'd hoped it would be. Lots of information, basics that would set one on the right path, and competition which would help challenge one's own notions of skill. Like with any other school there were enough and more students who weren't really serious about doing anything. They were out of school, away from home, free and waiting to discover themselves, and much energy got exempted in that. There were also those who had saved and taken huge loans to get to this point and were determined to make it all count. These were the people I became great friends with, because there was always so much to teach each other. What I loved about the attitude of the chef instructors was a simple philosophy: You will get as much as you put into this place. So I gave it all I had.

What transpired post this and much through school is a different and entertaining story in itself, perhaps for another time, but what became apparent when I stepped out into the proverbial 'real world' was how much I had been shaped as a chef by my growing years. Even the smallest things, from sarees to studying history in college, helped define the way I viewed and perceived food and tastes. I did the avant garde food trends and techniques and continue to in some form or the other, but it was the little details of developing flavour that still has me more excited than a visually stunning plate with multiple components. The years have taught me that there is never one right way of cooking or preparing a dish, and the more ways you can learn from and experience, the better you become at your trade. That ignoring what is around you to focus squarely on your own craft is foolishness, because nothing works in isolation and perspective often comes from outside the chopping block.

I often wonder where I stand today, and how time and experience and the patronage and friendships of scores of people coupled with my past have helped mould my own trajectory as a chef. It gradually became apparent that those simple yet balanced dishes from my growing-up years had enabled me to find wider success and get people across several markets excited. I learnt to play on old favourites by way of presentation and aesthetics, introducing to the repertoires of the dining public dishes or ingredients they had never had or even heard of but had been under their noses all the while—but never packaged in a way that would interest them. What I did was bring perspective to scores of young diners the way I had discovered it myself, and this was far more gratifying than merely trying to show off my skill sets to a select few. I created food with more integrity than novelty, developing a style that is deeply personal yet marked with the hallmark of quality that one comes to expect from a professional. In making people think about what they eat and yet enjoy without over thinking a dish is what has brought me full circle.

A Journey through the World of Slow Cooking

JEROME MARREL

Forty years ago, in June 1974, at the end of our first year of catering college, we escaped to the French countryside near Toulouse for what is called 'finishing all the goodies'—a tradition that involves clearing the larder before buying new geese and ducks and canning all the products.

We arrived at Castelnaudary, where our friend lived. This southern French market town is the seat of La Grande Confrérie du Cassoulet de Castelnaudary, or The Brotherhood of Castelnaudary's Cassoulet, an organization that was formed to retain the purity of a tradition and the quality of a dish that dated back to 1355.

Before unpacking, we were treated to a sumptuous lunch of foie gras, stuffed goose, duck magret and confits. It was delicious and we were ready for a well-deserved siesta. Our host, however, told us that it was now time to start preparing the cassoulet for the next evening. We reminded him that we had over twenty-four hours before it was to be served, but he impressed upon us that the dish *must* cook for that long. So off we went to the market to buy the finest white beans, pork meat and sausages.

We lit a wood fire and put a clay pot on it. In went a generous dose of goose fat and finely chopped onions. We sautéed the beans a bit, then added the various pork meats, sausages, duck leg confit, some tomato paste and a large helping of water from the nearby well. Then we covered the pot for a twenty-four-hour cooking—the *real* way to cook in the countryside.

Our host was pleased to see that hardly any stock remained from the previous year in the garde manger. We had indeed finished all the jars of liver, neck, pates, fat and confits, and they would be refilled as soon as the goose and duck markets opened the following week. The next evening, all of us gathered in the garden to open the clay pot. Lovely aromas emanated from within, and we were excited to taste the succulent meats that had been simmering for more than a day. Our host, however, had something else in mind. He opened the pot and started piling the pieces of meat on to a plate. We asked him why and he simply said that the dogs of the house would make a feast of them. We gaped at him in open-mouthed horror. Is that what was to become of our day-long cooking? He laughed at our shock and explained that this was the right way to eat a good cassoulet. The meats would have imparted their flavours to the beans, so now we could enjoy a simple dish of white beans flavoured with goose, duck and pork. It was heavenly. Thus content, we went back to finish the college year dreaming of the next cassoulet we would cook.

A parallel can be drawn, closer home, to the Goan prawn curry from which the prawns can be removed easily after the cooking as the gravy absorbs all the flavours. Often visitors just drink the curry without bothering about the ingredients inside.

This is of no surprise to me as the masalas are ground for hours and then put in the mixer with coconut milk for another couple of hours, making the curry extremely flavourful—a kind of slow cooking done the Goan way.

I often learn new recipes while cooking with Aunty Chlo, a sweet Goan lady who has transformed her passion for cooking into an art. I recently visited her to learn the Portuguese-Goan recipe for pork solantle, one that requires a lengthy preparation. We started by cutting the pork belly into one-inch cubes, ensuring we retain all the fat. Then Aunty Chlo added garam masala, cumin, turmeric and black pepper brought from my garden, and cloves, and cinnamon ground into a fine powder. She then poured in a large dose of vinegar. I was up and raring to cook, but she ushered me out of her kitchen, saying, 'Not yet. This has to mature overnight, so come back tomorrow.'

I was promptly back the next morning at ten. We now added quartered onions, garlic, broken dry red chillies, kokum and salt. Then the mixture, without adding water or oil, went into a large clay pot that was put on a low fire for six hours. When we removed the lid, a beautiful smell wafted out, and when we tasted it, the pork had taken on the flavours of all the ingredients. Aunty Chlo instructed me to keep it for a day and warm it up on the following day to derive an even better taste. I did as she told me, and sure enough, the solantle was much appreciated and enjoyed by my partner and a few of our friends the next day.

Slow cooking is a great way to enjoy certain dishes; cooking a dish and re-heating it over days is another great experience. Take, for instance, the Goa sorpotel with a large dose of feni in it. On the first day it is a nice dish to look at, having a raw taste and the feni still stands out. By the second day, the feni settles in the meat and the gravy thickens. Do not eat it as it is not yet ready for you. Cook it a third time to get the subtle taste of feni in a rich, thick gravy.

This is another approach to slow cooking, very common in Goan diet, be it with vindaloo or with pork assado. But, unfortunately, a lot of people do not have the time for such elaborate cooking, or think that if a dish is cooked and re-cooked, it loses its freshness. Do not believe the detractors; instead indulge in your taste buds.

It is true that such dishes require a long preparation time, which most people do not have today, but it is worth it to sacrifice some leisure time for the pleasure of one's body and mind. Slow-cooked food packs all the flavours into a dish, particularly when the pot is kept sealed for long hours. The aromas are trapped in, and when the crust is broken open, a wide range of tastes and smells will greet the senses.

Modern life has, unfortunately, altered food habits for the worse. Hassled with the trappings of their daily lives, people have little patience for their food and how it is cooked. Ready-to-eat dishes, fifteen-minute home recipes and poor quality takeaways dominate meal patterns, and the abomination that is fast food is the default option for most. Why are we all right with having lost touch with our native cuisines? What is it about fast food that appeals to so many people across the world? They are all just industrial products, inelegantly mixed together, fooling the consumer into thinking that there's a recipe hidden somewhere in there. A key ingredient in any recipe, however, is love. If palates and senses are to be appealed to and pleased, a more personal approach is vital, which is, of course, absent from all the fast food outlets of the world.

All hope is not yet lost, though, as there is still a lot of traditional cooking in practice around the world. The appeal of these preparations lies in the fact that they are so intrinsically a part of their traditions. Even though the rest of the world may not understand them, they are inextricably tied to the culture of the place they originate from.

We had an amazing experience in Mongolia eating roasted marmot and drinking airag, which is fermented mare's milk with 2 per cent alcohol content. Admittedly, it was not the best experience in terms of taste, but knowing that I was engaging in a tradition that dates back to Genghis Khan won me over! The marmot was roasted to perfection from inside and outside. Mongols, in fact, do a lot of cooking by stuffing their animals with hot stone, which yields a very tender meat. They even use hot stones to boil their stew, placing the stones inside the pot and letting it cook for hours.

I ate my first bat on a trip to the Seychelles years ago, only to find recently that it is a delicacy in Goa, where people cook it slowly in xacutti. They are very tasty animals as they feed on fruits: the best time to prepare a bat is during the mango season when the taste of the fruit has permeated into the meat, lending it a sweet flavour.

Cooking and eating a cat's head might sound horrific to most, but while working in the Middle East, I discovered that it is a delicacy for the Filippinos, and tastes similar to rabbit. They would feed the cat for weeks from their own rations in order to have the dish prepared once a month. Imagine the smiles on their faces when the dish was brought out!

The bugs, worms and insects sold near the temples of Angkor Wat are amazingly tasty. Of course it takes a strong stomach to even look at them as food, but once the psychological barrier is crossed, one finds that they taste like regular fried prawn or whitebait.

The fafaru in Tahiti is a kind of pickled fish prepared by leaving the raw fish out in the sun with sea water till it is nearly rotten. It is sure to make those with palates unexposed to it extremely squeamish, but is considered a delicacy by the locals, and is eaten at every meal.

The list is endless, but I must mention here the Carnivore restaurant in Nairobi, which used to serve an assortment of grilled game meats. It has now been closed down due to growing awareness about the need for the protection of wildlife.

While Carnivore may have had to close its doors to customers due to ecological concerns, my search for other traditional places that are still cooking like in the past has left me with mixed feelings. These are increasingly difficult to find, as labour costs have begun to hit the roof. The small bistro on a street corner in Paris, the food stalls in Singapore, the excellent churrascaria in Brazil, the real paella on wood fire in Spain, a pizza on a piece of bread in Italy, the last Ottoman cuisine restaurants of Istanbul, an entire traditional meal at a private home in Georgia—will these soon become unfamiliar token memories of times past? We can still find them today, but they are rapidly disappearing as technologies and tastes continue to change.

Bistros in Paris now order vacuum-packed dishes that try to look authentic on the plate. But, on a closer look, it is possible to still find superb bistros that have a good chef behind the 'piano'. Here, we may relish what our mothers used to cook at home: simple, unpretentious dishes that transport one to heaven. I do make sure we visit a couple each time we are in Paris, and taste tripes, gratin parmentier, quenelles of pike fish and usually a simple apple tart for dessert.

The food stalls of Singapore have more and more products mass-prepared in central cooking units and the days of the Newton Circus Food Centre are gone. It is difficult to find fresh fish there any longer, but you can still get a decent plate of fried noodles straight out of the wok.

In Brazil we now find salmon and prawns on the list of a place known only for grilled meats, the churrascaria. But it still remains arguably the best place on earth to have a meat dinner.

Imagine the setting: your table has a small paddle that is green on one side and red on the other. The waiters glide around it with dozens of offerings. If you turn the paddle to green, you are served a large helping. Turn the paddle to red till you are ready for more, and you are left to enjoy the juicy pieces.

The contemporary paella of Spain is a disgraced cousin of the original recipe. Nobody remembers that originally it was made with green kidney beans, not rice. I learned this quite by chance myself, over a Cognac and cigar on a cruise ship in Western Africa. I was in conversation with a man from Catalonia as we wanted to order a paella the next day. He recounted his mother's cooking and his story revealed to me that our collective perception of a dish we consider traditional is so warped and distorted. Of course the ship was unable to produce such a delicacy.

Pizzas are topped with industrial ingredients, the first being canned tomato puree. So I will dwell instead on the original pizza still served today at my sister's house near Laggo Maggiore. A large, thick slice of bread with pure virgin olive oil, fresh tomatoes, a few olives, anchovies and basil—to die for at the beginning of a meal.

Ottoman cooking is so labour-intensive that traditional restaurants of Istanbul are fast disappearing. But if you visit the Topkapi Palace, you can still indulge in traditional Ottoman preparations seated peacefully above the Bosphorus. It's definitely worth a try on a hot day, as you can enjoy your meal under the shaded canopy of centuries-old trees.

For how long will the Georgia family open its doors to tourists even while the chefs keep ageing? We had a wonderful experience in a Georgian home, where everything was cooked right before us on a wood fire. We downed the food with vodka.

Perhaps in another generation or two, we will all eat a standardized version of every dish prepared industrially.

But instead of throwing up our hands in despair, a more constructive approach would be for us to continue our traditions at home. This would entail not eating out too frequently, but it is fully worth it. The pleasures of going to the market, making preparations in the kitchen, and cooking slowly while sipping a glass of wine or champagne will compensate for the changing world and its poor tastes. Imagine a cooling Champagne Sangria as you start cooking a beef bourguignon. It is a forty-eight-hour process: selecting the meat with the butcher, buying two nice bottles of Shiraz wine or rich Burgundy if available, and then going to the market for fresh herbs, carrots, spring onions, mushrooms and potatoes. But this is just the beginning.

Once you have returned to the kitchen you need to cut the meat, wash the vegetables and carve them in the shape of olives, then tie the herbs in a nice 'Bouquet Garni'. Put everything in a large bowl, pour the wine slowly on top before adding some rock salt and black pepper. Et voila, you are ready for a twenty-four-hour marination.

While the beef is marinating, I want to make a point about the horror of dieting. If you eat healthy and in reasonable quantities, you should never have to diet. The food scene has become completely dysfunctional with various kinds of diets that offer quick-fix, temporary weight loss accompanied by a painful experience. The best diet is made of fresh products, cooked at home and eaten slowly without reaching for second helpings. You should be able to control your weight and feel good about yourself. Add to the menu a vegetable coulisse made only with roasted capsicum, fresh tomato and basil, nicely pureed, together with a tinge of chilli and a few pine seeds. Or a green salad with apples, emmenthal and walnuts. These could be the perfect start to a slow-cooked dinner.

Let's return to the kitchen for the Beef Bourguignon. It is day two, and a chilled glass of Chardonnay will accompany the cooking. Fry the beef in a mixture of equal parts of olive oil and butter so that it doesn't overheat. When it has turned light brown, sprinkle a large spoon of white flour till all the pieces are well coated. Then pour wine on top and let it thicken on a low fire. Add the vegetables, herbs and seasoning and cook for about thirty minutes. No, it is not done yet! Seal the pot with plain flour dough and place it in the oven for the next twenty-four hours on the lowest temperature. When you smell the aromas coming out of the dish on opening the seal the next day, you will definitely adjudge those forty-eight hours as having been well spent. You may say that it is a waste of all that time for a mere twenty minutes of eating, but when you see your guests' faces, you will feel rewarded for the time and effort spent.

So far I have used only traditional ingredients. It is worth trying new, unusual ingredients and adding them to an old recipe. Have you ever tried clams on the barbeque with a slight dose of Pernod and served with saffron-flavoured mayonnaise? It is divine. Or you can pair fresh mangoes with tender chicken meat to make an unforgettable salad with olive oil and homemade wine vinegar vinaigrette. What about wasabi added to slightly pureed potatoes to give that spicy taste? Cube potatoes sautéed in goose fat are enjoyed even by the staunchest vegetarians. Morel mushrooms from Kashmir stuffed with a nice French goat cheese are also a delicacy, especially if they are nearly a metre long. Prawns sautéed with fresh cream and Dijon mustard are a must try, as is the barbeque fillet of beef sprinkled with single malt.

And most importantly, to accompany the food, you need a group of close friends with whom you can share the delicacies.

The Bengali Bonti

CHITRITA BANERJI

How big is the difference between sitting and standing? A cultural universe, when you examine posture in the context of food preparation. In the kitchens of the West, the cook stands at a table or counter and uses a knife. But mention a kitchen to a Bengali, or evoke a favourite dish, and more often than not an image will surface of a woman seated on the floor, cutting, chopping or cooking. In India, especially in Bengal, this is the typical posture. For centuries, the Bengali cook and her assistant have remained firmly grounded on the kitchen floor, a tradition reflecting the paucity of furniture inside the house. A bed, for both sleeping and sitting, was usually the most important piece of furniture, but outside the bedroom people sat or rested on mats spread out on the floor, or on square carpets called asans. In the kitchen they often sat on small rectangular or square wooden platforms called pinris or jalchoukis, which raised them an inch or so above the floor.

From this closeness to the earth evolved the practice of sitting down both to prepare and cook food. Enter the *bonti*, a protean cutting instrument on which generations of Bengali women have learnt to peel, chop, dice and shred. Despite the recent incursion of knives, peelers, graters and other modern, Western-style kitchen utensils, the bonti is still alive and well in the rural and urban kitchens of Bengal.

A Bengali lexicon compiled by Jnanendramohan Das reveals that although the term bonti has been in the Bengali language for many years, it is actually derived from the language of the ancient tribal inhabitants of the eastern regions of the country. Das traces the word 'bonti' back to ancient Bengali narrative poems such as Ghanaram Chakrabarti's 'Dharmamangal', composed during the reign of Dharma Pala (775 – 810 AD), the second ruler of Bengal's Pala dynasty. In his definitive history of Bengal, *Bangalir Itihash*, the historian Nihar Ranjan Ray presents compelling evidence of the proto-Australoid people who settled in Bengal long before the Aryans came to India and whose language, customs and ritualistic beliefs still permeate the cultural life of Bengal. Ray also notes that Buddhist terracotta sculptures from the days of the Pala dynasty depict people using the bonti to cut and portion fish.

Basically, the bonti is nothing more than a curved blade rising out of a narrow, flat, wooden base. Sometimes the blade is mounted on a small iron tripod to increase its height. Its versatility comes from the many different types and sizes of both the blade and the base, as well as from the various uses to which it is put. The bonti's uniqueness comes from the posture required to use it: one must either squat on one's haunches, or sit on the floor with one knee raised while the corresponding foot presses down on the base. As in other 'floor-oriented' cultures, such as the Japanese, the people of Bengal were accustomed to squatting or sitting on the floor for indefinite periods of time. An 1832 volume by Mrs S.C. Belnos, *Twenty-four Plates Illustrative of Hindoo and European Manners in Bengal*, depicts a Bengali kitchen complete with utensils and a woman seated in front of a low stove, cooking. The author comments: 'Their furniture consists of low beds, small stools, a chest or two, perhaps an old-fashioned chair on which the master sits with his legs crossed under him, [and] a Hookah of cocanut [*sic*] shell on a brass stand ...' Even today, in rural Bengal where many cottages are sparsely furnished, people—especially men—squat comfortably on porches or under the shade of large trees as they smoke and chat. Only after the European presence was well established later in the nineteenth century did the living room or dining room, equipped with couches, chairs and tables, become a part of the ordinary Bengali home.

The bonti also appears in Kalighat paintings, a body of indigenous works produced in the vicinity of the Kalighat Temple, built in 1829 on the banks of the river Hooghly (a branch of the Ganges) in Calcutta. As Calcutta grew under the British rule and its Bengali residents developed a semi-decadent 'babu' culture, the Kalighat painters focussed their attention on urban rather than the canonic rural life.

To use a knife of any size or shape, the cook must bear down on the item being cut with one hand, while at the same time holding it with the other hand to prevent it from slipping. But unlike the more familiar knife, the bonti uses horizontal, rather than vertical, force. The cook positions herself in front of the tool, one foot pressed firmly against the wooden base. She then uses both hands to slide the vegetable, fruit, fish or meat, against the curving blade that faces her. To those used to working with a knife, the delicacy with which the rigidly positioned blade cuts seems miraculous: it peels the tiniest potato, trims the tendrils of string beans, splits the fleshy stems of plants, chops greens into minute particles for stir-frying, and even scales the biggest fish. At the great fish markets of Calcutta, fishmongers sit tightly packed together as they dismember giant carp and hilsa on huge, gleaming bontis, all the while engaging in jocular repartee about who has the better fish.

Like knives, bontis come in many different sizes, with blades varying in height, width and shape. Women using the instrument at home generally have two medium-sized bontis, one for cutting vegetables, the other for fish and meat (the animal products collectively known as 'amish'). This separation of vegetarian and non-vegetarian food was rigidly practised in all traditional Hindu homes until fairly recently and led to the term *'ansh-bonti'* for the tools used to cut fish or meat (ansh means 'fish scale'). Professional cooks dealing with large volumes of food use considerably heftier bontis than housewives. Their ansh-bontis must be strong enough to cut a twenty- or thirty-pound carp, and the blades are proportionately wider and higher. The bonti blade is generally made of iron rather than stainless steel, and it tends to rust if not immediately dried. Repeated use blunts the blade, so itinerant experts roam the cities with special gear for sharpening bontis and knives.

An interesting blade is found on the *kuruni*, a bonti used for the specific purpose of grating coconuts. In this type of bonti, the blade curves out of the wooden base in the usual way, but its tip is crowned with a round, serrated piece of metal. The cook sits in front of the kuruni with the front end of its base on a woven mat or tray, or even on a piece of newspaper. Holding one half of a fresh coconut in both hands, she scrapes it with circular motions against the metal disk as the coconut flesh rains down in a stream of white.

Such are the day-to-day uses of the bonti in the Bengali kitchen. But as with any instrument with a long history, this tool is endowed with a wealth of associations reaching far beyond the mundane. Although professional male chefs use the bonti, it is inextricably associated with Bengali women. The image of a woman seated at her bonti, surrounded by baskets of vegetables, is a cultural icon. Holding the vegetable or fish in both hands and running it into the blade makes the act of cutting a relatively softer, gentler motion than the more masculine gesture of bringing a knife down with force on a hard surface: the food is embraced even as it is dismembered.

In the days when most Bengalis lived in extended, multi-generational families, women had to make large meals every day. Usually the elderly grandmother or the widowed aunt was responsible for cutting the vegetables, while the younger women took on the more arduous task of cooking over the hot stove. This ritual of cutting, called *kutno kota*, was almost as important as the daily rituals carried out for the household gods. Some of my fondest childhood memories involve sitting near my grandmother on the floor of the large central space in her Calcutta house as she peeled and sliced the vegetables for the day's main afternoon meal. A grand array of shapes and colours surrounded her: purple and greenish-white eggplants; green-and-white striped *patols* (a favourite gourd-like vegetable of Bengalis); leafy greens of the *noteshaak* with their fleshy, rhubarb-like stems; yellow crescents of pumpkin; pale-skinned potatoes. During holidays and school vacations I would always sit beside my grandmother and watch her at the bonti ...

She takes a long, purple eggplant and dexterously halves it against the blade, then starts cutting one of the halves into smaller pieces. I pick up the remaining half and inspect the white, seed-studded flesh. Something is moving. A worm, secretly embedded in the flesh, is now forced into the open. What kind of insect is it, I ask my grandmother, what kind of insect lives hidden inside an eggplant and what does it eat? She smiles at me, takes the eggplant from my hand and cuts off the infested portion. Then she embarks on a story from an ancient Hindu text about a king who lived inside a glass palace without any openings to protect himself from the wrath of the snake king who had become his sworn enemy. But one day, when the king bit into a mango, a tiny worm came out from inside the flesh and within seconds was transformed into a huge serpent that bit him to death. I look down at the still-crawling worm in the discarded bit of eggplant with new respect ...

The woman at the bonti, however, is not always an elderly narrator. The young, nubile daughter of the family or the newly married bride sitting at the bonti are also part of Bengali iconography. As she joyfully manipulates food against the versatile blade, the young woman epitomizes feminine skills. When marriages were arranged in rural Bengal, the bridegroom's family would come to look at the prospective bride and ask to see her kitchen skills, noting how well she could chop with the bonti. In the southern district of Barisal in Bangladesh, it was not enough for a prospective bride to chop just any vegetable. Her future in-laws often demanded that she sit at the bonti and cut a bunch of *koloishaak*, the leafy greens of the legume *khesari daal*, whose fibrous leaves and stem have to be chopped very fine before stir-frying. The ideal bride had to be able to reduce the resistant bunch into minute particles of green. Yet, handling the bonti well had another advantage in Barisal. The local women used their bontis to defend themselves and their homes against gangs of armed robbers who attacked prosperous homesteads when the men were away.

Bengali literature contains many references to another, less domestic, aspect of the woman at the bonti. Recurring images portray her as young and demure, sitting with her head bent, concentrating on her hands as she moves the vegetable or the fish towards the lethal blade. Often a married woman is pictured, her head modestly covered with the shoulder end of her sari whose colourful border frames her face and hair. But the discreet posture and modest covering were a foil for a flirtatious element in extended family life, which offered virtually no privacy. Men—whether a husband or a romantic interest—could expect many eloquent, sidelong glances cast with surreptitious turns of the head as the woman went about her domestic tasks with the bonti.

An extension of this mild titillation is found in *Shobha*, a fascinating album of photographs by Gurudas Chattopadhyay, published around 1930. His photographs portray some of Calcutta's best-known prostitutes and are obviously intended for erotic stimulation. But this is no collection of *Playboy*-like nudes. Instead, each woman has been photographed fully clothed and seated before a bonti! Here is a study in body language: the straight back, the bifurcated legs (one crossed, the other raised), the coy eyes peeking out from under the sari covering the head. To the Bengali viewer/voyeur of the time, the bonti, by enforcing this posture, created a uniquely erotic vision of the female figure, rich in implication and suggestiveness.

Despite its long history, it is probably inevitable that in the new global century the bonti will eventually vanish. The kitchens of Bengal are rapidly changing. Knives rather than bontis are becoming the cutting implements of choice. Tables and countertops are triumphing over the floor; chairs, tables and couches are becoming as integral to the home as the doors and windows. Women no longer live in extended families, nor do their mornings consist of the leisurely ritual of kutno kota, when several women worked together, forming a sisterhood of the bonti. Now women are likely to work outside the home, which leaves little time for that kind of domestic fellowship. But for those of us who remember, the bonti will continue to be a potent symbol of multi-faceted femininity.

Burmese Day

KAI FRIESE

Tamu (A Myanmar Border town with India). The town is restricted to the foreign travelers due to the occasionally outbreak of robbery. This has become a story for the present generation because the Myanmar regime managed to incorporate all the arms group to the legal fold. Today Tamu is prevailed with law and order that is attracting the third party citizen. To tell it true, traveling through the demarcation is sampling the two different tastes in one dish. Burmese travel website http://www.7daystour.com/tamu.htm

I have an appetite for border districts that my stomach doesn't appreciate. The indecipherable scrawls in my travel journals from these culinary marchlands are illuminated by a few exuberant passages of clear block print, representing something I knew my future sedentary self would savour—but it's never the food.

Often it's a conversation, sometimes a visual epiphany, occasionally a narcotic, and quite frequently a beverage. The hot, sweet goat milk of Nirda, the pepper tea of Munsiari, the effervescent cold chhang of Kaza, and welcome tots of 'defence' rum all over the place. And though there have been a few gastronomic adventures that left me too shaken to record, I can recall these bilious madeleines at will. I wish I could forget them. The clumpy thukpa with a whiff of donkey ordure that induced projectile vomiting on the snows of Parangla. The tuna and Orange Tang tea on the plains near Hanle—which I quite enjoyed at the time, but then again, that was almost a beverage. The boiled macaque that I hurled over a campfire in Arunachal.

It's alimentary: the closer you get to the border, the more you miss Maggi noodles. Except that, as with all good axioms, there's one exception. Which in my case was the 25th of February 2000 when, relaxing in a grubby hotel room in the Manipuri border town of Moreh, in a clear hand and an exultant green pen, I recorded the following: 'Delicious lunch at Kabaw Hotel in Tamu. Menacing/ingratiating proprietor wearing khaki pants, banyaan and a big pistol. Works for the Myanmar Immigration Department. Tried to bully us into taking a room for the afternoon. Escaped by ordering everything on the menu: crispy venison, fish curry, chicken curry, steamed beans, veg soup with greens, drumstick soup with meatballs, salad, garnish, rice. Stella Artois and Murphy's Irish Stout. Rs 180 for two!'

It really was exceptional. But I was also very relieved. My wife and I had spent the previous day in Moreh listening to the melancholy tales of Burmese Tamil refugees, sinister rumours of SLORC spies disguised as beggars, and learning the grandiose acronyms of the various underground armies patrolling the denuded forest on either side of the border: UNLF, RPFPLA, KCP, KYKL, PREPAK, KNF, KNA ... It was a creepy little town, with nothing much to recommend it. The only entertainment was one cinema hall and a large video parlour with speakers broadcasting the soundtracks of Bhojpuri, Nepali, Meitei and martial arts sex films on to the streets. I was drawn into a screening of *Lethal Panther* and was stunned by the sight of entire families, men, women and suckling babies, watching a nude ninja straddling her gurgling lover—and then disembowelling him in media res.

But the cheap thrills on screen were only the penumbra of Moreh's main attraction: the smugglers' market of Namphalong Bazaar, ten feet away from the Indian border checkpost Gate No. 2. And for Rs 10 you could get a day pass to visit Moreh's Burmese twin, Tamu, a short tonga ride away in the Kabaw Valley. 'Neater and wealthier than Moreh' was my first impression, '... and even sulkier'.

All that changed that afternoon at the Kabaw Hotel. Memory has magnified the delight of that meal to such an extent that even the seedy streets of Moreh, its sleazy hotels and shady characters acquired a crepuscular glamour. I thought of Moreh when I watched Orson Welles' grimy classic *A Touch of Evil*. And I saw myself in Mike Vargas (Charlton Heston!) taking his American bride Suzie (Janet Leigh) through the mean streets of Los Robles. 'All border towns show the worst of the country,' he said comfortingly. I thought of it more recently when I read Raymond Chandler's last great novel *The Long Goodbye*. 'Tijuana is not Mexico,' says the world-weary Philip Marlowe. 'No border town is anything but a border town.'

In December 2006, I talked my way into an assignment to revisit Tamu–Moreh. It was for a culinary piece (you're reading it) but my real agenda was to savour the *noir*-ish charms of Tijuanaland again. After the flight to Imphal and a four-hour road journey, I reached Moreh too late to visit Tamu but with plenty of time for a recce of Namphalong Bazaar, now bristling with everything from power tools to iPods. I befriended a liquor stall owner who told me that the pistol-packing proprietor of Kabaw Hotel was dead. '*Char number se mar gaya,*' he said, which turned out to mean AIDS. We discussed his whiskies, which ran from Thai-bottled Vat 69 (750cl, Rs 350) to Scotland-bottled (Rs 600) to Burmese Two Dog and our own RC. 'Everyone wants to drink foreign liquor,' he said sagely. 'Two Dog is foreign in Moreh and Bagpiper is foreign over here.' Then he recommended three restaurants for me to visit in Tamu the next day. One Chinese, one Tamil, one Burmese.

Dusk fell as I made my way back down Moreh's main street and the Assam Rifles were on patrol. Perfect strangers warned me not to stay out late. The town was still skittering from the murder of an Assam Rifles, JCO by an UNLF assassin in July 2006. Every storyteller was fascinated by the same ghoulish detail: He had been shot in a PCO while he was talking to his wife. His name was Tuk Bahadur Pun. '*Do phool wala,*' someone said. A subedar.

I repaired to a lamp-lit bar and ran through a peg of Two Dog, another of Cutty Sark and a can of Dali beer from Yunnan. That's right, one Burmese, one Scotch, one beer—accompanied by tapas of boiled mustard stalks and small fish called 'fiftin', cooked whole and served with onion and salt.

I was up at dawn the next morning—5 a.m. on this fringe of the country—and by eight I was in a motorcycle tuktuk on the road to Tamu—except that it was nine, Myanmar time. Ten minutes later I walked into the Float restaurant, a Tamu landmark ('any national, any religion can come and have'), only to find a raucous wedding party in progress. The groom himself invited me to join them, but I wasn't dressed for the occasion and departed with directions for Meik Li Yint a few minutes away in a sidecar cycle-rickshaw. Though later in the day I did have an honest Tamil spread (complete with fish, mutton, pachadi, muzhagapodi and more) and a small Burmese meal of sesame chicken noodles with broth and spicy cabbage (Sankhaoswe, Heiyi and Kofi Chen), it was the Yunnan cuisine of Meik Li Yint that made my day this time. The menu ranged from 'Pig Ear Salad' to 'Seramblod Egg' but I had 'Rahoit Greens', which were stir-fried Chinese broccoli spears (leafy with tiny florets) with a few blanched tomatoes, spring onions, chillies and garlic. I pointed at 'Meet with Sour Mustard' on the menu but was served a more mundane chicken dish instead. Soup was served last, an enormous two-litre vat of 'Twelve Young Vegetable Soup'. I tried counting the vegetables swimming around in this pellucid aquarium, but after the snow peas, broccoli, cauliflower, baby carrots and greens, I snared some brown tofu and then boiled quail eggs, and decided to just eat instead.

When I left for Imphal the next day, my notebook was sated with its usual complement of coversation, anecdote, alcohol and a *silent* porn film called *Love Is Poison*. Look, the food is great but Tamu is no culinary Mecca. It's just a border town. Still, if you want some *noir*-ishment with your nourishment, you really do get two different tastes in one dish.

The Things I Will Put in My Mouth

SRINATH PERUR

An Indian's omnivorousness is characterized by his or her place on an intricately notched scale. Through some complex intersection of place, religion, caste, income, health fiendishness, moral conscience, degree of cosmopolitanism or tendency to social reform or asceticism or adventure, a person's diet can range from hipster veganism and no-root-vegetables to lacto-ovo-vegetarianism to eating fish and/or chicken (except on certain days of the week and/or killed only in a certain manner) to eating mutton (but perhaps not cooking it at home) to not eating pork to shunning beef (and forcing you to do so too) to eating just about anything. In heartily prejudiced common terminology, one end of the scale corresponds roughly to 'pure veg' and the other end to 'hardcore non-veg'.[1] I happen to have done some confused sliding along this scale, and since I'm curious about the process by which people arrive at the set of foods they'll put into their mouths, I might as well begin with myself.

Family legend has it that I was a mean hunter as a toddler. I'd be crawling about desultorily on the floor when I would spot an insect at a distance, and freeze. Then, in a frenzy of slapping and sliding (fond aunts recount), I'd make my way to the prey, bring down upon it a small but heavy hand, and eat it before the adults could intervene.

Hunting-gathering has been how we humans have fed ourselves for most of our time on this planet, and I might have continued in my foraging ways if not for the fact that I was growing up in these times in a vegetarian Brahmin home. The instinctive omnivore in me went dormant once I turned properly bipedal. At home there was plenty of milk and curd, but not eggs or meat of any kind; grain and vegetables, but not onion and garlic. I didn't realize it at the time, but the pungent charm to my adolescent self of food eaten off pushcarts or at restaurants had much to do with their containing onion and garlic. After I returned from these excursions, my grandmother would clutch the edge of her saree to her nose if I entered the room she was in, sometimes even the day after.

Looking back at my childhood, I marvel at the transparency and resilience of the cultural bubble I lived in. My family, friends, neighbours, classmates were almost all 'upper'-caste, middle-class Hindus. It took no effort to be vegetarian in this world. When

---

1   There's also the school of thought that 'hardcore non-veg' is not just about the range of animal flesh consumed but also about how integral it is to one's diet. There's probably a good deal of overlap between those two categories, and it's perhaps not worth getting all hardcore about it.

I was in high school and would eat out, there might be a few omnivores[2] present, but there were always enough vegetarians around to ensure that we could stick to what we were used to. Someone would go, 'Okay, so let's order two veg and two non-veg dishes', and there would be a reconfiguration of the table so all the vegetarians ended up sitting together, solely (we believed) for the ease of sharing food.

I'm somewhat ashamed now by my lack of curiosity as a boy. How could I be perfectly content to leave an entire category of food untasted? I did have friends who were vegetarian at home but went to great lengths to eat chicken or fish or eggs outside. Perhaps I didn't join them because I was never too consciously aware of the fact that those foods were forbidden at home. They were, of course, but in so entrenched a manner as to be unnoticeable. I suppose my attitude was that being vegetarian was a default setting that didn't require thinking about; it was just the way we were. No one told me not to eat meat, and so I didn't. It was more clear that alcohol and tobacco were forbidden, and I wasted no time in trying them.

I was sixteen or seventeen when I had my first taste of animal flesh (after, that is, the insects of my early foraging days). Five or six of us friends had gone to a Chinese restaurant where we ordered Veg American Chopsuey—a dish that is neither Chinese nor American. A sweet, red, starchy slop arrived, and it was a few blistering mouthfuls later that I realized that amidst

---

2   While it's common usage to say 'non-vegetarian', it seems silly to define a category as the negative of a smaller category. That is, the term makes it appear as though vegetarianism were the norm while in fact many more people in the world, and in India, are non-veg. Plus, the Indian use of 'non-veg' has connotations of dissolution and loucheness that are both undeserved and unearned. For example: 'Let me now tell you a non-veg joke.'

the fried noodles and chopped vegetables was something that looked like shredded cabbage but was softer and chewier. It had to be chicken. I looked up at the one regular meat-eater among us and he motioned to me to stay quiet. (To keep the Jain girl in our midst from throwing up, he told me later.) Then someone voiced the concern that we had been served the chicken version of the dish by mistake. The resident omnivore only shrugged non-committally. (Why waste food and money, he said later.) A couple of us finished our plates; some others, who had been eating happily enough until then, gave up after sifting through the mess with a fork. The waiter looked confused when asked what we'd been served, and we were in any case too meek to argue. We later came to see it as an adventure—except the Jain girl, who it seems did go home and throw up.

Not long after, I went to college where I spent four years living in a hostel. The campus had messes veg and non-veg, and I was in one of the former. Breakfast was a particularly disappointing affair unless you ate eggs, which were served in the veg messes too, and I started eating eggs one morning without any thought. We all got tired of mess food quickly enough. We'd go out to restaurants in groups when we could afford it or get someone else to pay. This was when a broader range of diet preferences gathered at one table. There wasn't much discussion about *why* each one ate whatever they did. It was all too complex to get into. A dismissive remark might be aimed at a vegetarian, or someone else might be asked, 'You're not eating chicken today?', to which, 'No, it's Thursday', was a perfectly adequate answer. There were some who turned omnivore during those years away from home, either from curiosity, or to fit in with a new set of friends, or because they were going to the gym with less-than-ideal results and someone had told them that nothing could happen without animal protein. Most graduated with their diets relatively unchanged.

It was not until I was in my mid-twenties that I began to give active thought to the matter of my being vegetarian. I was then living in Mumbai and the people I was meeting came from more diverse backgrounds. Dinner hosts would groan and ask, 'Do you at least eat egg?' Perhaps the assumption was that no meal is complete without some form of animal protein or that offering only vegetables was a shameful way to treat a guest. While meeting someone for the first time at a party or a restaurant, the question occasionally intruded mid-meal out of nowhere: 'Are you veg out of choice or ...'

The part that remained unexpressed, I learnt with time, sought to find out if I was vegetarian for puritanical reasons. If I was, that might mean I was also capable of other forms of appalling orthodoxy—who knew, perhaps I believed I was superior by birth; perhaps I was even devout. After all, diet in the Indian context has much to do with caste and religion. But I often got the feeling that the question was intended not to identify my own beliefs, but either to work out my antecedents or to determine the extent to which my hedonism was repressed.[3] The pity or puzzlement of those who grew up in a culture of meat-eating I could easily stand. But I could not decide which group I found more annoying: the vegetarians who felt active relief at finding me to be one of their kind, or the former vegetarians who had bucked their background and now condescendingly said things like, 'Want to try a piece?'

Another factor came up in my twenties. I knew I wanted to travel widely and experience different cultures—and what is food if not culture? It's rooted in a land, its climate and

---

3　'But you drink?'

history, the sensibility of its people. What use was going to a place if I had to subsist on theplas and bread and cheese? Not unrelated to this was a somewhat romantic aspiration: that I should be able to partake of anything that a fellow human being considered food.

I was vegetarian by habit. I had no personal revulsion towards meat-eating; it was just that I wasn't used to it. So I began to train myself to be an omnivore, starting with the occasional small portion. It took some effort at first. Meat felt faintly alien in my mouth, mostly because it was far chewier than anything else I'd called food. It also filled me up faster.[4] The intervals between my meat-eating got shorter, the circumstances less exceptional. I'd just begun to leave behind my socially inexpedient vegetarianism when another beast began to raise its head: now that I was actively working towards eating animals, there was no way I could not reckon with the moral implications of doing so.

It's usually simple enough to regard meat as a food substance detached from its once-living source. Chunks, pieces, slices, slabs, mince—they are all conveniently familiar and disembodied. But I'd receive occasional reminders of the fact that what I was eating used to be a living animal whose body worked not so differently from mine: the accusing hard-boiled eye of a fish in mustard gravy, a pointlessly articulating joint left after a chicken leg had been consumed, the ferrous tang of a well-chewed piece of meat.

---

4   On a couple of occasions I'd tried eating nothing but fruit for the whole day and found I had to spend an inordinate amount of time feeding myself. The experiment proved fruitful in other ways: I realized that grain was dense, and therefore a more efficient way of sustaining oneself; also, the density of their food explained why cows felt compelled to eat all day and why carnivores in the wild could go days without feeding themselves.

To be able to extend such moral consideration to non-human animals is a luxury. We were foragers for most of human history (around 200,000 years), obtaining nutrition from a variety of plant and animal sources. It's likely that only after the advent of agriculture—some ten or twelve thousand years ago—was a reliable supply of plant-based food possible. Even in today's hyper-connected, well-supplied world, there are those in cold or arid areas who would find it difficult, or at least terribly expensive, to subsist without animals as part of their diet. When it is manageable, there's always something else that makes it inconvenient: tradition, culture, tastes, bodily rhythms attuned to a way of eating. But it is also true that more people than ever before can now consider not eating animals. Where the motivation is other than personal or planetary health, the quandary is likely to be on the lines of whether it is all right to take animal life when it is not absolutely necessary.

It's not an issue that's regarded with much consistency. In most societies around the world today, kicking a pet dog is likely to be met with outrage, perhaps even brief imprisonment, while the systematic daily killing of thousands of animals is unexceptionable. The difference seems to be that the latter category of assault is seen as a human need, not just a whim or indulgence.

To think that non-human animal lives matter at all comes from our perceiving something in them that's common with us. We can't seem to help seeing ourselves in animals, especially mammals, which are biologically closer to us, but still the whole matter is fraught with selective empathy. Some will be repulsed by the idea of eating dogs or cats because they know them better by virtue of their being common pets. Presumably it is easier in the case of these animals to see at least an essential rudeness to killing something that clearly has an appreciation of life.[5]

In my case, some of these questions about taking animal life as well as an answer of sorts crystallized early one Mumbai morning. I had worked all night and was in the grip of that strange high that comes from not sleeping. I was making my way through a network of narrow lanes to a place that served pre-dawn breakfast. I heard shouts as I got there. A goat had escaped from the butcher shop next door. When I reached the scene, three men had confined the goat to the arms of a t-junction of lanes. The goat ran from end to end in a frenzy, turning back when it found one of the men blocking its path. The men converged on it, caught it, and dragged it to the butcher's. I may be anthropomorphizing, but if ever I've seen a living being that wanted—was desperate—to live, it was that goat.

The moral question for me was a different one than for most omnivores. I was entirely used to living on vegetarian food, and quite content to do so. I had no deep-rooted cultural associations with meat eating, so there was no prospect of missing my mother's cooking or anything of the sort. I'd also travelled a fair amount by then and found that it was possible to get by in most places as a vegetarian. The question for me

---

5   Neuroscience has been invoked to weigh in on whether or not certain animals can feel pain, and if they can, whether it is a dumb reflex, or whether they are capable of dread, anxiety and the entire gamut of distress that we humans call suffering. To spare the reader pain and nuance and cut a long story crudely short: yes, many non-human animals seem capable of experiencing pain and suffering in ways similar to us. With many other animals, we simply don't know what's going on, but it seems significant to note that the harder scientists look the more they find going on. Why, even plants are now believed to have rudimentary forms of memory and the ability to feel pain.

was more about whether to take up eating animals rather than whether to give it up. The answer was clear: no.

But it would have to be a qualified 'no'. Soon after, I went to a friend's house for dinner. I had enjoyed her mutton biryani on a previous visit, and she was feeling particularly good about the one she'd made this time. To refuse to taste it would have been churlish.

It's always partial, the consideration we extend to animals. Even people who feel strongly about killing animals will seldom value one animal life as equal to one human life. There aren't many (though they exist) who disagree that it's okay for someone to kill an animal in self-defence, or for animals to be killed or put to discomfort in the process of developing life-saving drugs for humans.[6] We will stand by our own. But even in this regard, we are only barely coming round to treating humans humanely.

In India, the modalities of eating—what people eat, are allowed to eat, with whom, in which order, off what plates[7]— have long been used to dominate, marginalize, impose hierarchy and exclude. Being vegetarian in India is too often accompanied by smugness[8] and a revulsion for the food of others, which is in

---

6 My writing was interrupted a couple of sentences earlier by a swarm of winged termites. At times of the year here, in Bangalore, they emerge from colonies in the ground and, primed as they are for flying towards light, invade houses in the evening. I closed the doors and windows of my room and found their number continuing to proliferate. Investigation revealed that there was a nest in an electrical box inside the room that teemed with tiny grubs and larger winged fellows that emerged at intervals into the light. I've sprayed some insecticide, and even as I continue writing in another room about moral consideration for animals, I am hoping that thousands of insect lives come to an end.

7 And even head-clutchingly messed-up stuff such as who gets to roll over whose leftovers for currying divine favour.

8 Why is it that no restaurant saves on signage by dropping the 'Pure' preceding 'Vegetarian'?

itself a form of violence.[9] To be able to sit with someone and share a meal is a small sign of human fellowship, and one I'm unwilling to abandon out of consideration to animals.

And so mine is a confused, compromised position when it comes to being an omnivore. I do consume milk and eggs, both of which I might cut down on at some point seeing that those industries are responsible for plenty of animal suffering.[10] Apart from that, I'm almost always vegetarian, though I'll eat animals when there's no other reasonable option or when I'm sharing food with others and don't feel like making a fuss. The thumb rule I try to follow is to not add to the demand. Sometimes I make an exception when I'm travelling and want to try something I've never eaten before. On those occasions there's really nothing that I absolutely won't put in my mouth (though it's been a while since I ate an insect, unless you count that caterpillar from a couple of years ago). On that scale that goes from pure veg to hard-core non-veg, I suppose I'd count as some sort of hard-core non-practising non-vegetarian.

---

9 For instance, Ambedkar has argued convincingly that the roots of untouchability lie in the caste-Hindu horror of beef and those who consume it.

10 But what would I do without chai and curd rice I don't know.

The Sound of Flowers

JHAMPAN MOOKERJEE

'When Bada Dev, the great god, created earth, he also made the tree of life. He called it mahua. It gives us food, timber, it shelters birds, insects and animals. Only good spirits live on it, for it gives us the water of life.' On the edge of Kanha National Park, Bagh Singh Dhurwe, a Gond tribal, told me this story many years ago.

And as with popular folk tales, I have heard many variations of this theme over the years. It seems when Bada Dev, who is a formless top-god spirit for the Gond and Baiga tribes in central India, created the world, he also created Nanga Baiga and Nangi Baigin. These first naked Baiga humans, like Adam and Eve, were the progenitors of the entire Baiga race. But having done that, and being a caring godfather, he was genuinely concerned: 'What will these guys drink, and more importantly, offer us gods in their shrines?' he worried. So he called a few animals that happened to be around: a tiger, a dove and a parakeet, and a mouse and a pig; he then asked them to turn into mahua trees.

When these trees started flowering in spring, birds and animals ate the flowers and became loud and happy. The humans noticed this and got hooked on to it as well. 'Mahua has a way with you. If you have a few, you feel happy and chirp like a parakeet or coo like a dove, laughing a lot, saying the same things over and over again. If you drink a little more, you become a tiger, full of courage and bluster and you roar. But if you drink even more, it turns you into a pig or a mouse, sniffling and rolling on the ground, wallowing in mud or looking for a hole to hide in. Such are the ways of mahua,' Bagh Singh said.

Ten years ago I thought this was a quaint lesson on the etiquette of rural drinking, little knowing that this tree is so primary to life here that on the central Indian deciduous landscape an entire forest can get wiped out but no one will touch a mahua tree!

There is another charming story as well. It seems a couple was in love, but could not marry as they were from different tribes. Rather than break this union, they went deep into the forest and killed themselves. It is said that watered by their blood two plants grew on that spot. God was so moved that he named one plant ganja (or cannabis) and the other, mahua. It is believed that mahua and ganja are family.

My first drink of mahua was a bit of a shock. Having run out of rum on a long assignment in the interiors of Chhattisgarh, I asked our local assistant if there was anything that he could get for us. He came back late in the evening looking very happy, with a dirty mineral water bottle filled with an opaque fluid. It smelt strong as I took a swig from it, but it was surprisingly smooth and had a flavour like nothing else I had ever had before. It is difficult to describe the flavour of mahua if you have not smelt it. The closest I can think of is a cross between musk, ripe jack fruit, guava and rice wine, but many might disagree.

After three swigs I was slurring, but it was a nice, benumbed feeling. By about seven swigs I was happily immobile, I am told, with a smile fixed on my face. My eyelids and limbs felt leaden and everything around moved as if in slow motion. I have since had mahua regularly and it always makes me relaxed, slow and peaceful. But it takes getting used to. There are very few people I have introduced mahua to, and they have loved it from the word go. I usually serve it at home with some fizzy lemon drink or even soda with a slice of lime. But in the forest I have seen people dancing rhythmically, drinking through moonlit nights around warm campfires in spring or autumn after the harvest. They dance and drink, and drink and dance till they collapse in a stupor. Someone else then takes their place till they wake up again and start dancing. It's a part of their lives.

In 1861 James Forsyth, an English civil servant, was assigned to be the Acting Conservator of Forests, Central Provinces, to survey a large patch of forest around what is today the Pachmarhi Biosphere and the Satpura Tiger Reserve near Hoshangabad in Madhya Pradesh. Basing himself at Pachmarhi, he travelled around this rich stretch of almost virgin forest with its Gond and Baiga people for a little less than a decade. A keen hunter himself, he enjoyed shooting tigers and other game as he rode through the territory. He took copious notes which he later turned into a book that was posthumously published in London in 1871 as *The Highlands of Central India: Notes on the Forests and Wild Tribes, Natural History and Sports.* In a style that is very Victorian evangelist, full of reformist posturing that was typical of those days, this book is the only one I have come across that compares mahua alcohol to Irish whisky. 'The spirit, when well made and mellowed by age, is by no means of despicable quality, resembling in some degree Irish whisky.' He was a keen observer of village life and must have imbibed mahua regularly as he is the only one who has written with some affinity and erudition on the subject. But more on that later.

Mahua alcohol is regularly offered to forest spirits and gods. It is a must for celebrations around births, deaths and weddings. Among Gonds the boy's parents go to the girl's with an offering of good mahua as an engagement ritual. On the wedding day two young boys from the groom's family are sent to the forest to collect small branches of mahua. They are then sent with these to the bride's house where an elderly lady receives them. She washes the branches and their feet with water and turmeric. These branches are then kept at the wedding location as celestial witnesses to the marriage. Of course a lot of mahua is drunk as well.

In another corner of the country, near the infamous Godhara in Gujarat, live the Rathwa Bhil tribals who paint a temple to their god, Pithora Baba, on the main wall of their house. Every Rathwa Bhil tribal family is expected to do this once in their lifetime. It is an elaborate and expensive nine-day ritual which includes daily feasts with drinks for the entire village community. People collect in hundreds for it. Preparations begin well in advance with large drums of mahua being made as excise officials look the other way in this predominantly tribal zone of dry Gujarat. Local Pithora painters are booked for the ceremony with gifts that vary according to the intricacy and the number of gods that need to be drawn. The goats and chickens that are to be sacrificed are also in direct proportion to the gods being painted. The gods look like humans and ride horses across the wall, along with vignettes of daily life in the villages and surrounding forests full of wild animals. Among the recurrent motifs are a chameleon, a spiky sloth bear and one toddy tapper climbing up a date palm in a lower corner of the wall. Traditionally, the colours used for the painting are made of local dyes mixed with milk and mahua alcohol. The painting has to be completed in nine days, with the prayers, drinking, singing and feasting going on simultaneously, and consecrated on the last day. Once created, these paintings are never touched, even if they fade or the wall crumbles.

Contrary to what the Internet will tell you, mahua is a slow grower with low survival rates. But once it crosses the first few years, it starts gathering speed depending on how nutritious the soil is. In thick forests it tends to grow straight, but on open land the tree spreads out with a big and handsome head. It can grow over 20 metres and easily survive for over a century. Found on the edges of Gujarat and Rajasthan bordering Madhya Pradesh, it extends as far as the plains of Nepal through the Gangetic basin and then through Uttar Pradesh, Bihar, West Bengal, Odisha, Andhra Pradesh, Madhya Pradesh, Chhattisgarh, Maharashtra and Karnataka all the way down to the edges of Kerala and Goa through Tamil Nadu. The central Indian species has rounded leaves, but further south a sub-species with elongated leaves takes over, though the flower and fruit are really no different. The tree starts flowering after about ten years, which is a long time.

Called mahua or mahwa in Hindi; mahuda in Gujarati; irupa, mohu and idu in central Indian tribal languages like Durva, Halbi and Gondi; mahool in Oriya; ippa in Telegu and iluppai in Tamil, the tree does not cross over into Northeast India, though it is found in Bangladesh and Myanmar. According to Amirthalingam Murugesan, the author of *Sacred Trees of Tamil Nadu*, it survives as *sthala vriksha* or temple tree in many Shiva temples.

The story goes that Shiva asked the mahua tree to grow at a particular corner of the Sri Neelakandeswarar temple in the Nagapattinam district of Tamil Nadu. Why Shiva zeroed in on an iluppai in his backyard, I don't know, (Nanditha Krishna and Amirthalingam Murugesan, who wrote the *Sacred Plants of India*, do not elucidate), but the tree did exactly what he wanted, and flourished. Shiva was so happy that he granted the tree two wishes: that its oil would be used to light the temple lamps and that mahua would be the most popular tree in that area. The temple seems to be at least a thousand years old and I am unable to confirm if its lamps are still lit with mahua oil, but as testimony to the second wish, the area apparently became so dense with the species that the temple town was named Iluppaipattu or 'the land of the mahua tree' and even now has an illupai as its *thala virutcham* (temple tree). The name *madhuka* or booze-lover is also a synonym for Shiva, which may have been a reason for his wish.

⋐

As winter slowly gives in to spring, the mahua tree yellows and sheds. For the uninitiated, a bizarre ritual now begins. When I saw this for the first time in Barkot, Odisha, six years ago, I did not know what was happening. Women and children were going around in groups tying colourful strips of old sarees to the bare mahua trees that stood in forests or even on common land. A few old trees were left alone. 'This tells others that the tree is taken,' Manju told me. 'We know which trees are ours, but this is just to make sure that no one else lays claim. The ones without ribbons are ancestral family trees on private land. Everyone knows that so no one will touch them. The tree, which can live over a hundred years, is shared by many generations of a family.'

Manju's family, which had three old trees, now cleaned all the land under the spread of the trees. The undergrowth was cut, fallen leaves swept away and then, to give the land a distinct ash colour, the stubble on the ground was burnt. The tree was then anointed with prayers.

As spring sets in (usually March-April), the naked trees burst into buds that hang like olive green tassels from the ends of the branches. Soon these turn into light yellow-green succulent, hollow, grape-like flowers rich in sugar and nutrients that bloom and drop usually between 2 and 6 a.m.!

James Forsyth noted in the 1860s something that must have been known to the people forever: 'The value of the Mhowa consists in the fleshy corolla of its flower, and in its seeds. The flower is highly deciduous, ripening and falling in the months of March and April. It possesses considerable substance, and sweet but sickly taste and smell. It is a favourite article of food with all wild tribes, and the lower classes of Hindus; but its main use is in the distillation of ardent spirits, most of what is consumed is made from Mhowa.'

I trekked with Manju's family, including her three young children, to the trees after dinner. We walked through a fairly dense forest patch in the dark. Her sister and two brothers carried axes and the children carried baskets to collect the flowers. Her husband was away on a road project in the neighbouring district. They were all barefoot and carried lanterns. I was wearing boots and my bright headlamp lit the way. 'Aren't you worried about snakes while walking barefoot?' I asked in concern. 'Why don't you marry and settle down in our village—we can always use your headlamp then,' said Sarju, her brother, and they all doubled up in giggles. 'Ummu's brother died last year,' Manju said in the middle of all this laughter. 'A bear got him in the night. We just did not see it in the lantern light.' I was suddenly a little more alert and flashed the light around and they all rolled up in laughter again. I remembered my colleague Debobroto Sircar's study on human-bear conflicts in Madhya Pradesh. Almost 70 per cent of bear attacks are during the season when both bears and people eagerly wait for the mahua trees to blossom. Entire villages, mostly women and children, are out in the forest at night. Lactating mother bears with young cubs need the food and are more aggressive around this time. Clashes are inevitable.

I quote Forsyth again: 'The luscious flowers are no less a favourite food of the brute creation than of man. Every vegetable-eating animal and bird incessantly endeavours to fill itself with Mhowa during its flowering season. Sambar, nilgae and bears appear to lose their natural apprehensions of danger in some degree during the Mhowa season; and the most favourable chance of shooting them are then obtained.'

We reached Manju's trees a little before midnight and lit a fire to keep the animals away. At a distance I could see other fires. Some people were beating tins and drums. Even then an average of ten human and unaccounted-for bear lives are lost every year in Madhya Pradesh alone. This competition for mahua flowers has disfigured, maimed and paralysed thousands of people and led bears and their cubs to brutal deaths.

Debo took me to the Chaura Dadar village near the famous shrine at Amarkantak in Madhya Pradesh, known as the source of the Narmada river. We must have travelled 20 kilometres through rough tracks, climbing up to a mesa where the village was. On one side was a gorge through which the Narmada flowed and on the other side was a mix of forest and terraced farmland. There was not a single mahua tree in the vicinity, but twenty-seven attacks took place in the past few years with two deaths, the highest in any village in central India. I sat dumbfounded in a victim's house surrounded by twelve completely disfigured human beings straight out of a horror film. 'During the season we have to walk more than 10 kilometres across the Narmada into Chhattisgarh in the night to collect the flower, for we have no trees near the village.' Why not plant mahua if there are none around the village, why do you need to walk so far away, I asked. 'Your forefathers had planted so many other trees in the village, so why not mahua?' They were a bit surprised by this dumb city question. 'How can you plant mahua? It grows on its own. No one plants mahua,' one of them said, and they all nodded, whatever remained of their mutilated heads, in a frightening display of collective agreement.

Ten years ago, when I started taking a little more than a cursory interest in mahua, I would find it odd that no nurseries stocked this plant. The forest department, which focusses only on trees that can be cut and sold, may not have had an interest in this species. But even the Van Samiti (village forest societies), which harvested the flower and the seed for substantial profits, did not grow it in their nurseries. If this tree was economically so important for the people, why did they not plant it?

In December 2012, I bumped into Nishikant Jadhav at a lodge near Tadoba National Park in Maharashtra, where he was supervising the afforestation of its grounds. A retired forest officer from Madhya Pradesh with intense eyes, long peppery hair and an abiding interest in botany, N.J. told me of a forest department mahua plantation on the Chhindwara-Nagpur road. 'It's quite old, I can't remember the details, and I don't know if it still exists, but you can check. It's the only one that I know of,' he casually said. My antennae went up and thus began my search for the only known mahua plantation ever planted.

My first stop was the forest department in Bhopal and there everyone drew a blank. No one seemed to recall such a thing. 'Can't be,' they said, echoing what I had heard in villages. 'Why would someone plant mahua? Try the M.P. Forest Research Institute, they might have started something.' MPFRI in Jabalpur was working on some quick-yielding mahua strains, but was so

cagey that I felt they were building a nuclear bomb. It was finally
a tiger researcher working at the Pench National Park, adjacent
to Chhindwara, who came to my rescue. When Aniruddha
Majumdar, the researcher, heard about this plantation, he was
intrigued. 'Strange, this is in my area and I have never heard of
it. Let me talk to a few people,' he said. We were at a workshop
in Pench and I did not hear from him for three days. On the
fourth day, he came back with a eureka look in his eyes and we
set up a visit once the workshop ended.

We exited Pench through the Jamtara gate watching a large
pack of wild dogs en route—their muscular red bodies sprinting
effortlessly through tall, yellow grass swaying in the breeze as
their loud whistles rang through the air. We drove through the
beautiful countryside that alternated between yellow, red and
black with patches of bright green. The Chhindwara-Nagpur
road rolled up and down through hills and valleys with what
looked like deep canyons in the distance till we reached the
Sillewani forest rest house. Built in 1934, it was large and looked
like it had been recently restored with garish new furniture and
tiles. 'Not too many people come here,' the caretaker said, as he
gave us chai. 'Politicians camp here during elections, officers in
passage, sometimes there are parties.' Walking around, I noticed
a swimming pool. Yes, a swimming pool! It's probably the only
forest rest house in India with a swimming pool.

The forest guard, Gangaram Sanodiya, of the Khutama
Beat in the Sillewani Forest Range of the South Chhindwara
Division, was dressed in his best and confused. He clearly
expected someone of note, who wouldn't be excited by silly
things such as mahua plantations. 'You want to see the mahua
plantation,' he very politely murmured. 'Sure I will take you,
but you passed it on the way here. There is a board right on
the highway, didn't you see it?' Strangely enough, we had not,

but once we went back there, I could see why we had missed it despite the signage. It is a small two-acre plot screened by other trees on the highway and it did not look any different from other patches of forest except it had a lot more mahua trees which were exactly 65 years, 8 months, 3 weeks and 2 days old on 23 April 2013, the day we were there. Probably the only bunch of old mahua trees in a central Indian forest where you can tell the exact age to the day.

It made me even more curious. To be fair to Gangaram, once he got interested he spent time and dug up old records. Three months later, he sent me a copy of the original planning file with the help of his Range officer, M.K. Solanki. It was a revelation. Forest officers in 1948, just a year after Independence, had recognized the worth of the mahua species. The file written in cursive long hand titled *Experimental Mahua Plantation* began thus: 'The Central Provinces government in its forest department has ordered that artificial regeneration of mahua should be undertaken on an experimental scale as it is desirable to adopt measures to increase the number of this valuable species.' It defined the objectives of this experiment as 'primarily to evolve a suitable technique for the artificial regeneration of mahua (*Bassia latifolia*) which will ultimately be utilized for augmenting the individuals of the species in localities where it is scarce.'

On 19 June 1948 Sillewani Forest Range Officer S.A. Sayeed went with an assistant to collect dry seeds of 'healthy and mature mahua trees' from the nearby Nandudhana and Amla forest villages. The next day, he planted 120 seeds in clusters of four or five at a distance of 30x30 feet in four patches. The seeds started germinating around 4 July and continued to do so till 7 August. It must have started raining heavily during this period, but weather conditions are not recorded on the file.

Planned painstakingly at an estimated cost of Rs 196 in May 1948 by Sayeed and Divisional Forest Officer, N.I. Kurian, this mahua patch was closely followed by the department till 1954. The total expense till then was 973 rupees 15 annas and 3 paise. I could not trace either of these officers or their families. Interest seemed to fade after 1954 and there are no records to show if this experiment yielded anything of note. Today ninety-six surviving trees on a two-acre patch stand desolate by the roadside tended to by a man from the Amla village across the road. He gets to collect all the flowers and seeds in return for this service.

In July 2012 I was looking for plants at a forest department nursery in a mining town called Ukba, about 30 kilometres from Kanha. I asked the person in charge if he had any mahua seedlings.

'Now that you ask,' he said, 'I am actually desperately looking for seeds. It is so late in the season, most *goollis* (pronounced *gool-lees*) have been used up for oil. I just can't find any. Do you know anyone who can give me a few hundred?'

I was surprised. Why would he suddenly start planting mahua?

'You are right,' he said. 'We don't do mahua, but the government has declared this as the "Year of the mahua" and informed us late. Even the funds have arrived so late that we can't find seeds.'

Exactly sixty-three years after this experiment in Chhindwara, the Madhya Pradesh forest department, after ignoring one of its most useful trees, did an about-turn and declared 2011 as the 'Year of the mahua'. Throughout 2012 I looked for places where the department was planting mahua, but could find only a few miserable patches. In 2013, I met the Additional Principal Chief Conservator of Forests in charge of Research and Development in Bhopal, who kept track of such things.

'We must have planted a few hundred thousand nursery-grown trees across the state. We have not collated figures as yet, but will mail you once we do so. You see, our minister likes to adopt one particular tree every year and encourage it. Last year was bamboo, before that was mahua. Just routine, nothing special really.' And I thought someone was finally righting a historical wrong. Of course, I never heard from him.

ଔ

We sat around the warmth of the fire waiting for the flowers to fall. 'The tree seems to follow a distinct cycle. Two years of good flowering followed by a lean season. If the rains aren't good for a few years, the yield automatically declines. When there is a drought, the trees don't flower as much. In those years our crops fail as well and we actually cook and eat the dried flower that is stored in the house. Very little *daru* is made during those years. Before our village got a ration shop, most poor tribal families had mahua in the dry summer months, when there was no other food in the forest,' Manju said.

In Barkot, Odisha, I must have been in a deep sleep for Sarju's urgent taps woke me up with a start. 'Listen,' he said dramatically. A bit groggy, I first thought he was pointing to a bear. And then it came to me: in the silence of the night, a steady pitter-patter of light rain, but with big drops. But though the April night had cooled down considerably, this was certainly no rain. So what was that sound? 'Flowers falling ...' We both listened to this rain in silence. Round and fleshy grape-like things which hardly looked like any flower that I knew of steadily plopped on my head. I put one in my mouth. It tasted musky, refreshing and very sweet with a bit of grit.

All around women and children slept while men kept watch. On the edges of a few trees some ghosts began to move. I flashed the headlamp and noticed a spotted deer and a wild boar seeking their share. As tins clanged they melted away. Slowly the skies lit up. Women and children awoke, stretched and started picking the fallen flowers one by one, bodies bent double. The flowers stopped falling around 7 a.m., but this meticulous and painstaking collection went on till almost 9.00. And then, with baskets full and heavy, we slowly walked back.

At the village there was no rest. The courtyard was swept and the morning's collection spread out to dry. Next to it was yesterday's lot, already changing colour. The dried flowers looked brownish red. These were thrashed to take off the dust and then stored in nylon sacks. There was enough work to keep them going twenty-four hours without a break. The leafless mahua tree flowers continuously for nearly three weeks before rich red leaves erupt and the flowering stops. As the flowering cycle varies, for a little over two months thousands of villages and millions of people in central India get busy going through this ritual every day, perhaps for thousands of years. The local markets closely watch this activity as they eagerly await the harvest.

Each of Manju's adult trees yield around 150 kilos. In a good year she could end up with 600 kilos, if not more. In a bad year she could get less than half of that, but the prices would go up. She will at best store around 50 kilos at home and sell the rest in the local market. In 2013, the prices started at Rs 16 per kilo and went up to 21. Manju held her stock and made over Rs 10,000—a substantial amount in that economy. Larger households, which have the ability to harvest more trees, can end up with much more. 'This is ready money used to buy a lot of our household needs. Storage trunks for clothes, grain and so many other things, even jewellery. In my grandfather's time, dried mahua was exchanged for salt. In some areas they do so even today,' Manju told me.

I visited the bustling weekly market at Keswahi in the Shahdol district of Madhya Pradesh during the season. Groups of women in colourful clothes were streaming in, carrying sacks of mahua flowers which were being weighed by shop hands on traditional, manual and also electronic scales. Traders sat watching the activity, noting down the weight and doling out the right amount immediately. For small change there were bars of soap, which the women happily accepted. By the evening there was easily more than 50 tonnes collected in that small market. 'On a busy day we collect more than a hundred tonnes by the evening,' one trader said. At nightfall I counted twenty-two large trucks laden with dried mahua flowers driving out of that market. Forest department sources said that although no clear records were kept, the Keswahi market alone could be buying between 3-5000 tonnes of dried mahua. At least a hundred markets of this size or larger exist in Madhya Pradesh alone, excluding the smaller markets, not to talk of Odisha, Chhattisgarh, Andhra Pradesh and Jharkhand, which are the largest mahua-producing states in central India. There are no federal records of this activity and very inaccurate state records, but we are easily talking hundreds of thousands of tonnes of dried mahua!

'Where does it all go and what is it for?' I could not help but ask one of the traders I had befriended. 'It's a long chain and we are the smallest unit in it. There are mid-level buyers between us and the cold storages. At all levels the margins are a rupee or two per kilo, but we deal in say 50 tonnes in a season and make a few lakhs. In the mid and top levels the quantities are mind-boggling. In the larger cold storages in Raipur and Bilaspur, where most of the mahua is stored, the quantities could easily be 7-8 lakh tonnes in each cold storage. And 98 per cent of this is distilled alcohol,' he said.

Mahua is in the cold storages by May-June. It remains there till September and then it starts moving back. 'Bastar is the largest market. Probably 25 per cent of the collection goes there. But the product moves all the way up to Rajasthan and UP for bulk use in distilleries. However, the largest amount of what is kept in cold storages is consumed in retail. Probably, the same wholesale merchants who bought the produce in the first instance will be selling it to retailers or shopkeepers in villages, who will then sell it to the very same people who collected it from the forests and sold it to them, but at prices (in 2013) which will now vary from Rs 25-30.' The turnover can run into billions of rupees and this economy is almost completely cash.

Things were just the same just 200 years ago as Forsyth observed: 'The trees have to be watched night and day if the crop is to be saved; and the wilder races, who fear neither wild beast or the evil spirit, are generally engaged to do this for a wage of one half the produce. The yield of flowers from a single tree is about 130 lbs, worth five shillings in the market; and the nuts, which form in bunches after the droppings of flowers, yield a thick oil, much resembling tallow in appearance and properties. It is used for burning, for the manufacture of soap, and adulterating the clarified butter so largely consumed by all natives. A demand for it has lately sprung up in the Bombay market; and a good deal has been exported since the opening of the railway. The supply must be immense; and probably this new demand will be the means of greatly increasing the value of these trees.'

ॐ

It was a very wet December in Redhakhol, Odisha, when I first reached Michael's house. That was in 2009. It was raining heavily. We were drenched and shivering. There was ankle-deep water all around and we saw smoke rising out of his hut. We were on a wildlife survey and our local guide said that this was a friend who could give us some tea.

A lanky man with a boyish smile opened the door and welcomed the five of us in. He took one look at us and said, 'Tea not good, I have something better.' He came with glasses of warm mahua and we were instantly revived. That first meeting turned into a party!

We slowly found Michael to be one of the best animal trackers in the area and promptly hired him. And Michael adopted me as his distillation assistant. If he was preparing a new batch and I happened to be around, he would call me. 'Saar, new batch, need free labour,' he would say with a mischievous smile on his face. We would first clean the dry mahua flower, beating it with a stick to get rid of the dust. Simultaneously, large quantities of water would be set to boil. Next, it would be soaked and washed, making sure that the residue at the bottom is thrown away. Then in a ratio of five kilos to five litres, the mahua would be soaked in a large aluminium container in cool water. Before covering and consigning it to a dark corner, one small ball of dried rice flour, yeast and herbs were crushed into the mixture.

I gradually found out that this was a Jharkhand and Bihar technique, as Michael and Bina were Oraon tribals from Jharkhand whose forefathers had settled down in Odisha at Redhakhol near Sambalpur. The Gond and Baiga tribes of Chattisgarh and Madhya Pradesh or the Kondhs of Malkangiri in Odisha did not add this starter called *ranu*. Mahua flowers, like grapes or apples, self-ferment, which is universally considered a sign of good raw material that produces healthy alcohol.

In the summer the pot starts bubbling on the second day as the yeast gets going and by the fourth day, it is ready to be distilled. In winter it takes a few days longer, but they know it is ready by the look of it and by putting a few drops in their mouth. At this stage it emits that heady mahua fragrance which is unmistakable. Ants and other insects claim their share and are seen swimming in the froth. Many a time, while walking through villages, I have caught a whiff of this and got drawn to its source. Sure enough, the owner was distilling. He would happily call me in, force me to stay on for a few drinks before sending me staggering on my way. It is only in Bastar that they also drink this brew by straining out the liquid at this stage. It is a summer drink, called *landa* (pronounced *laan-da*) thought cooling for the body.

Michael's distillation technique was simple and similar to that practised across many tribes in central India. The fermented mahua is set on a very slow fire. On top of this a similar sized pot with holes in the bottom is placed. Inside this, on a raised surface so that the holes don't get choked, a smaller sized clay pot is inserted. The second pot is then topped by another large vessel filled with cold water. The two joints between the three pots are sealed with strips of wet cloth dipped in fine clay picked up from termite nests. When the pots heat up, the clay and cloth dry and harden, sealing the joints tightly.

As the brew in the bottommost pot warms up, vapours rise up through the holes in the second pot and hit the cold bottom of the third pot on top. The vapour condenses to drip into the clay pot kept inside the second pot. In some parts of Madhya Pradesh, I found this top pot made of copper. The heat remains steady and low and as the water in the top container heats up, it is replaced with cold water. A 5 kilo mash takes about four hours to finish, with the water being changed at least five times.

What comes out of this clay pot is called mahua, mahuli, mahuda and other names in various parts of central India. The technique varies mildly in terms of innovations for draining the alcohol as it condenses. Clay and bamboo tools have slowly given way to aluminium and plastic, but the alcohol and the distillation apparatus have remained essentially the same from perhaps before the Christian era, making it arguably the first recorded distillery in the world.

To get around this effort of changing the water repeatedly, many people set up their stills next to a river. The flowing water provides constant cooling and distillation becomes easier and better. In the interiors of Baliguda in Odisha, I met Nupur, the local tribal hooch queen. This stunning beauty ran an almost industrial-sized illegal distillery within the forest next to a waterfall. We trekked a few miles to get to the location. She and her ragtag gang of seven were very suspicious to begin with, but once the ice broke, we had full access.

A 40-litre aluminium pot sat heating on a raised mud platform from which two bamboo pipes descended on to two mud pots in the river. This was mid-summer. It was hot and the waterfall had almost dried up. A bamboo pipe directed a steady flow from the little that remained, splashing water on the two condensing pots. On a ledge above was a fermentation station where many large terracota containers embedded in the earth full of bubbling mahua were getting ready for the pot still. Down the stream was a herd of nineteen buffaloes wallowing in the mud with their faces turned towards the still, nostrils flared and quivering, sniffing the heady aroma.

'My husband was a distillation worker and doing very well. We were a happy family. Many people were jealous of us and then someone put an evil spell on him. We tried everything by going to the best shamans, but he simply wasted and died. I was left alone with two children. I had seen him doing this and had worked with him, so I thought why not take over where he left,' Nupur told us over glasses of fresh mahua. She first joined as a worker, but others soon realized she was smarter than the others, so she started handling the business and became the boss. She now had the largest share of investment in that group and took care of police and excise as well. 'Ours is the best mahua you can get in these parts. We give the best quality and get the best prices. People queue up to buy our stuff,' she said with pride.

Meanwhile, the batch on the flame was ready. The alcohol was poured into truck tyre tubes for ease of storage and transportation. The big pot was carried over to the waiting buffaloes and overturned. The brown liquid slowly seeped in the muddy water as smoke rose from the pile of mash. The animals drew a semicircle around this mound patiently, waiting for it to cool and then started eating voraciously. Mahua-flavoured milk, I thought.

It is a travesty that mahua, which is so much a part of the social and cultural fabric of central India, is outlawed in Odisha, Andhra Pradesh and Maharashtra. At least Madhya Pradesh and Chhattisgarh respect the traditions and allow the tribals to brew and distill for personal use.

We were at Michael's for a drink one evening. A chicken had been freshly killed and fried with salt and chillies in mahua oil. It was a delicious snack. We were all laughing and joking when his elder brother arrived, took one look at us, and went inside. He emerged a little later and said, 'Oh, I thought you were Biharis,' and everyone started laughing. 'The government gives out mahua distillation licenses every year in an auction. This is controlled entirely by the Biharis. The investors are Marwaris from Bihar or Jharkhand and the workers, usually Rajputs or Brahmins. They run an informer network in the area. The distillery manager gives free bottles for information, which they then follow up with the help of the excise department. There are raids and people are harassed, their stills broken and utensils taken away, sometimes they are arrested and jailed. Why should the government force us to drink that mass-made stuff when we can make the best quality at home? Now when I have to make large amounts for family weddings and rituals, I go deep inside the forest and distill where no one can find me,' Michael said.

I visited three licensed mahua distilleries in Barkot, Odisha. Each of them was producing between 500 and 1000 litres daily in huge copper pots. There were rows of 300 litre plastic fermentation drums in a covered yard. But what caught my eye was the size of the staff. Each one of them was over 6.5 feet in height, built like a wrestler and together they looked like a private army. Every one of them was from Bihar or Jharkhand.

'Why do you think we choose people of this size? Why do you think we need to keep this *fauj* here?' the distillery manager, Manoj Kumar Dubey, asked me and started laughing. Tall and well built himself, he sat on a chair in a vest and lungi inside a large courtyard piled with wood and pieces of steel. In the middle of the courtyard was a huge still that sat on a medium-sized brick and cement furnace. Made of copper, it looked like a scaled-up version of a copper pot that people use in homes to store water. Five people could easily stand inside it. In fact that is what they did to clean it. Dialogues and background music from the popular serial *Ramayana* blared on cable TV at the back. Everything about this distillery reminded me more of a strict ashram than something to do with alcohol.

Dubeyji has spent over twenty years in the business. 'I started as a sixteen year old in the owner's country liquor distribution outlet in Raipur, Chhattisgarh. After working there for about ten years, he must have found me reliable for he moved me here to Barkot where they were just setting up in 2002.' The business is owned by a Sahu, originally from Ranchi, now in Jharkhand, but he is now settled in Bilaspur, Chhattisgarh, where his family runs a string of businesses.

'I slowly learnt to distill, to extract the best quantity and the quality, but this is not a great business to be in, there is too much *chik chik* here. People get drunk and violent, and the biggest menace is illegal distilling. These tribals think they can get away with just anything. I am permitted by the government to distill; I have to pay for a license. The excise department regularly checks my quality, but these people set up their dirty stills just anywhere, mix all kinds of things in the wash and then die.' I slowly realized that his six-feet-plus fauj were the rural equivalent of urban bar bouncers. 'I need these people for security and to keep things under control. I can never stop illegal distilling completely, but at least I can minimize it. My staff keeps in touch with the people and finds out where the trouble is, and then we conduct raids with the help of excise and police. There is also a bit of pressure from these departments to get them a quota of cases every month. They have their targets too. Now you know why I need to keep an army,' he laughed again.

'Do you bribe people with liquor to get information?' I ask.

'*Arre sahab*,' he started laughing again at my naiveté, '*kya kya nahin karna padta*. I am a Brahmin and I have been here for many years. I am there for the people in their *sukh dukh*, I do puja for them, everyone knows me here and calls me Pandeyji. They come to me for help, that is how we keep in touch. *Par kuch lene ke liye kuch dena to padta hi hai.*'

'A Brahmin, really?' I said. 'I thought you were a Bhumihar.' A land-owning community of farmers found only in Bihar and eastern Uttar Pradesh, Bhumihars consider themselves Brahmins, but are looked down upon by the latter. Tall and well built, and with a lot of political muscle as well, Bhumihars practise some of the more violent politics in Bihar and are feared. Dubey was indignant.

'*Kya bat kar rahe hain*, I am a Dubey. I am a high-caste Kanyakubj Brahmin.'

'Oh, I was told I am a Kanyakubj Brahmin as well.'

'Really,' he sized me up with a new look. 'One of us. Why didn't you tell me before? What is your gotra?' This stumped me completely as I just could not remember.

'You can't remember your gotra,' he towered over me like an Oxford don who had summarily lost faith in his star pupil. 'People like you will ruin our caste.'

'So how come a high-caste Brahmin like you is working in the liquor business?'

'*Arre sahab*, this is *kaliyug*. If a Brahmin like you can't remember his gotra, anything can happen. Do you think I like this *chik chik*? I am forced to do this for it gets me a decent salary and I can look after my children. It is my misfortune that I have to live in this environment, but I don't touch this stuff, not even a drop. Every one of my staff does puja with me in a temple that I have built inside the distillery, every day, without fail, and none of them are allowed to drink.' No wonder, the place looked like an austere ashram.

'But how do you gauge quality, then, if none of you touch this stuff?'

'I have spent so much time doing this *paap* (sin) that I can tell just by the smell and the consistency of the distill,' he told me with some pride.

Each 300 litre blue plastic drum, that had once housed some intensely corrosive chemical and had a skull and crossbones on it with a few strands of lightning added for effect, held 35 kilos of dry mahua. This was topped with 50 litres of mildly warm water. A few hours later the brown mahua would start rehydrating and swell up to look like raisins. 'We don't add anything else to it and we are not permitted to do so either. This is the purest mahua alcohol you can get. But yes, some unscrupulous people do sometimes add molasses or jaggery to give the wash some strength when dry mahua is in short supply, but that usually makes the process more expensive. The only thing we sometimes add is a few mugfuls of active wash from other vats to speed up the fermentation in case it is lagging, but that is about it, nothing else,' Dubeyji said. He reminded me of the Brahmin equivalent of a Trappist monk, isolated in his monastery distillery, immersed in what he considered a disgusting craft with some of his senses trained to abhor this work but others so finely attuned to excelling in it.

I asked for a taste on the way out. It seemed sweet compared to what I was used to drinking in village homes. Dubeyji was disgusted. He refused to shake hands with a Brahmin who drank.

ය

For many years, while travelling through Odisha, Madhya Pradesh and Chattisgarh on various assignments, I would hear of sweets that were made with dried mahua, but never found them. Nobody makes them any more, I was told. 'Maybe during festivals some people might, but it is not as common as it used to be. I sometimes see it being sold at a village fair, but it is getting to be rare,' Alikh Kanhar of Banigoccha, Odisha, told me. 'In fact, we used to just roast it on a griddle and eat it as a snack. It had a smoky sweet taste. I can't remember when I had it last. I think people have lost the taste for it, now that they have Bikaner *bhujiya*,' he smiled. He spoke fondly of *mahul peetha*, *kakra pitha*, *mahul chokoli*, *mahul seejha* and *latha*.

On my last day in Banigoccha in Odisha, I walked a few kilometres in the evening to the Phalpaju village to meet

Chanchala Behera, who headed the local village forest society. Sitting in the courtyard of her spread-out mud house, I found her and her daughter Manasi eating a large, round roti-like thing that had an utthapam look, but was certainly not an utthapam. '*Seejha*,' she casually told me. '*Mahul seejha*?!' She was amused by my excitement. 'Can I taste?' I asked. They were most embarrassed that I wanted to try a piece from their plate and Manasi rushed inside to make a new one for me. Made from dried mahua soaked overnight and boiled to a pulp, then kneaded with besan or soaked *kuluth* dal (channa or gram), raised for a few hours and lightly fried, seejha was coarse. It was not so sweet either and I found it difficult to finish the big one she had lovingly made for me. But I could see that it was full of energy and could keep a person going for long.

In parts of Madhya Pradesh the juice from the pulp is squeezed out, kneaded with wholewheat flour, seasoned and fried like a parantha. 'We call it *mahuari*. It stays in a closed box for a few days and travels well. We mix the same juice with rice flour and steam it, like idli. That's *kachi* (kaa-chee), very tasty. In fact, this same juice is boiled to a thick syrup and they cook coarse, home-made wheat or rice noodles in it. We call it *farah* (fa-raa). That's a dessert. Sometimes we roast wheat or rice flour on a griddle, cook it in the syrup and as it thickens just let it cool down. We then set it in trays and cut it like barfi,' Samar Singh from Satna, near Rewa in Madhya Pradesh told me. 'Twenty years ago it used to be made at home and as young boys we used to love it. I don't think my children will even touch it. Tastes have radically changed. There is even a stigma attached to eating or drinking mahua.'

Mahul peetha, I was told, was more sophisticated. Mahua was soaked and boiled to a pulp and kneaded with rice flour and *khoya* (milk solids). Then rolled by hand into oblong pieces, stuffed with dried fruits, then fried a deep brown and dipped in syrup. But in Odisha, the land of *pithas* with hundreds of amazing variations, this one is almost unheard of.

Latha (laa-taa), in fact, is common to almost all of central India with mild variations. Dry mahua is cleaned of grit and roasted. It is then pounded with roasted black or white sesame seeds or peanuts or both to a point when they fuse together. In some places they add roasted bajra or pearl millet and dry fruits as well. It is then rolled into laddoos by hand and stored. If kept in air-tight containers, it stays for long. It reminded me of an energy ball as opposed to a bar. In Shahdol, Madhya Pradesh, they keep it as a powder and call it *bhookha* or hungry. 'It is for the elderly who can't bite into a hard laddoo.' In ten years I have not seen it anywhere.

'*Raanb* (rna-aab) was the rage in our growing years around Rajnandgaon,' senior forest officer and botanist B.P. Nonhare reminisced in Raipur. 'Our roots are in Marathwada, but for generations we have been here. My mother would take 5 kilos of dried mahua and thoroughly clean it. She would then put it into a *degh* with double the amount of water so that it was fully covered. This would soak for a while and then put to boil on low heat. It would keep boiling like this for 16-17 hours, sometimes overnight, while someone watched it carefully to ensure it did not burn and there was enough liquid in there. After about ten hours a kilo each of dried coconut and cashew were added to it. By the time it started to look dark and took on a viscous consistency, the coconut and cashew had almost dissolved. This was cooled and strained with a cheese cloth, squeezing every drop of goodness out, and stored in glass jars in our store. I remember being given a breakfast of raanb, milk and roti almost every day in the winter during our childhood and we would very happily eat it. It must have done something for our resistance because we almost never had coughs and colds. For the elderly who had gout or aching joints, my mother would add dried ginger to this.'

'I remember this vividly as an elaborate winter ritual. There was great excitement in the house. Mahua would be bought and we would all help clean it. Then a fire would be lit in the courtyard and we would sit and watch the degh bubble away. As my mother grew older, we would have less and less of it, till one day she stopped. She said it was just too tiring and her joints ached. I don't think I have seen this anywhere these days, but in the fifties and sixties, it was common on the borders of Chattisgarh and Maharashtra.'

His children have not tasted it either.

If Food Be the Food…

KARTHIKA NAÏR

Sangam House Triptych

WORSHIP

Guru and Swami
and Thampi-with-yearning-ears
lie on the suburbs
of my fingers' arc, lips bared,
eyes fixed in unnerving hope.

If a dog could speak,
he would drawl: 'Here is the trick:
I let you believe
you are God, divine, adored.
Now feed me more bread, my lord.'

REPAST

We feast all the time
eat like emperors
each meal a banquet
sip the smell of rain the stubbly moon
spread uneven fingers over trees
drink in the quiet of pooled thoughts
divide light with moths, mites, crickets
and the odd visitor toad
devour the music of words
words in eight voices and accents
and moods sometimes ten or twelve
toast to the exuberant delight
the laughter of a mama bear laden
with honey and meat dip long
into the magic of revisited tales of beginnings and ends
filled with a Danish bumbling god with no sense
of shape and heroines with a predilection for puns
and one cranky rhino who will save the world
once glimpse the quicksilver
puckish god of poetry

Now multiply them the laughter the words
the thought the delight the sorrow this time
leave some in the alcoves on eaves
beside windows sprinkled on butterfly
wings stray sunlit free verses
on the grass and carry the rest
in wallets and pockets dangle
them from ears you'll still find a few
in the hollow of a throat

FARE THEE WELL

Shed layers of night,
Sky, patch by uneven patch.
Day shivers within,
still tender; and teal, claret,
the words we won't spell: goodbye.

For we meet again,
surely and soon on the shores
of other mornings,
around crisp toast dipped in mist
or within fresh, warm stories.

The Invaders

Feasts and hallowed days spin on orbits
seldom grazing mine, till your voice swings
past meridians and meteorites
(Insat 2-B and Mobistar abetting)
this Saturday noon to hum Happy Holi
into the unwary whorls of a left eardrum.

I could weigh the vernal sunbeams
in those notes, bronzed on a bonfire
where good blooms in twice-born glee;
count the koel warming up behind –
the first chamber music concert this year
on a fourth-floor South Delhi balcony;
nearly touch flecks of gulaal tinting you
into a metonym for tropical spring.

The call ends, like other things.
But echoes of a koelled clarinet,
of your voice and its joyful salute,
snag on the woven blue rose stems
shading my kitchen window, perch on high
pelmets, recoil, reproduce and let
loose dissident whims:

To sift ochre, emerald, indigo
from the festive phonemes and smear
an ashen, unshaven sky above;

find water-balloons to hurl at chimney-potted
rooftops, a mass christening in cerise;

teach thumri to ungainly pigeons lumbering
on the girders outside – for a mehfil in mid-air....

I switch off the cell, and reheat tagliatelle
instead, adding paprika, pesto,
carrots and capsicum for a whisper
of insane flavour – it's Holi, after all.

Blood Moon Rising: Poorna with Vyaasa

पूछे जो कोई मेरी निषानी रंग हिनना लिखना
गोरे बदन पे उंगली से मेरा नाम अदा लिखना
कभी–कभी आस–पास चांद रेहती है
कभी–कभी आस–पास षाम रेहती है
आओ ना, आओ ना, झेहलुम् में बेह लेंगे
वादी के मौसम भी एक दिन तो बदलेंगे

Should anyone ask for my keepsake, my sign,
write the colour henna, sign the name grace
with your finger on my fair body.
Now and then, the moon dwells here.
Now and then, it is gloaming.
Yes, come. Come, let us flow away in the Jhelum.
The seasons in the valley will change too one day.

– Gulzar, Naam Adaa Likhna (Yahaan, 2005)

Begin with the labia, Lord. Make me
a word, swift and feather-light, a flurry
beneath the philtrum nuzzling the upper,
then lower lip, teasing teeth apart, swirls
on tongue-tip and blade and root that carry
ribbon lightning to the brain, the smokey winesting
of caresses on a hard palate.
Transform from noun to verb these lips. Savour.
Brush. Sip. For tonight, we need no food to dine.
Should anyone ask for my keepsake, my sign

of birth or station, tell them, Lord, nothing matters
but this nightsong: with *alaap* of twined tongues; tatters
of pulse that will *drut* in *teentaal*; the *raag bahaar*

of your breath deep within my throat; hip and thigh, shaft,
pubis—in long *bandish*, flesh to flesh, that shatters
thought and time. For mating, like music, is no race:
no clocks await at start or finish, pleasure shared stays
the sole prize—and keepsake, as faces change, voices drift,
signs wilt. Save its five-chambered heart, treasure misplaced
by gods. Write the colour henna. Sign the name grace.

Name its fragrance earth. Colour its music
midnight. Label the shape Desire—relic,
once more, from heaven. Measure its weight
as sunlight, but also planet. (Add
a fifth veda, Lord, penned in euphoric
verse, on kama – unnamed melody
that lends harmony to both virtue and wealth –
and spell how kama, dharma, artha usher
as one moksha, the last remedy.)
With your finger on my fair body,

resume writing, My Lord, define
your landscape of pleasure. Your spine
arches: permit my hands maiden
journeys, let one graze lush terai
around a chest, scale the incline
of collarbone, then reappear
on the nape of a neck, curving your
head towards my breasts. The other hand
trails your behind, tracing half-spheres
now and then. The moon dwells here,

twin demilunes, tight and perfect
to light a yoni. For reflect,

Lord, a flame must burn both blue and golden.
Thirst requited is key to coitus,
more so if the desired effect
is healthy sons, lust loaming
the womb, attest our midwives. Men must bring,
not just seek the pinnacle. So, rouse my
seed. Set hands and tongue roaming
now. And then, it'll be gloaming

again and again, the blessed moment when night
and day merge to stain skies in many-hued delight.
Continue, Lord. Unfurl my petals, taste
and quaff, trace and stroke the whorls till they come
alive, enflame, throb and bloom to complete this rite
that spring enjoins. Penetrate, then thrust. Thrust. Succumb
to the pain, explode future selves, lose your being.
But do not lose me, for it isn't over yet.
Not till I surge and pound and flood, till I become,
yes, come. *Come, let us flow away in the Jhelum,*

the night or the Milky Way, you plead, *leave the land,*
this world—how dear, how absurd are lovers' demands
in bliss, even those of ascetics. I came, Lord, in aid
of a distressed lass. I came to bear a wise, robust child
for this clan. Ever afters, you must understand,
are not for maids. Nor life, should the queen wish to flay
defiance in its bud. You'll forget me too, though perhaps
not this night. For nothing forever remains, whether thirst
or royal norms. Even the sun must melt away.
The seasons in the valley will change too one day.

Unseen Food

NILANJANA S. ROY

At Brigade Ground, the buses had started to come in from mid-morning; by afternoon, there was a thick, orderly mass of people from Bengal's districts and villages, streaming in for one of the many rallies held by Mamata Banerjee, the West Bengal chief minister.

Political rallies and bandhs had punctuated the daily life of citizens in Calcutta for so long that it was only the foreigners in our hotel who found it strange that half the city would shut down, the traffic funnelled off the roads or slowing to a crawl, until 5 p.m. I had grown up in Calcutta, but lived away from the city long enough to be curious about the rally itself. It was a short walk away from the hotel, the crowds pressing in but friendly enough, and as I passed the Victoria Memorial, I began to notice the changing landscape of street food.

That part of Calcutta had always been famous for its phuchkas, the East's answer to the North Indian golgappa.

Chola vendors, bhelpuri and jhaal muri vendors selling variations on spiced mixtures of puffed rice or various green and brown grams were common enough.

But what sprang into view, because of the sheer number of hawker's stands that had sprung up to service the crowd, was the other kind of street food, so everyday that it barely registered to the Indian eye and that most food writers and historians didn't consider worth noting—vendors who sold utilitarian, cheap and often nutritious meals.

A rapid survey demonstrated the range of snacks or full meals that you could buy for under Rs 20, sometimes even under Rs 10: litti-chokka, plates of red rice and watery dal, thick rotis made from mixed grains with several variations on ragi, basic khichdis, spicy omelettes (among the most expensive dishes) with the cheapest sliced white bread, thin gruels with fermented rice as the base, and from different districts variations on the sattu.

There was a separation between these hawkers and the vendors who sold the more familiar street foods of Calcutta melas—fat, frilled, oily 'kabiraji' cutlets and Mughlai porotas, spiced aloo doms—potato curry accompanied by luchis (made from white flour) or radha ballabi, luchis stuffed with peas, or dalpuri, luchis stuffed with a paste of ground and fried spiced lentils, assorted pakoras and bhaajis, and the familiar range of sticky, syrupy sweetmeats.

The latter were patronized by locals from Calcutta, for whom Mamata's rally was another excuse to come out on a winter's day and stuff their faces. The prices of these dishes were not high at all by restaurant standards, but they were not Rs 10 or Rs 15 either. The former had an eye on customers who had come in for the rally without their own food bundles, who were looking for a cheap but filling meal.

The same separation was apparent in so many other Indian cities. When we spoke of 'street food', we meant the wide range of savoury and sweet delicacies every Indian city boasted of, from dosas, idlis and buttermilk to golgappas, bhelpuri and papri chaat, from bread pakoras to bedni aloo. But the rickshaw-pullers who hung around Humayun's Tomb in Nizamuddin or waited for fares in Chandni Chowk in Old Delhi rarely ate from the chaatwaalas or the jalebiwaalas; even when priced within reach, these foods were not sufficient for a working man's meal.

They patronized the small stalls that sold home food on the street, sometimes meals as simple as leftover rice fermented through the night and warmed up with a little green chilli and oil, sometimes rotis with one mixed vegetable curry, often grains that the affluent middle classes had abandoned in the pursuit of white flour—a rise in the price of ragi (millet) was far more catastrophic for labourers and rickshaw-pullers than a rise in the price of potatoes. A glass of sattu or a blended ragi drink provides more energy than a plate of rotis and potato curry, and it is much cheaper; where ragi is available, it is often the preferred meal.

But it is hard to see what is right under your nose. In the popular descriptions of Indian food, the distinctions between home and restaurant food are sometimes discussed but it is not so easy to look at what we mean when we say 'Indian food', and what we leave out or skate over. Many years ago, travelling in Sikkim, I'd been struck by the cheap tsampa, roasted barley flour, and the ease with which it could be mixed with nothing more exotic than water to make a filling meal that would take you through the high altitudes of Gurudongmar or Yumthang.

But when Sikkimese food is described, it is the momos, delicious pork dumplings served with soup, or thukpa, a thick broth of meat and vegetables served with tiny and delectable variations all the way from Sikkim to Darjeeling to Nepal. Tsampa is too everyday, too monotone, too commonplace to be described, and perhaps it is too much the food of the masses as well.

Yet, everywhere you look, in almost every Indian state, there is some variation on the tsampa and the sattu, and in their ubiquity these mixes are probably as well known, if not better known, than chapattis, rotis and naans. When I read Anjali Purohit's *Ragi-Ragini*, a quirky collection of ragi recipes, songs and rhymes that accompanied women's work in the kitchen and stories around this humble grain, I began to understand how the twin binaries of rice and wheat should not be the default setting in modern Indian households.

Recipes using ragi (also known as nachni or finger millet) are scattered through the book—savoury and sweet porridges, different kinds of sweetmeats—and linked with Bahinabai's poems and the narrator's sharing of the histories of the women in her family. The omnipresence of ragi reminded me of how Delhi's older households almost always served bajra rotis, not wheat flour rotis, in a previous generation. A year or so after reading Purohit's book and experimenting with ragi recipes, I came across very fancily packaged boxes of finger millet in an organic food store, reinventing the old, almost forgotten, recipes for a new generation that liked the idea of eating healthy.

That need for the comfort of non-white flour grains persist in strange ways, as with the curious Bengali passion for Horlicks, which is malt-based, or the haunting survival of lemon-barley water across the country in an age of colas—its viscous goodness pressed on children with the admonishment that it is good for their health.

The question of what an Indian thali is and what doesn't make it to that plate could have far more disturbing overtones though. Many Indians who are not from the Northeast, for instance, carry their general ignorance of that region to the foods of the Seven Sisters. The distinctions between Nagaland's cuisine, the subtle differences between Khasi and Garo cooking, the pleasures of a Mizoram feast or an Arunachal-style pickle are lost on the mainland, who often see all of these layered and separate cuisines as foreign.

Yet, in terms of flavour, the distance should not have been that great: the full-bodied aroma of anishi—fermented Colocasia leaves ground with chilli—and other spices used extensively by the Ao Naga tribe and the heavy richness of asafoetida (commonly used in Benares cooking) are not that far apart; the fire of Bhut Jolakia, the famous chilli ubiquitous across Assam, Nagaland and Manipur, is a close cousin to the bite of Andhra chillies.

But at wedding banquets in Delhi's increasingly lavish nuptial celebrations, there are some troubling omissions: you might find counters of Thai food, or of Chinese food, but rarely would there be a Nagaland counter serving anishi or akhuni, and the containers brimming over with biryani from Lucknow or Hyderabad or even the Syrian Christian style would almost never have a Khasi jadoh rice served with tungtap, a dried fish pickle.

Some of this have to do with meat taboos (chicken is the 'safe' meat of India, given the number of communities that object to pork, beef or even have a distaste for goat meat), but much of this also has to do with a deliberate invisibility. The lack of exposure to food from the Northeast is only matched by the lack of mainland Indians' interest in finding out that these cuisines— which have lasted for centuries—go well beyond momos.

In personal histories from the Dalit community, the most painful of memories, and the most chequered of experiences, concern food. And many also raise a blunt question: why aren't the staples of the Dalit kitchen Indian enough to feature in mainstream discussions of 'our' food? From the segregation of glasses and plates to the feeding of leftovers, food has historically been a way to exercise control, a constant reminder of caste lines. But Dalit food is also secretly coveted, and along with other non-Brahminical communities, the freedom to eat all kinds of meat is often envied.

That envy, and the status of meat as covetable in different contexts, can be glimpsed in Indian fiction and in popular music, though. The two men in Premchand's classic short story, 'Kafan' (The Shroud), celebrate the sudden arrival of riches with a feast. The money is intended to help them buy a shroud for Madhav's wife who has died; but shrouds are upper-caste, affluent luxuries. Madhav and his father, Ghisu, reminisce about a wedding banquet where they were once fed puris cooked in 'real ghee', and spend the money for the shound without compunction on the food of the affluent: 'two sers of puris, a meat stew, spiced liver and fried fish'.

Meat confers status, but it is also used as a symbol of corruption, an appetite for power run amok. The band Indian Ocean used lyrics from Maharashtrian folk protest songs in 'Boll Weevil'. They sing about the government official who comes in demanding a bribe from the locals in the form of expensive chicken: 'Makhedar aave, kukri maange re.' And in Uday Prakash's short story collection, The Walls of Delhi, the absolute corruption of the police and of intellectuals who have sold themselves to the lure of the soft life is indicated by food and drink. 'You can smell the stench of liquor coming from the words they write. And underneath their sentences lie a pile of chicken and goat bones, and the skeletons of the innocent ones.' The police inspector in his story orders a bottle of Royal Challenge and a 'big plate of chicken'.

As abhorrent as the practices of ritual untouchability are, the lines between pure and profane are often easily crossed, the boundaries more porous than they appear. The Dalit writer Chandra Bhan Prasad writes about an incident from his childhood when his uncles working in Burma sent a large bronze cooking vessel to the family in India. His uncle Baldev, having acquired 'a privileged bronze vessel identified with upper-caste landlords', held a feast to celebrate, and cooked forty kilos of pork in the vessel.

At night, the local zamindar arrived in stealth; instead of riding in on his horse, he had walked there so that he would not be identified. He had heard about the bronze vessel from Burma, and on seeing it, offered to give Mr Prasad's uncle some land in exchange for the cooking dish. Baldev, perturbed, told him that they had cooked pig meat in it already.

'Since pig meat is the only-Dalit-meat in my part of the country, my uncle couldn't anticipate that the zamindar would still want the vessel. "Who knows that the vessel was used and pig meat cooked except your family and relatives," the zamindar is said to have reasoned with my uncle.' The Burma bronze vessel was cleansed with ash, and the bargain made, the zamindar left with his prize.

In recent years, increasingly ugly wars have broken out, pitting vegetarian and often Hindu upper-caste communities against others. The meat versus vegetarian wars are intensifying in India, setting one religion against another—and also setting one caste against another. There is little clarity on the issue, because while India has a long history of vegetarianism, it has never been a predominantly vegetarian country, nor is the abjuration of meats other than chicken and mutton uniformly prevalent across the land.

Dalits, tribals, Other Backward Classes and in many regions, even savarna or privileged caste Hindus, have often argued that they have a history of eating pork and beef that goes back for centuries, and that their meat and vegetarian dishes belong to the mainstream platter as much as any other apparently 'Indian' dish. Meat-eating in India has its visible, public side—as jokes about tandoori chicken being the national bird testify—and the hidden, backdoor history.

In the Delhi of the 1970s and 1980s, it was not uncommon for meat and bread to be delivered directly to homes: the milkman would come around with his clanking tin cans, the breadman would arrive with a tin box strapped onto the back of his bicycle, and the meatman would bring the day's cuts in a similar tin box.

In Sarojini Nagar and Chanakya Puri, the meatman would bring the meat, chicken and mutton around to the front doors of the middleclass in the morning. Another butcher would come around later, cycling through the back lanes with cheap cuts of pork and beef contained in a similar tin box. The division of meat was a demonstration of the division of labour—most domestic help in those days came from tribal communities or from castes who had far fewer taboos on eating different kinds of meat than their employers did.

But it is not just meat that is hidden. In INA market, where the vegetable stalls cater to local households as well as to restaurant chefs and members of New Delhi's large expat community, I was surprised to see a selection of unusual greens one winter. They were unusual because they were so humble—red spinach, wild chekor saag, and what used to be called jungli lahsun or wild garlic—and because they were rarely seen in fancy markets. Unlike palak saag and sarson ka saag, Delhi's two favourite forms of spinach, these were not so easy to find. Bengalis used them in the ceremony on the day just before Diwali when fourteen varieties of greens, some bitter, are served, and fourteen lamps lit in the home; otherwise I had not seen them in Delhi's mainstream markets.

The seller told me that one of his suppliers of organic vegetables had been packaging these greens along with the rest. At first, none of his usual customers would buy these 'weeds', he said. But then he had the clever idea of placing them alongside kale and endive, and packaging them in the way many supermarkets were packaging rocket and mesclun—in large, loose plastic bags. He drew immediate interest from Korean and Chinese shoppers whose assessment of greens was fairly sophisticated, then from other expats who liked the idea of cooking with 'local Indian stir-fry greens', and then from a few Indians who remembered the mixed saags and sabzis of their childhood.

It took some research to understand why these greens had disappeared from the market and from many people's memories. Foraging for plants that are often classified as weeds, but have a high nutritional value is retained in some communities. In a key paper, Sundriyal and Sundriyal document the survival of the practice of harvesting edible wild plants across Sikkim, for example. The Gujjar tribes in Jammu and Kashmir, the millions of tribals in Rajasthan, Chattisgarh and across the Himalayas keep alive the practice of gathering these plants.

But in more urban settlements, the idea of harvesting wild plants has all but disappeared as spaces in cities have shrunk. If the wild 'commons' is replaced in small towns and cities with markets, malls and parks, people's relationship with the land inevitably changes. It takes just one generation of forgetfulness to lose the habit of foraging, though it is now becoming fashionable again in the rest of the world, thanks to the prominence of restaurants like Rene Redzepi's Noma in Copenhagen. Redzepi, one of the world's best-known chefs, explained the pull of foraging in an online interview: 'In a very basic sense, you're connected to your place—that's what foraging gives you. You understand what's edible and you start seeing nature not just as a beautiful thing—as a picture-perfect thing to move in, but also as a very delicious resource.'

A few communities still forage—mostly tribals—but there is a fine commonality between tribes as distinct and sometimes as geographically far-flung as the Santhal, Sounti, Gond, Juang, Kol, Bhumiz, Oraon, Munda, Kharwar and Chero. Many forage for the same leaves and plants—pittha sag might be called kointho in a different part of the country, pok arkha might reappear as chimti saag—but the method of collection remains the same: these nutritious plants grow not just in the wild, but in urban and rural ditches, and often in the rows between cultivated plants in tilled fields.

From the point of view of farmers, and also tribals and often Dalit communities, cultivators of fields are either wasteful or blind: the surprise that people would throw away or not notice edible, tasty and nutritious plants echoes from Punjab to Bihar to Assam, if you talk to local foragers.

ɞ

It is growing harder and harder for me to nail down 'Indian food' in any way. Some of the not-seeing is common to those who live in cities and have lost touch with the seasons of growing, or do not know the alphabet of edible plants (or insects and small molluscs, for that matter).

Some of the food that is never talked of as 'Indian' is excluded because of deep, and disturbing, biases in favour of the mainland and the mainstream; in some cases, for both vegetarian and non-vegetarian, community taboos mask larger insecurities, angers and fears. And when you begin to add in the food and plant varieties brought in by travellers who came and settled here, asking what 'authentic' Indian food might be feels like an absurd project: authentic in which century, for which community?

But some day, perhaps someone will write a history of unseen or overlooked or secret Indian food, spending time with the migrants, the foragers, the cooks excluded by either Brahminical or regional bias. It would have to be a very capacious history, but it would also be a very tasty one.

A Table for Three

SUMANA, JAYADITYA, BIKRAMJIT

Over the past 20-25 years, among the three of us, we've lived in six cities across India: Kolkata, Ahmedabad, Baroda, Chandigarh, Delhi and Bangalore. It wasn't planned, of course, but our lives on wheels have fashioned us in unforeseen ways, taken us closer to parts of the country we'd have never known otherwise, and also kindled a thirst for travel and all that it brings.

But first, some background. Joy's (as Jayaditya is known) and Bikramjit's families were friends from way back but the two weren't really friendly, given the four-year age difference. Sumana met Joy at The Statesman, Kolkata, which was the first place of employment for both. A year or so down the line, Joy and Sumana had moved to Ahmedabad with new jobs at a newspaper. Bikramjit, meanwhile, was also dabbling in journalism in Kolkata. When a position opened up in the newspaper in Ahmedabad, he, too, made the cross-country trek. (And lest one thinks this is an unholy menage-a-trois, let it be clarified that there were at least two other members of the travelling circus; it just happened that some of us hit it off better than the others. Oh, *and somewhere along the way, Sumana and Joy got married; Bikramjit missed out on the wedding because their common boss wouldn't give him leave.)*

We've driven each other mad with our idiosyncrasies, fought over perceived slights and injustices but always been bound together by the love of food. This is how it happened.

Joy: I think our first common food experience would have been cooking in our chummery in Ahmedabad. This was in 1995. Which is funny because none of us really knew how to cook (or maybe Bikramjit did but he didn't let on). But we had to cook because it was cheaper than eating out—and, crucially, because cooking gave us a smidgin of familiarity in an otherwise totally alien terrain. If I had to pick out the a-ha moment, it would probably be the rice that we left on the burner while we went to watch *Khamoshi*. Halfway through the movie, and halfway across the city, we remembered it was on the stove. I think that was the first and last time we burnt anything to a cinder.

I don't think Ahmedabad is given enough credit for being a food city. It was great for us, living away from home on a few thousand a month. We ate well—veg, non-veg and everything in between and beyond.

Sumana: Even before we had the gas stove, we had a kerosene stove. I have some nightmarish memories associated with that: one, I couldn't cook; two, I had no idea how to control the heat on the stove; and three, the aloo in the aloo dum was just not behaving the way it was supposed to—half of it was burnt and the other half raw. So much for my surprise for my flatmates. I still recall my sense of relief when they breezed in, summed up my plight with one look and announced that we were going to eat out (to celebrate some completely fake occasion).

Bikramjit: I think the first thing I remember about the chummery was the stark, bare kitchen, something I never really got used to. I did not cook much probably because I wasn't in the mood.

Sumana: If we managed to finish work at a respectable hour, though, there was only one place to go: Aunty's. Her tiny eatery had a formal name, La Bella, but we never knew the name of this little, wizened lady in a blue dress who ran it with an iron hand and a Man Friday. She had four tables, a blackboard menu, and if you came late, you went hungry. And that was that. Her menu wasn't inventive: chicken masala, mutton masala, rice and fish (fry or gravy), but it was wholesome, filling and almost ridiculously inexpensive. No wonder anyone who ever studied in Ahmedabad—and it had a lot of institutes even then—has a special corner in their heart for Aunty.

Bikramjit: Besides La Bella, I especially remember Bhatiyar Gali (the cooks' lane) and sweating in the summer heat while consuming large helpings of spicy food. I was introduced to La Bella by my brother, but I really became a regular with Joy and Sumana. I think for me cooking came more gradually, as I got to know my friends better.

Joy: What helped us in our culinary adventures was the relative safety of Ahmedabad, a city that came to life at sunset and was very safe to explore even at the dead of night. We could take an auto from the new city—where we lived—to the old, fill up on the cheap and delicious food in the gallis there, and come back, four in an auto. Sometimes we went to the Cama (the posh hotel across the Sabarmati), and on a Rs 100 per head budget eat 'shroom steak' and Death by Chocolate.

Bikramjit: Ah, the Rs 100 per head splurge after night duty. As far as I remember, it came to a little over Rs 100, but I had generous friends who 'lent' me the cash.

Joy: Despite all those attractions, we learnt how to cook. There are two dishes we cooked that cling to my mind even today: a beef buffath and a prawn curry. And both because of the excellence of the raw protein. We got the beef from a tiny shop in the old city whose main business was selling auto spares, and we got the prawns from the main fish market (which was a revelation—the seafood was fresh and relatively cheap).

Sumana: I think the random eating out we did on lean budgets in the early days of our friendship cemented our bond, besides laying the foundation for future food adventures. We realized we liked good food and had no compunctions travelling for or spending—or not spending, given our perpetual penury in those days—on it. Our likes and dislikes were still being formed, but we began to appreciate and respect each other's opinions and suggestions.

Bikramjit: And we picked up ideas from everywhere. I remember being told by a colleague of ours how to find out if the fish were really fresh by looking at their anuses. It's pretty failsafe. We cooked largely vegetarian food at home, except when we had a party. I remember making crab malai curry once: we used buckets to cook the crabs because we didn't have utensils large enough! But things looked up when we moved to Baroda (all three of us quit the Ahmedabad newspaper and our new job took us to Baroda, barely two hours away). For the first time, we set up a proper kitchen. Our parents came over and, deeply moved by our impoverished state, generously bought us utensils and implements, including decent serving spoons. On a friend's recommendation, we employed a middle-aged Marathi lady, Muktabai; she brought her mother, daughter-in-law and granddaughter (four generations in all!) and they cleaned and cooked for us, so our chummery began resembling the home we had left behind. It was in Baroda that we started cooking for the sake of flavour, not just to fill our tummies. We started taking lunch to office and Sumana started baking in an oven.

Sumana: I still have that oven! It's only about twenty years old now and still in regular use. I agree, Baroda was the turning point: it's where each of us took baby steps into our specialized areas. Bikramjit, we realized, was brilliant when he was in the mood and had to cook for parties. I found out that I could follow a recipe. And Joy we treasured for his knife skills and his palate. A balance that works very well for us many years hence.

Joy: It's possibly in Baroda that we all realized how important food was to our lives, to be seen not merely as a daily necessity but as something to plan the day around. Muktabai would cook Gujarati/Marathi/Sindhi dishes, largely vegetarian and very seasonal. The cooking implements Bikramjit's parents bought us made the kitchen more personal, and what definitely helped was the plan of the kitchen itself—large, airy, with two huge windows that looked out to the horizon, where in the distance you could see the hill of Pavagadh. A kitchen to spend lots of time in. And we did.

Bikramjit: Baroda was also the time when Sumana and Joy got married and I moved to a tiny flat nearby, much to their chagrin. And it was where Sumana and I began our cookbook collection, which still exists, though now broken up between two cities.

Joy: The one other food-related function of Baroda in our lives was that we started having favourite restaurants and favourite dishes. San's Sizzlers was where we first had iced tea and teppanyaki (or what passed off as it). Sandeep, the avuncular owner, indulged us and was a reason we kept going back. Down the road was the Welcomgroup Vadodara, which is where we would go after night shift for their mutton curry. That's also where we had our first taste of Mexican food: two chefs, Roberto and Antonio, had come down for a food festival. The standout dish was a chicken cooked in chocolate, which was mind-bending in terms of understanding how chocolate could taste so different. It was in Gujarat that we learnt that the smaller cities can surprise you with the variety and quality of food.

Bikramjit: We then moved to Chandigarh, in 2000, which is where Sumana came into her own as a cook; without Muktabai and with specific ideas of what she wanted, she had no option but to start cooking on a daily basis. That Chandigarh stint was quite idyllic; the mountains were only a couple of hours away and we would drive up for lunch to Giani da Dhaba on the Shimla Highway and get back in time for work. We were often unaccountably delayed and our boss soon got used to the excuses of flat tyres and jammed highways.

Sumana: Despite Bikramjit's evident talent with meat and fish, the most memorable meal he ever cooked for us was purely vegetarian and, ironically, in the land of butter chicken. I remember Joy and I were on night shift and starving. It was winter, the kind of quiet, crystal-clear, bone-freezing night that's common in northern India, when all sane people ensure they're tucked under multiple blankets by 9 p.m. Bikramjit cooked us a hot meal of dal and rice. It was simple and it was superb.

Joy: What stood out in this meal was the freshness, the simplicity and the authenticity, and I think that has been our 'food philosophy'—if one can use such a grand phrase for such a basic activity—in the years that followed. We enjoy eating together because we look for the same things in food. It means that we are very fussy about where we eat out, preferring places that specialize in a particular cuisine and have a reputation for authenticity; multi-cuisine restaurants are only a last resort. Of course, we argue and differ over choice of cuisine and though that rules out some cuisines from common meals, especially Middle-Eastern, there's still enough to go around. A chicken sandwich at Koshy's in Bangalore or a roti and dal at Giani's dhaba has given us as much pleasure as the sashimi at Megu in Delhi.

Sumana: Which is why one of the things we really enjoy doing—be it singly or together—is discovering markets and shopping for food, be it at home or abroad. Over time, we've learnt to identify and pick good vegetables—the whole exotic-organic trend of produce began on our watch—and meats. I remember the excitement when the first organic vegetable store opened in downtown Baroda around the turn of the millennium; there was a sense, even in that small town, that this was the beginning of something new.

Bikramjit: I have always loved the process of putting together a meal. Like looking for a specific cut of meat or a size of prawn, and then building up the dish from there, with the various herbs and spices. For a majority of the time we were in the same city (from 1995 to 2006, give or take a few months), shopping on Saturday with Sumana was a highlight of sorts. We had sussed out the shopkeepers and got ones with whom we vibed to source the produce we wanted.

Joy: Going to the market was a part of my childhood. From the age of eight or so I would accompany my mother and grandmother to New Market in Kolkata every Saturday morning—to the meat section (where the butcher had those huge mutton-chop whiskers), the chicken stalls, the fruit and veg, the grocery store (where I would sometimes be plonked down and given a cold drink while the store owner and I chatted at length about Mohun Bagan and East Bengal). Our childhood holidays used to be in Kalimpong, in the Darjeeling hills, and the haat there was full of fungi and ferns that one never saw anywhere else. I still try and squeeze in a Saturday-morning market trip when in Kolkata; I'm always blown away by the sheer variety of produce, especially the greens. And I realize the importance of building relationships with the stall-holders, some of whom have nothing more than a plastic sheet spread on the ground. They will always give you their best stuff.

Sumana: My family had a holiday home in Madhupur, in what is now Jharkhand. While the shopping in Kolkata was largely left to our old cook, who'd been with the family for years, in Madhupur my father made a morning ritual of going to the market. I loved tagging along with him. In the 1980s, Madhupur was the quintessential heartland town, with a market overflowing with the freshest produce, be it locally grown rice or locally reared goats. My father had a good eye for vegetables, meat and fish; he also loved his sweets. Normally a reserved man, he always enjoyed a good banter with the shopkeepers, who, I think, also appreciated a connoisseur. Unlike many parents nowadays, he never shied away from exposing me to the blood and gore of the fish and meat markets; I think it was important for him that we see where our food came from, so that we respected it and made the most of it.

Our house in Madhupur also had a large orchard of mango, litchi, banana, custard-apple, cashew and other fruit trees, besides a front flower garden. I remember him taking me around, pointing out the various varieties and teaching me to distinguish between one and the other by the leaves. In retrospect, I know this is why I've always associated food with farming.

Bikramjit: Shopping done, cooking is the easy part. Because we cook for each other, we have a fairly good idea of each other's tastes. If I eat something I think is amazing, I can recommend it to either Joy or Sumana, because I can predict whether they will like it or not. Similarly, they are also good at knowing what I like to eat or enjoy doing in the kitchen. I think the culmination of our food interests was our trip to South Africa in 2010, where we had what is now called a curated holiday. Where we went and what we did was decided to a large extent by what we wanted to eat.

Joy: Sumana's grouse is that we didn't have any 'South African' food in South Africa, but I think we went one step ahead—we had some of the freshest produce served in the most interesting and innovative ways. That was the first time I tasted sorrel, which was an unexpected explosion of flavour in the palate. And it was there that we realized that the best food (and these were some of the world's top-rated restaurants) is not necessarily served in grand settings by snooty waiters and with a black-tie dress code but is accessible to anyone who takes an interest. At La Colombe, the atmosphere is of a farmyard kitchen; the waiters are friendly and helpful. We went after a day's traipsing round Cape Town but our slightly dishevelled look didn't seem to raise any eyebrows. Most gratifying (apart from the food) was to see a man sitting on his own, very much at ease, reading a book and slowly making his way through his meal, in complete communion with his senses. That is true fine dining.

Sumana: I was a solo diner, actually, at Central, Lima, in 2014. But we saw several of them at fine dining places in many cities. There's nothing quite like eating with like-minded people, but sometimes—especially for business travellers—your own company is all you can fall back on. And rather that, than someone who doesn't appreciate the food!

Joy: The informality in South Africa suited us, given that we are notoriously unable to subscribe to time and dress codes! But it opened up a new world for us. A couple of years ago we were in Edinburgh and had reservations for dinner at The Kitchin. Sumana had bust a toe that morning and was in obvious distress when we reached there but the staff were wonderful, helping her along and finding a suitable place for us to sit. At the end of the meal Tom Kitchin, the chef, came out and signed our menus. That was a lovely personal touch that immediately lifted an already great experience several notches higher. It's something that we're seeing now in India too, where managers no longer act like Carson the butler (of *Downton Abbey*) turning up his nose at black tie instead of white for dinner!

Bikramjit: I think one reason we work (or eat) well together is that we have very defined strengths. Joy is good with flavours. I have an idea of quantities, be it ordering at restaurants or cooking for parties at home. Sumana likes things Just So when it comes to cuisines she is familiar with. Of course, we do enjoy doing things that are not conformist and, sometimes, that works out wonderfully for everyone.

Sumana: As precious as these fine-dining memories—and there are several others, in Istanbul, London and elsewhere—are our walkabouts in farmers' markets. All of us love discovering indigenous produce, talking in whatever language possible with shopkeepers and farmers, admiring gross-looking seafood and strange fruits, and sampling peculiar stuff wherever possible! At the Neighbourgoods Market in Cape Town—a must-do for every visitor—we had different vendors every few feet, selling everything from home-brewed beer to seafood paella, fresh cheeses to honeycombs (and some beautiful and wildly expensive, and heavy, wooden chopping boards).

Joy: I had been to Cape Town a few weeks before the other two came and I remember going to Neighbourgoods one Saturday and immediately thinking, 'This is where we have to come together.' I think our love for fresh markets wherever we travel is only outweighed by our extreme laziness so that we don't actually end up cooking much while on holiday. I look at all the varieties of mushrooms, the rows of greens, the hunks of beef and shelves of seafood and wonder what it would be like to cook with such good produce. But it rarely happens. So we end up eating excellent food but we miss out on the Masterchef experience, using all the wonderful produce (and possibly great kitchen equipment) ourselves. We spent a couple of nights in this town called De Kelders, which is on the South African coast where the whales come in. It was a homestay with a fully loaded kitchen but it also had lovely people in charge who organized everything for us.

Sumana: Going back a bit in time, I remember our first trip abroad for a friend's wedding. We were very gauche, very wide-eyed, though we were in the UK, which is familiar at so many levels. Our friends took us to a seafood restaurant in Mumbles, Wales. And I was blown away by how lightly the fish was treated, with just butter and lemon juice. I remember thinking, 'Wow, no wonder the spice trade was so important to these guys.' I also realized how we smother our food with masalas, possibly to disguise inferior produce or to guard against spoilage in our tropical heat. That very simple meal suddenly connected a whole host of dots for me.

Joy: The Istanbul trip was special for another reason: we were very lucky to meet up with Aylin Oney, who, apart from being a warm, funny and super-helpful friend, is a local food historian. So we got to see bits of Istanbul we would probably not have otherwise seen. We ate like locals at Ciya in Kadikoy, we shopped in the tiny stalls surrounding it, buying honey fresh off the combs and the best Turkish delight. We met Bilge, whose shop at the Spice Market was like Aladdin's cave for food lovers.

Sumana: Yes, I think that the organized food tour in Istanbul really opened our eyes to the huge difference local knowledge can make. In Peru, my hosts were well aware of my interest in food, in not just eating it, but related history and agriculture as well. I was lucky enough to get a tour of an organic farm at the foothills of the Andes (it's the most spectacular farm ever, with the mountains seeming to rise right up from the clearing of the farm), see various fruits and vegetables growing in the fields, go around local markets (very like our Indian haats, actually) and see quinoa heaped up for sale, just like rice is, in our bazaars. I believe prices have gone up five times at the ground level since the quasi-grain suddenly became popular worldwide. It was another indicator how food cannot be a single-point interest; everything in our lives tie up with it.

Joy: When we went to Rio, hotel rates were far too high and all we could afford was a homestay; our host, Eliana, was a wonderfully spirited Chilean in her seventies, a former professor of political science. She had a lovely house straddling five levels with a huge and well-stocked kitchen that she threw open to us. On the last day of our stay she decided she was going to cook a moqueca (fish stew) for us so we set off shopping. She took us to this local market where no one spoke anything other than Portuguese, and inside that to her favourite grocery store to buy the oils and spices we'd need. It was no more than a neighbourhood kirana store; I've seen them across India, and their treasures are known only to locals. We bought rice, a special palm oil, various powders (including cocoa sold loose)—the sort of stuff no tourist would get to see, and far more authentic (and cheaper) than what they sold in the department stores. On the way back home we took a short detour to the Confeitaria Colombo, a really grand nineteenth-century café that specialized in pastries. Off our beaten track, for sure. That evening she made the moqueca and as she made it she told us stories of her life, which seemed to be interwoven with the moqueca. All of that (and some good wine) made for an unforgettable dinner.

Sumana: The moqueca story was very special to me: I had first read about it in Jorge Amado's classic novel *Gabriela, Clove and Cinnamon*. And as it happens, a television adaptation of the novel is where Eliana learnt to cook the stew, though over the years she had made it her own.

Joy: My discovery was not a coincidence, it was planned. Months before our Brazil trip I'd seen an episode of Anthony Bourdain's show where he went to Sao Paulo and ate feijoada, which was originally slave food, a stew made with the offcuts and tripe, with beans and a lot of accompaniments. I was fascinated by it, by the story and the elevation of slave food into the national dish of Brazil. We had feijoada in Goa a few weeks before our Brazil trip and it disappointed me: is this what the fuss was about? I needn't have worried; we had it on our second day in Sao Paulo, and it was everything I'd expected: full of flavour, with layers and textures to it, and bits and bobs of meat that you weren't too sure about (was that an ear or a snout or something else?). We had it several more times on that trip, including on a rainy and chilly afternoon in Rio and it was soul food, just like it said on the bottle.

Bikramjit: Simultaneously, we've had the good fortune of meeting people who have helped grow our interest in food. I became friends with the late Jacob Sahaya, when we met at a dinner. His knowledge of coastal Tamil food, Kongunadu food, was something he was very proud of. A couple of years after that meal, I got to meet and work with Jacob again and met his family as well while cooking up some very intricate Nadar dishes. It was a community (and cuisine) I'd been unaware of. For someone who was a star—Jacob had a hugely popular cooking show on Sun TV—he was very close to his roots. Like me, he believed the food made by the aunts and mums was unbeatable. His restaurant, which I visited shortly before his sudden and tragic death in 2012—he was just thirty-eight—was a fantastic homage to all the home-style recipes he had collected over the years.

Joy: I remember that first dinner (and also a meal several years later at his restaurant in Chennai). There were many things we learnt from him that we apply even today.

Bikramjit: He was the first person I knew who had researched food through ancient Tamil texts. It spurred me to investigate and read about food because I realized how little I knew. Jacob introduced me to Indian food without foreign influences: no chillies, no potatoes, no cane sugar. It's amazing what we have been able to make Indian. It makes me think every time I look at a dish.

Joy: One of the privileges of being on the fringes, as it were, of the food business—writing about food, eating out frequently—has been the proximity it gives us to the creators of good food, insights into their philosophies, an understanding of how the business works. They are primarily chefs—putting good food on exciting menus—but their stories and their world views go far beyond what they put on the plate.

Bikramjit: The person who inspired me, especially while he was in his experimental stage of cooking, is Bakshish Dean. I met him while working on my very first food review in Delhi—a review of his restaurant Fire at the Park—and we clicked almost immediately. I was in awe of his knowledge of food; we had both read Harold McGee and Bakshish has used this knowledge in a practical sense. That first menu was fresh and extraordinary; he looked at the food, the ambience, the service, the crockery and cutlery as part of a whole experience. And his food really stood out. I still feel Bakshish is one of the best culinary minds in the country. I remember those long conversations I had with him sitting in his tiny office in the kitchen, tasting bits of different dishes and just talking about food non-stop. It was like sitting in on a lecture, and it helped me think out of the box. I still remember a meal that he had invited me to where he made this pulao with green methi seeds and rice from a recipe he had borrowed from his Muslim neighbours in Shimla. My decision to go and hunt authentic recipes from across India, which I turned into a TV show, was largely inspired by what Bakshish fed me right there in Delhi. He made me realize the importance of sticking to the original flavours of anything one is cooking.

Joy: What has always fascinated me is not the chefs but the domestic cooks, the bawarchis. How they mastered alien meat, fruits and vegetables, alien flavours and processes to produce gourmet dishes—it's fairly mindboggling when you come to think of it. We had a cook called Sunil from Purulia, one of the poorest districts of West Bengal. He came to our house as a raw teenager but within a few years he was making souffles, soups, roasts and stews; most amazing was how he cooked beef perfectly even though he didn't eat it (and could barely touch it). Even a kebab would have been alien to him as also the process of grilling. I wish I had asked him how he had picked up all this: did he merely replicate instructions perfectly, did he understand what was going on, or was it pure instinct? I never did ask, of course; we just took it for granted.

Sumana: Talking about cooks/chefs we're impressed by, I have to bring in my grandmum. She was the classic Indian matriarch, never measuring anything but by andaz, producing the most finely cut vegetables on the Bengali bonti and cooking only a few signature dishes herself, usually sweets. The family cook produced the daily meals on her directions; she'd be telling him about the tempering and the timings from one room, and he'd be sweating it out over the coal fire in the kitchen. Yet every single dish and every single meal that we ate while she helmed the household bore her stamp. Typically, she never used recipes, nor did she leave behind any and, as typically, I was never interested in following what she did as a child; food was something that just appeared at the dining table, though the talk of food was always all around. The thrill when I managed to approximate a particularly favourite dal years after she had passed away was indescribable.

Joy: My interest in food came from my mother. As a child I would be in the kitchen while she baked (always in the afternoon, when she had the kitchen to herself); I would pass the ingredients and operate the mixie, and as reward I would claim the scraps of dough (my favourite was the dough used in apple pie). This was the 1970s, when you didn't get most of the ingredients that are so freely available today, and my mother was an expert in substituting and making use of local produce in Western food long before it became fashionable in the top restaurants. Her curiosity about food—willing to try anything just once, to travel for a taste or a recipe—has rubbed off on me. I wish I had her ability to approach perfect strangers at the fish stall or the fruit market and ask them how they were going to cook what they had bought.

Bikramjit: When I was allowed to go out with the family to eat (I was a very, very badly behaved child), I always managed to sweet talk my way into various kitchens, my favourite being the kitchen of our neighbourhood Chinese restaurant, Chung Wah. It was a fascinating, dark, smoky kitchen with flashes of fire from the woks. The chefs wore vests (ganjis) and almost played with the food. This was possibly the beginnings of my desire to become a chef. And yes, I wanted to be a Chinese chef. The first person who encouraged me to begin the process of cooking was my aunt Shona, who I remember came to spend time with the family in 1977. I vividly remember Chhotopishi, as I called her, using an element heater to cook up pork chops with apple sauce. From scratch. She even took me to the market and that's when, I think for the first time in my life, I saw a dish coming together from start to finish.

Joy: When Bikramjit comes to stay with us, there is an obligatory visit to the local fish market where he will buy vast quantities of seafood and then proceed to cook. By the end of the evening he uses up every single cooking utensil (and some that aren't), but in the end turn out some incredible dishes. I remember he once bought a whole seer fish. We brought it home and all he did was add some soy sauce, ginger, coriander and lime, and steam it. It was simple and it was perfect. We have actually planned our big parties around his visits—he is happiest when left alone in the kitchen to create havoc and turn out a never-ending stream of freshly cooked finger food. This has often been preceded by a visit to the market to buy a carload of stuff from crockery to implements to raw material to the best cheeses/sausages/meats, and you can sense Sumana's tension levels rising when he walks through the door with the baskets, bags and boxes but by the end of the evening there are a lot of very happy, if overstuffed, guests who walk, or roll, out of our door. He loves an audience. The flipside is that if he has to cook a simple meal for the three of us and is not in the mood, it could go horribly wrong.

Bikramjit: I think Sumana's cooking has evolved the most in the past twenty years. From knowing very little about food or cooking and, frankly, having very little interest in it, she is today the most knowledgeable, in the deepest sense, among the three of us and can turn out gourmet meals as well as very good everyday rice-and-dal lunches. And the latter is actually the mark of a good cook; gourmet meals, with good ingredients and fancy recipes, are often easier to replicate than simple food made to taste very good. Joy and I have been exposed to food and cooking from an early age so in some ways it is more innate but Sumana has learnt it almost from scratch later on.

Joy: I think we've all evolved in different ways. I think more about food than before, and I analyse differently, perhaps a bit too much, as well as plan and execute differently. I've been exposed to more of, and have learnt to appreciate, Bengali food; ditto with Sumana and 'Western' food. Bikramjit, who always straddled both worlds, has learnt to be more discerning (especially in our company). The landscape around us is far more democratic than before; everyone has more defined tastes, even twenty-something colleagues will know clearly what they like and dislike and are not shy of articulating it. But after all that travel, all those top restaurants and Masterchef dishes and fancy ingredients, there's one truism that stays with us: The best meals are those shared around a big table with family or friends. Nothing makes a meal more complete and more satisfying than the company of those close to you, the conversation stretching the mealtime for hours. A bit like this chat!

Sumana: Time to end, with this quote from Virginia Woolf that sums it up: 'One cannot think well, love well, sleep well, if one has not dined well.'

Cook It Slowly

MAMANG DAI

'All day we are doing nothing, but we feel hungry,' says my mother, laughing.

Yes, I hanker for grilled octopus, cheese and olives, but I also remember the serene faces of a group of women sitting around a fire where a pot is on the boil. Their conversation goes something like this:

'Don't let it boil too fast.'

'Hai, take the lid off.'

'Hai, the taste will evaporate.'

'Cook it slowly.'

'This is the best time, when the red ants are seen on the leaves.'

'Hai, it is a sign.'

'The ants are clever ...'

It is a quiet, languid conversation in a village house on the art of cooking the popular On-giin leaf, or Clerodendrum Colebrookianum. It is a tall, vigorously growing perennial shrub of broad, dark green leaves with a hint of bitterness. As children we used to hate this stuff but ate them because we were told it would make us grow tall, especially if we held up the greens, stem and all, and tilted our heads back to eat them. Now food scientists have analysed that Clerodendrum contains medicinal properties for the treatment of diabetes, rheumatism and hypertension. I go to the market and buy bundles of the leaf. They grow in the garden too, and I look out for the red ants to appear.

What is khautek, tongtep, khau-laam and dungpoo?

In case you are wondering, these are all rice preparations—steamed, wrapped in leaf, powdered, mixed with sesame seeds and flattened into cakes. They are then rolled into balls or cooked in bamboo tubes. Rice is the most widely consumed staple grain in Arunachal Pradesh. In fact, it is believed to be of divine origin. One story goes that rice is a gift from the gods that came to a race of sky dwellers in the land of fish and stars. It happened during a great hunt when the faithful dog of a legendary hunter lost his way and strayed into the kingdom of the Great Earth Mother, the Goddess of Grain. The dog told her how he was lost. The goddess heard him out and then sent him on his way with a few grains of rice, which the faithful dog carried back to his master in the crease of his ear. Today, rice is cultivated throughout the state and many varieties are grown—they can be classified into two broad categories: that of highland or mountain rice, which is grown in the cyclical jhum fields of shifting cultivation, and the lowland or wet rice cultivation. A hardy species of mountain rice, known locally as 'Mipun', is believed to be the original seed that was brought back from the granary of the Earth Mother.

Rice preparations are required on many occasions. Rice cakes using red, short-grained sticky rice wrapped in leaf are an essential item at weddings. Rice is also the chief ingredient for the local beer that, according to popular folklore, makes men equal to the gods and restores health and laughter in this world.

Khau-laam or bamboo rice is a clean, convenient way of packaging cooked rice that can be carried easily when out on a journey. The ingredients are simply rice and water. I am using the word 'khau-laam' of the Khampti people where the variety of bamboo used is known locally as 'khaulam-ba'. It is a soft bamboo with a thin membrane that coats the rice as it cooks, allowing the cooked rice to be removed in one cylindrical piece. The rice is left to soak overnight and filled into bamboo tubes, leaving enough space for expansion. A little water is poured in and the bamboo is sealed with a leaf of arrowroot. The rice-filled bamboo tubes are cooked over an open fire, and a good deal of attention is required to ensure that the rice is thoroughly cooked and not burnt. Bamboo rice can be eaten by simply pulling back the soft bamboo, or by slicing the bamboo into pieces. It's flavour is unparalelled and can be savoured best while sitting in the shade by a river with the breeze on your face. Then nothing else is required except khau-laam and maybe a little salt.

Khampti cuisine is also famous for a raw fish soup traditionally prepared only by men, and like gazpacho, served cold. It is called paa-saa. This soup is laboriously prepared using all parts of a popular freshwater fish called Ngopie. However, the key ingredient is a leaf called khum-phat, identified as Bischofia javanica,[1] of which almost 3 kilos are required to extract a litre of juice. The leaves are pounded in a large vessel and steeped in water. The juice is extracted by squeezing out the excess water, then mixing the leaves with the finely chopped raw fish along

---

1   Source: Dr. K. Haridasan, former systematic botanist, Arunachal State Forest Research Institute.

with coriander, chilli, garlic, ginger, watercress and white basil. The stock for the soup is prepared by boiling the dry roasted scales and finely pounded bones of the fish and then filtering it through a fine sieve. This stock is used as long as a fine layer of fish oil is visible. The soup is of a fresh green colour, and in taste paa-saa is a masterpiece of subtle flavours and elegant seasoning. The traditional accompaniment to paa-saa is a chutney made of the roe and edible innards of the fish, stir-fried in a little oil with chopped garlic, scallions, salt and chillies. The result is a dark, rich paste that is the perfect combination with the soup. Paa-saa is an invention for the winter when the harvest is in, and a connoisseur would consider it a sacrilege to have anything else on the table if there was the unbeatable triad of fragrant new rice, the dark chutney and a bowl of paa-saa.

Like rice, bamboo is the other life-giving plant in Arunachal Pradesh. It is used for fuel, fodder, shelter and food. This will be evident to any visitor to the state, who sooner or later is likely to be assailed by the distinct aroma of bamboo shoot that is used daily in a variety of local preparations. Pickled, dried or cooked bamboo shoot is that tastemaker that is believed to possess curative properties with protease activity which helps in the digestion of proteins.

Bamboo shoot is the new growth of culms and in season it is available whole. The popular edible varieties range from the coarse root clumpers to the ivory yellow, pinkish and pale green tender runner shoots. Generally households buy these in bulk, and after peeling off the protective sheath, chop the fresh culm and pack it into jars or even plastic buckets. This becomes the fermented bamboo shoot that is used to flavour meat and vegetable dishes. Bamboo shoot can be stored for long periods in air-tight containers. Sometimes these are lightly burnt or pressed with a heavy stone to drain out excess moisture and the shoots are stored whole. In rural Arunachal, bamboo shoot is traditionally stored in large bamboo tubes which are then stacked in a cool place like a water point or a small stream. Another way of storing it is by sun-drying. This is an arduous process that involves a lot of chopping. The finely chopped bamboo shoot is spread out on a large mat and allowed to dry completely. This type of bamboo shoot is preferred for cooking with smoked fish, though it is also used in a number of meat dishes and chutneys. It is light, easy to carry, and a dose of dried bamboo mixed with a little water, salt and chilli can really perk up the appetite.

Like most food in Arunachal, bamboo also has its mythical origins. Traditional local cuisine is simple. It is linked to the environment and with what is available, with special festivals and rituals associated with the agricultural cycle. Contrary to popular perception, traditional communities do not usually eat meat. The hunting and fishing traditions do not provide meat at all times of the year, and they are also associated with rituals and food taboos. Meat and fish are generally dried, smoked and preserved to tide over lean periods.

The energy of a village is concentrated in the cultivation of rice for which large clearings are made on the hillsides. Wet rice cultivation was introduced in the late 1950s to boost production, and in the foothills every fertile plot of land was used for growing rice. However, wet rice cultivation, of which my home district is at the forefront, is now perceived as the culprit behind the increasing number of diabetic cases which were fairly unknown in tribal society before. A higher-yielding variety of ginger, another essential ingredient in local preparations, was also introduced, but I heard that in some villages people began to suffer dental problems which they thought was due to the larger-sized but fairly tasteless hybrid ginger. It may be speculation, but it has made me think about food in a new light.

Of course, Arunachal lifestyle and food habits have changed over the years. In the old days, food was for sustenance and survival. The relationship between food and medicine was also quite clear. In homes today the table is usually laid with a mosaic of cultural combinations. There's saffron rice, instant noodles, the western equivalent of our local black pudding, a suggestion of Haggis and KFC.

The simple food of bygone days cooked fresh over woodfires can now only be enjoyed in the villages, and specialized preparations can make a comeback only perhaps if they are on the menu for visiting tourists. The influence of Continental, Chinese, Asian and Indian curries and spices has also helped to modify local dishes. There is information technology too that has changed the food scene. Food is visible and ever present, just like when we were in school laboriously copying out recipes in our prized notebooks, the equivalent of being on Facebook back then—never mind that Cornish pasties and clotted cream were a dream away and we would never get the ingredients, at least not in Arunachal then, to conjure up such heavenly delights. World cooking is now at our doorstep.

Yet one thing I have never seen, not even on TV shows about wild places and esoteric food, is the small, edible insect called tari. When the weather is cool and the sky is overcast, a dark, buzzing cloud settles softly over the dry riverbeds and disappears into the gravel and naked stones. This is the season of the tari, a blackish-brown river beetle that arrives in the months of November and December, presumably to hibernate. An acquired taste makes the tari prey to groups of villagers, especially women, who scour the riverbeds and overturn stones in search of this delicacy. Tari is eaten raw, cooked, boiled, fried or roasted. The only thing to watch out for is the tiny red centre on the chest of the beetle which causes a burning sensation if eaten inadvertently. This portion is plucked out easily, but stains the fingertips like nicotine. Not much is known about this beetle except that it belongs to the class Insecta and the species name is Nazara.[2]

The addiction to tari-eating is also hard to explain. To my mind it is quite tasteless, but aficionados go into raptures over it. In many cases people have literally gone mad eating the tari. This is a strange disorder that is believed to attack a person who unfortunately eats a tari that is already dead, or one that dies before it is used in cooking. The results can be disastrous. The affected person can experience extreme hallucination and can take on the behaviour of the insect, shunning light and crawling under objects in search of a dark place. The illness is not fatal, but its effect lasts for days. It is a strange sight to see someone lying in a hospital bed yanking back the cover over their head and body whenever anxious relatives try to take a peep to see how the patient is doing. One year, so many people were hit by tari consumption that the district administration imposed a ban on its procurement and sale. Yet, every season, the affair with the tari continues. Kept in bamboo tubes or in string bags and perforated containers, the tari can live for days and weeks without food or water, and such food parcels sent to friends and relatives where tari is unavailable is cause for great delight. Any takers, anyone?

---

2   Source: Dr A. Borang, ethno zoologist, State Forest Research Institute, Itanagar.

Inheritance

NAINTARA MAYA OBEROI

Every Sunday, we went to my grandparents' house in Rajendra Nagar for dinner. First the house was a red-brick one with a courtyard in Old Rajendra Nagar; later, a bigger plot in New Rajendra Nagar. In both neighbourhoods, there was a flourishing neighbourhood dhaba called Bittu's or Pappu's, which served chicken curry, mutton curry, rotis, black ma-ki-dal, gobi-aloo and a 'mixed vegetable' preparation that changed from day to day.

The rotis were my job, my father's and mine. We would walk down with my cousin to the dhaba and order the rotis for dinner. If it was very cold, as a great indulgence, we would drive down and wait inside my parents' Maruti. But I liked to stand, sweaty, right next to the tandoor to watch the roti man at work.

If I stood on tiptoe, I could see the red flame inside the tandoor and the air pockets rising in the rotis, which flaked and cracked when touched. The roti man had three assistants,

224

each ganglier than the last, who would lay out huge sheets of wholewheat dough, and cut and roll them into balls. They would then dust them with dry flour, flatten them, whirl them once or twice around in their floured hands, and hand them over to the artiste. He would lower the dough to the inner wall of the tandoor, which was covered in iron mounds on the inside, where the dry heat would blister and cook the bread. He always knew when the rotis were ready to be fished out with his hooked iron rod; if you ordered enough rotis, they would give you a plastic bag of raw red onions and some of the dal fry—'dal fly' as my father referred to it—free.

The neighbours would be out for their dinners, too: the officious lady from a few streets down who ran everyone's lives, the local beat cops, my grandmother's Arya Samaj cronies, and the next block's Balraj Kohli uncle who, every Sunday, treated himself to a fiery meat curry and one chilled bottle of beer. Men came to eat under the naked bulbs suspended from the rafters; women came to pick up food to take home. As they waited, people would fall into backslapping, into handshaking, into gossip.

Rajendra Nagar was one of Delhi's Partition refugee colonies, hurriedly created after 1947 to accommodate the millions of displaced people pouring into independent India. In Delhi, these neighbourhoods were named after Hindu Congress leaders: Rajendra Nagar, Patel Nagar, Tilak Nagar and Lajpat Nagar. Over time, the accents of its inhabitants mellowed 'Rajendra Nagar' down to the more rounded, affectionate 'Rajinder Nagar', just as Connaught Place became 'Knaat Place', and residential colonies all across South Delhi became 'c'lonies'.

Rajinder Nagar was, without doubt, a Punjabi c'lony. Punjabi villages and towns had always had common tandoors for baking bread; women would prepare the dough at home and then take it to the communal oven to cook. So tandoors sprang up in Rajinder Nagar too. In the afternoons or early evenings, my grandmother would make atta at home and take it to the tandoorwala who sat down the street, relying on the households of the neighbouring lanes for business. He had no counter, no tables and chairs, no awning—just five bricks and a clay oven.

☙

The Rajinder Nagar house didn't originally belong to my dada and dadi. My paternal grandfather was from Pind Dadan Khan, in the arduous Potohar Plateau region of West Punjab, and his family had moved to Rawalpindi and he to Lahore. My grandmother's family, though, originally from Fatehgarh Churian in East Punjab, had lived in a village that fell across the new border, now in Pakistan. They came in 1947, like many other Partition refugees, on the trains from West Punjab carrying whatever they could salvage. My grandmother's brother wangled a job exchange as a government clerk in Delhi, and this came with a flat in Panchkuian Road, to the west of the city then. For a few months, seventy people squeezed into its three rooms, waiting to find work and somewhere to go. My grandfather, who'd lived in university accommodation in Lahore, wasn't eligible for any kind of house allotment. Still, in 1947, they counted themselves lucky. He was a teacher and he managed to find work, first in Rohtak, then in Ajmer, then in Dehradun. Others languished in refugee camps for years.

'Don't be silly,' Professor Aziz, my grandfather's colleague at Government College, Lahore had told him. 'In a little while you can have a permanent position here. I don't know why you're going off to God-knows-where. All this will pass.'

Most people were of the same mind. No one thought the border was about to become impermeable. My mother's mother locked her treasures and books in her school desk when she left Lahore; she didn't know she wouldn't be back for the new term in July. My grandfather journeyed back in September 1947 to track down his niece in a tuberculosis asylum.

Not understanding the danger they were in, his sister Channo Devi and her husband refused to leave Murree, where they owned a curio shop; eventually, in September 1947 they were sent to an army-run refugee camp in Rawalpindi, and in October, lifted out to India on a DC3 Dakota flight. Legend has it that Channo tried to persuade the soldiers to allow her to bring her prized tandoor with her on the plane.

In the early 1950s, land and houses were allotted to the refugees according to what they could prove they'd left behind; several old hierarchies were thus recreated. In Rajinder Nagar, the residents were mostly people with the same Punjabi middle-class background, often linked in a loose way to the reformist Arya Samaj movement, so friendships formed fast. Channo Devi's husband received a ninety-square-yard plot as compensation, three rooms set around a courtyard. This was the house that she would leave to her brother some decades later.

ॐ

The Partition refugees scraped a living out of small patri shops, hardware stores, taxis and phatphatiyas. Some people, like those of my family, became teachers, medical orderlies or joined the army; they became dry cleaners or restaurateurs, or opened textbook shops and ice-cream factories.

Others set up eateries. Some of these were restaurants like Moti Mahal and Chonas, but more often, they were dhabas. With low overheads and slim profit margins, the dhaba owners didn't have a lot of utensils. They concentrated on their tandoors: rotis toasted to a crackle, and whole chickens skewered and grilled in their red depths. There would be an assortment of pickles, and 'mukka wala pyaaz', a whole onion unmercifully smashed with a closed fist to release its flavours. Sometimes there were chicken tikkas, or seekh kebabs, or tawa-fried meat, like keema or kaleji. The remains of the fire were used to slow-cook whole black gram or sabut urad dal overnight, which gave the black lentils, the famous 'ma-ki-dal', its distinct, creamy, broken-down flavour in time for the next day (the swirls of cream that you see in restaurants turn it into 'dal makhani', but these were not part of the original recipe). A recognizable dhaba repertoire bloomed along the arterial roads of the new colonies, along the highways of the new India, and anywhere anyone could set up five bricks and an oven and sweat their way to a loyal clientele.

'Today, when Dilliwalas are a minority in their own city, it saddens me to see butter chicken, dal makhani and other roadside fares take over as delicacies,' wrote a peevish Sadia Dehlvi in a newspaper article in 2010. Butter chicken, the most famous issue of this era, is a restaurant dish, invented, so the probably apocryphal story has it, by Kundan Lal Gujral, the owner of Moti Mahal restaurant, in order to rescue some dried-out tandoori chicken. Punjabi ma-ki-dal is real dhaba fare, born out of necessity and enterprise. But both are products of the pragmatism and drive that, in the 1890s, led groups of Punjabi labourers to migrate to Canada, Kenya and California to better their lives (several of the Punjabis in California married their fellow agricultural labourers, who were Mexican— an unexpected but obviously rajma-based coming together of hearts). These same qualities helped the new arrivals thrive in post-Independence Delhi.

ℭℨ

Still, growing up in Delhi in the late 1990s, Punjabiyat seemed something to be embarrassed about. 'The only culture Punjabis have is agriculture,' went the Delhi joke, a caricature that consigned to the dust of another place all Punjab's poets, scholars, singers, artists and musicians. Punjabis were vulgar, dairy-swilling, glitter-loving yokels and, as Delhi historian Narayani Gupta sniffed in her *Delhi between the Two Empires*, contemporary Delhi was becoming a place where 'Tilak Nagars and Nehru Roads proliferate, and hardly anyone knows of the poetry of Mir and Zauq, the humour of Ghalib, the quality of life that Chandni Chowk once symbolized.'

I tried to dissociate myself from the caricature. It irritated me that everyone in my family said 'p'ronthi' instead of what I understood to be the correct Hindi 'parantha', and 'lassan' for what my friends from Delhi or UP called 'lehsoon'. Even now, I always pointedly say 'parantha'.

I didn't really think of myself as Punjabi anyway. My parents, having lived so long in Assam and Meghalaya, spoke Assamese between themselves, and to me. I couldn't understand any Punjabi, and I preferred rice to rotis. If my friends returned in the summer to families and ancestral homes here and there across India, I had Assam, all the leafy expanse of the tea estates around Dibrugarh, the unreal green of the paddy fields near Jorhat, the orchid-hung trees of Manas, the buttery early sun of Guwahati, the shifting islets of Majuli; I had the Brahmaputra, the angriest, most beautiful river in the world. I didn't feel dispossessed. When anyone at school asked me where I came from, I said, 'Assam.' Weaned on stubby joha rice like any good Assamese baby, and dipped at thirty days old into the raging Brahmaputra for luck, I didn't know where else I could be from.

છ

'*Jis Lahore nahi vekhya, woh janmya hi nahi*', goes the Punjabi saying. Those who have not seen Lahore, have not lived. Both sets of my grandparents, who came to India from Multan, from Lahore and from Rawalpindi, spoke of Lahore as if they'd lost a lodestar. Since Ranjit Singh's reign, Lahore, the capital of the region, had been the glory, the touchstone and the beating heart of Punjab, its hub of culture and politics. It must have been hard for anyone to imagine that this Delhi, this city that was both ruin and upstart, could take the place of a living Lahore.

I didn't think seriously about being Punjabi until the early 2000s, when travel between India and Pakistan suddenly opened up. My family trickled over the border one by one (my father, visiting for the World Cup, was accosted by strangers in cricket stadiums inviting him over for dinner; it took months to exorcise the memory of so much good-humoured gosht). When I went on a university trip to Lahore, I was expecting not only hospitality, but also a sort of homecoming. I wanted very much to find the house on Omkar Road where my family had lived, to parachute into an old Punjab that belonged to my grandparents, that I would now never see, a Punjab of planned towns like Sargodha and organic muddles like Lahore, the now-unmoored syncretic culture of travelling mirasi singers and trilingual scholars, the old worlds of Multan, Murree, Sialkot, Gujrat, Rawalpindi.

When I got there though, in 2006, it seemed more like the Amritsar we'd just crossed: a chaotic small town, equal parts middle-class swank and medieval confusion. Like Delhi and most Indian cities, its heritage is badly preserved, and its charms lie hidden beneath the modern cityscape.

I tried to squint to see if I could find a wormhole somehow, a window into what might have been my city. I thought that if

I could, at long last, manifest in Lahore, something of Lahore might well manifest in me. There were Oberois and Sanans and Sardanas and Mongias somewhere in Pakistan, but I couldn't find them. (There was, if I had only known it, my father said later, a famous Oberoi right there in Lahore, a Muslim mafia kingpin.) When I told people about my family in Rawalpindi, Lahore, Multan, and they tried to speak to me in Saraiki or in Punjabi, I was a stranger again. I was Punjabi, but I wasn't from either of the Punjabs that remained. I had lost something, but I wasn't sure what had replaced it. I was out of joint.

CB

Certain things are inherited. My grandfather was an exigent, uncompromising person. He worked hard, supported his four children and his brother's children. He was a well-read, intelligent man, a Fulbright scholar, an English teacher who wrote short stories in Hindi and translated Premchand into Urdu. He had no time for 'khaki-shorts-walas', or for organized religion either. Our family dinners were punctuated with stories, awful pun contests and borderline racist jokes, mostly about Punjabis themselves: their accents, their bumptiousness, their hirsuteness, their denseness. (Until I was ten, I thought that the Akali Dal was a kind of lentil, 'a kali dal'.)

My father told me that when his father received a small inheritance from his sister, he set up a library instead of building a house. When he died, we found out that he had, for years, stretched his resources to sponsor the education of two unknown schoolboys. His last present to me was a copy of *Jude the Obscure*, which he left for me in the bookshelf, among his collection of Urdu, English and Hindi novels. These were what I was fed on.

CB

Punjabi food is meant for those with an appetite. It is not a delicate cuisine, but a muscular, generous, backslapping one. It differs vastly from region to region: the aloo-bukhara koftas of Peshawar stuffed with plums from the hill orchards nearby; the stir-fried tawa meats of Amritsar; the Lahori seekh kebabs and besan-thickened kadhi; the khaam khatai kebabs of Patiala; saag-meat, or sarson-da-saag and makki-di-roti; the heavy, onion-laced biryanis; and the lighter kabuli chana pulaos. All of it is generous in portion and flavour; in its bastardized restaurant form, it can be nothing more than a delivery vehicle for cholesterol and the precursor to a nap on a manji.

But in Punjabi, even the most elaborate meal is called 'dal-roti', or just 'roti'. And there are always rotis: tandoori rotis, chapatis, paranthas, missi rotis, makki rotis, kulchas, bhaturas, puris, khasta rotis and khameeri naans. We ate them with pale kabuli chana dal with spinach or lauki in it, or small black garbanzo chanas, pink multani masoor dal or green urad dal, or kadhai-cooked chicken or dry keema.

Kanji was made every winter in my nani's house, with long inky black carrots, dark and mineral in taste, fermented in big pots in the sun. Peeling them stained your hands reddish-purple, and the sour, pungent smell lingered in the jars long after. Sweet red carrots were for gajar ka halwa, layered with almonds and crumbles of khoya. But I couldn't stomach either: what I liked best were the brown, crunchy edges of milk cake, sugar, milk and cardamom slowly cooked until solid, and my grandmother's suji halwa, like a gurdwara's wheat-based karha parshad, but lighter, fluffier and thicker.

My grandfather hated rajma, the beloved Punjabi staple. 'Rajma has no flavour of its own,' he would say, 'it's all that tomato masala that gives it a taste.' My father doesn't like rajma either, and I have internalized their dislikes, just as I acquired my father's horror of bananas, the result of a childhood at a boarding school where breakfast was mouldy bananas. I picture a Sunday lunch that may or may not have happened: rajma in the centre, quartered pink onions, methi, rotis and rice, and the three of us in a row at the dining table, sulking at our plates.

What my dada liked best were tandoori rotis. My dadi considered them too thick and heavy, something vaguely rustic that the northerners of the punishing Potohar liked, with their rough-and-rude culture. She preferred the thinner paranthas, which she thought were more refined. They were in agreement about rice. 'Khichdi?' they would ask solicitously when someone had an upset stomach, but otherwise, rice was a food for babies or sick people, decidedly inferior to a good piece of roti.

Towards the end of his life, my grandfather remained unbent towards chapatis, but still, a roti meant a tandoori roti, not a phulka or a naan made from refined flour. 'Chopad ke le aao,' he'd say, a soft pat of homemade white butter in the centre, the roti scrunched up in a bundle. At the end of the meal, he might have asked for 'ikk rukhhi', which was just a roti with no butter and no accompaniments, only the bread.

∞

Sometimes in Paris, where I live now, the young men who sell fake watches and Eiffel Tower key chains along the boulevards try to speak to me in Punjabi, recognizing in my features something from home. It's a thickened, theth village Punjabi, which is beyond my rudimentary Delhi phrases, gleaned mostly from songs and Bollywood dialogue. They share something with my grandparents though: the enterprising, resilient spirit of the Punjabis who crossed the Radcliffe Line in either direction, and who were met with derision by the inhabitants of the cities they arrived in, sometimes even by the people who sheltered them. (Both my grandmothers, if they read this, would be alarmed to learn they hold anything in common with these gold-chain-wearing, iPhone-flashing, sneakered guys in hoodies.)

I think about my dadi's dark-gold suji halwa, the only halwa I really like. When my father was a child, special occasions were marked by jalebis; by the time I was growing up, birthday cakes were indispensable, but even today I associate big days, both happy and unhappy, with suji halwa.

Last year I asked her for the recipe, and tried to recreate it in Paris. *One katori of suji and one of desi ghee, roasted slowly on the fire till brown, one tablespoon besan, sugar, saffron, water and raisins.* I had never cooked with desi ghee in my life, so I had to enlist my mother's help. Both genetically incapable of following a recipe, we looked at the sugar content advised, reduced it, and ended up with a kind of pale diet version. When I told my grandmother, an I-could-have-told-you-that expression appeared on her face, and she just giggled.

೮೩

I don't go much to Rajinder Nagar any more since my grand-mother moved house, but I know the dhaba and its attendant world have long since vanished, replaced by malls and multiplexes and plate-glass Punjabi baroque homes with Doric columns and Swiss chalet roofs. Perhaps the skyrocketing rents have driven Bittu out, perhaps he has moved up to a Swiss chalet too.

There's another Partition refugee colony in Delhi, farther south, built where there was once only scrubland: Lajpat Nagar. Since the early nineties, this chaotic, bustling neighbourhood, mostly Punjabi, has played host to an influx of Afghans and Iraqis, Tibetans and Turks, refugees, students and people needing medical treatment, who quickly took over rooms and flats in the homes of the original inhabitants. First one, then another Afghani bakery sprang up in the neighbourhood. They produce massive flat loaves of Afghani bread every day from a huge earthen oven on a platform. These snowshoe naans are hand-marked with a pattern of dimples when the dough is still wet. Every evening, the Afghans from the surrounding lanes queue up for their freshly baked bread. Sometimes I'd buy a naan on my way back from work, and eat it with kebabs from the Iranian restaurant a few lanes down.

In Kamla Nagar near Delhi University, a few years ago, I saw another tandoor. Chicken and veggie momos were being rubbed with an orange tandoori spice mix and a little chilli-garlic paste, then roasted in the clay tandoor in a Chinjabi restaurant. Parts of the glutinous white-flour skin blistered and puckered black while the inside remained a sturdy, juicy momo. You can see tandoori momos all over Delhi now, like an irreverent culinary metaphor sprung from its elbow-rubbing mix of displaced communities.

Delhi is a prickly, overflowing, unkind city that doesn't give up its secrets easily. But it expands to accommodate everyone who comes, and it no longer belongs to one people or another. People who were once looked upon as usurpers have become the new brokers of power, everyone inching up towards privilege, generation by generation, and new outsiders arrive, to be stared at and then taken in, traditions and all. The city doesn't buckle, but swells each year with all of them, always acquiring new layers.

I don't know what I inherited from Punjab. But I understand better now about appetite, and how bombast can signify the desire to stand on solid ground that will not suddenly shift from under your feet. The pugnacity of Delhi Punjabis didn't preclude injury or nostalgia or regret. Their neighbourhoods were sometimes enclaves of orthodoxy and conservatism and of pragmatic acceptance as well. If they were conspicuous in their appetites, all show and glitter and violence, it was perhaps bravado, like a counter-spell against the future. And if Punjabis transformed the city, it changed and sustained them too, both accumulating new traits rather than mourning what was lost.

○ʒ

Your history bears gifts. 1947 made migration a necessity for my grandparents, people who had never travelled very far before, but who acclimatized themselved to all sorts of places thereafter: Ajmer, Dehradun, Ranchi, Tawang, Goa, the Andamans and Shillong. Channo Devi, sans tandoor, opened a shop in Mussoorie. In their twenties, my parents chose to live in the remote, troubled Assam of the 1980s; they possessed something that allowed them to adapt to difficult lives too. I think of my father's mother, cooking on angeethis all those years in Ranchi, in Ajmer, in Dehradun. I think of my mother's mother, carrying her crockery strapped on the back of a mule up to Tawang. I think about my twenty-three-year-old mother in Assam, scouring Barpeta district for eggs, when the whole town was on fire, to make a birthday cake for my father, a cake she baked on an outdoor fire in a steel pateela.

I'm anchored in Delhi in a way that perhaps neither my grandparents nor my parents are. I inherited it: Delhi, the city that kept open house through everything, absorbed all these stories, nourished my family and soaked up their food. Delhi, the place that allows all sorts of people to belong, even while retaining the fiction that they are from somewhere else. In my tiny Paris flat, I cook suji halwa from one grandma's recipe, and biryani from my other grandmother's instructions. I try to replicate my mother's signature meal, the weekly standard of my growing-up years: green Thai curry, raw papaya salad and chicken satay. Where you're from is complex, but I inherited the assurance that you can carry your home anywhere; all places will feed you and take you in.

Not Just Dessert

SIDIN VADUKUT

Shortly after Narendra Modi was sworn in as India's prime minister on 26 May 2014, the Government of India did something that is close to the heart of every real Gujarati: it threw a huge, multi-course tea party. This might sound like I am falling back on some lazy stereotype. But I assure you I am not. Some years ago I lived in Gujarat briefly. And I came back superbly impressed by the average Gujarati's commitment to that gold standard of dietary health—frequent, small meals in addition to the regular three large ones.

Otherwise, why of all the problems facing British India did Mahatma Gandhi, the greatest Gujarati in history, choose to fight for salt? Because the Mahatma knew, like generations of Gujjus before and after him, that freedom and all is okay but if four o'clock bun maska has no salt then one will be in a bad mood till five o'clock dabeli.

So the lavish tea party that followed Modi's inauguration—an early dinner to be fair—came as no surprise. The menu probably

238

comprised about thirteen courses, mostly cooked in the kitchens of the Rashtrapati Bhavan.

I say 'probably' because no one is exactly sure what was really served that evening. Initially the rumours that spread were very Gujarati-centric and prominently featured dhokla, a steamed cake of chickpea flour that is to Gujarat what tax evasion is to Formula 1 racing, that is, non-negotiable.

Instead it appears that the meal was hosted by Pranab Mukherjee, the President of the Republic, and therefore featured, if anything, a tilt towards Bengali-ness.

But, overall, the menu featured excellent, even intriguing, dishes handpicked from many of India's varied ethnic cuisines. Through a combination of international, national and regional classics, it highlighted a rich diversity of ingredients, cooking styles and culinary heritages.

The first dish on the menu, for instance, was Chilled Melon Soup made of muskmelons. Which is kind of cool and a little 'global'. Melons, of course, are not indigenous to India at all. When the first Mughal emperor, Babur, arrived in the subcontinent he complained about many things. 'Hindustan is a country of few charms,' he wrote. 'There are no good horses, no good dogs, no grapes, muskmelons or first-rate fruits, no ice or cold water, no good bread or food cooked in the bazaars, no hot baths, no colleges, no candles, torches or candlesticks.' Thankfully India has since rectified most of these shortcomings, especially the muskmelon. Which is truly one of the better-behaved melons, what with its portable size and weight.

After chilling over the soup the guests moved on to Chicken Hazari. An excellent dish of marinated boneless chicken pieces cooked in a clay oven. Which nicely counterbalanced the 'firangi' melon soup, because every chicken in the world is believed to have descended from the Indian jungle fowl. However, the great food-historian K.T. Achaya says that despite having domesticated fowl, eating poultry or eggs remained taboo in the ancient subcontinent for many, many years. Perhaps our ancestors first tamed these birds for cockfighting. Thank god, then, for the first Indian, almost definitely a Punjabi, who looked at a chicken and thought: 'Bored of Gobi 65, I wonder ...'

Tandoori Aloo was the next item on the Modi Menu. A true classic dish of potatoes cooked in a clay oven. While potatoes form one of the bedrock components of Indian cooking, it is not a vegetable that is native to the country. No, really. Potatoes first arrived in Europe from South America in the mid-fifteenth century, and took another two centuries to become even a novelty food item in India. It was perhaps first consumed on the subcontinent with any relish by Europeans, before Indians developed a penchant for the tuber. Today India is one of the world's greatest growers and eaters of potatoes. There is even a Central Potato Research Institute with numerous branches. The tandoor oven, on the other hand, has been in use in India for centuries. Remains have been found in excavation sites belonging to the Indus Valley Civilization. Though, now that I think about it, I wonder why oven-cooking is so rare in the south.

But who has time for such thoughts when we have to launch into a plate of Galauti Kebabs? Tender, delicately spiced lamb-mince medallions cooked on a grill before you pop them into your mouth and wait for sweet death to envelope you because there is nothing else left in life to experience.

Galauti kebabs are that good. But they are also a relatively recent culinary innovation. One story goes that the kebab was invented for Nawab Wajid Ali Shah, ruler of the kingdom of Awadh in modern-day Uttar Pradesh, between 1847 and 1856. In his old age the nawab lost all his teeth so he could no longer chew meat. Thus his chef invented the meltingly soft galauti kebab for his culinary enjoyment. However, this story is almost certainly not totally accurate. But there is no question that the galauti is a hallmark of Awadhi cuisine.

But is it as good as the next two items—Kerala Prawn Stew and Kerala Vegetable Stew?

Hahahaha. No.

Broadly speaking, the southern state of Kerala has three culinary traditions: Hindu, Muslim and Syrian Christian. The stew belongs to the third. The Syrian Christians of Kerala are inheritors of an ancient Christian tradition that is almost as old as Christianity. Even though the community has since split into several branches who treat each other with the Christian virtues of suspicion and air pistols, they all trace their origins to the disputed evangelical journeys of Thomas, one of the original twelve disciples of Christ. What there is absolutely no dispute about whatsoever are the countless delights of the Syrian Christian kitchen. Syrian Christian cuisine combines local Hindu traditions with heavy influences from the food of the missionaries and the European traders and colonists. The stew is a staple of most Syrian Christian households. My grandmother's recipe involved leaving bits of little bone in and then cooking the stew for long hours over a coconut shell fire.

The vegetarian option is exactly the same as the meat/fish option without the meat/fish. I refuse to elaborate on this travesty.

No time to slow down for Mr Invited Dignitary! We still have many delicious delights to work through. Such as the world-famous Chicken Chettinad, one of Tamil Nadu's more famous non-veg contributions to world cuisine.

Chettinad in southern Tamil Nadu is the home of the Chettiars, who were great traders and bankers and maintained links with South-East Asia for hundreds of years. According to one food writer these links can be seen, for instance, in the use of the star anise in Chettinad recipes. The undisputed king of this local cuisine is Chettinad Chicken, a dish once described as 'a sinus-clearing black pepper chicken' by a Western journalist. That description is perfectly accurate.

Thank goodness then that your sinuses can relax while you indulge in some soothing bowls of Kadhi, or chickpea flower dumplings in a yoghurt gravy. Chickpeas originated somewhere in Turkey and then spread outwards via the Silk Route. Today India is the largest producer of chickpeas in the world. There are several versions of the chickpea in India. But the small, dark 'Desi' variety—it is actually called Desi—is believed to be the closest to the original Turkish variety that was first consumed some eight millennia ago. Do keep in mind, however, that while a good chickpea dumpling can elevate a good kadhi, this dish is all about the depth of flavour and texture of the yoghurt sauce. Too thick and it can quickly overwhelm. Too thin and it tastes like a demented buttermilk. Balance is the key to a good kadhi. Best served with good, long-grained basmati rice.

After that mild kadhi interlude we leap forward to a portion of Birbali Kofta Curry. This dish of vegetable dumplings in gravy is named after one of Emperor Akbar's most illustrious ministers. But it is not entirely clear why this is so. The Hindu poet, singer and raconteur Birbal was renowned not for his culinary exploits but his quick wit and close relationship with the emperor. Folktales involving Akbar and Birbal are essential reading for most Indian children. But wait. Was Birbal a minister by day and a dumpling maestro by night? We will never know.

Next up on the Modi Meal is Kela Methi Nu Shaak. Which sounds like the kind of phrase you find in a crossword anagram clue.

Order some Kela Methi Nu Shaak for the dude dancing in the cinema (5, 6, 5)

Answer: Human Talkie Shake

But, seriously, this is an excellent Gujarati delicacy. Plantain or banana is cooked with fenugreek leaves and what you get is a dish in which the bitterness of the fenugreek leaves plays against the sweet banana—a combination of flavours that is quite common in Gujarati food. K.T. Achaya says that the modern edible banana has two parent species—one of which, Musa Balbisiana, is 'truly Indian'. (Which means it still has the original packaging for the TV it bought in 1997.)

This species crossed with another, Musa Acuminata, which arrived from South-East Asia, to create a whole variety of edible bananas. Bananas were then taken across the world by traders and invaders.

In much the same way that Dal Makhani is now an international phenomenon.

This dish, on the face of it, is simplicity itself: lentils cooked in rich, dark buttery sauce. And while a good dal makhani is not impossible to pull off, a great one is a work of art. It is also the gold standard by which many people judge a good restaurant. Serve up a respectable bowl of dal makhani, and many customers will forgive many other failings.

Mind you, this mainstay of Punjabi food is both ancient and modern. References to lentils can be found in the Vedas, the ancient foundational texts of Hinduism. But the dal makhani as we love it today, Vir Sanghvi writes, is a much more modern innovation, invented and perfected perhaps in the last half-century. Remarkable, then, that it is now available in restaurants all over the world.

We now come to the dish that was most talked about afterwards: Potoler Dorma. Most people are convinced that this was a personal choice of the president himself. Thus the First Dish of the Republic is pointed gourd stuffed with vegetables and cooked in gravy. While gourds have always been a part of Indian cooking, this particular Bengali preparation is attributed by one cookbook to the once large but now tiny Armenian community of Kolkata. Armenians first came to India, it is believed, along with the armies of Alexander. Small communities popped up all over India from Kerala to Kolkata. In Kolkata the Armenian dolma, or stuffed vegetables, may have been the inspiration for the potoler dorma.

But you know what? I really hope one of the things Modi will take care of as part of his reforms will be a national ban on all forms of gourds. I hate them. Yuck.

Finally we come to Pineapple Halwa and Mango Shrikhand.

You see, when Vasco da Gama first set foot in India, the pineapple was unheard of here. Like the potato, it was yet to arrive from South America via the Portuguese. But by 1590, as K.T. Achaya says, it was hot property in the markets of Delhi. Within a century India had assimilated an entirely foreign and, let's be frank, bizarre-looking fruit. Mango, on the other hand, is as Indian as Indian can get. And Mango Shrikhand, a sweetened, strained yoghurt flavoured with mango, is a quintessentially Gujarati way to end a meal.

Shrikhand is a particularly versatile concoction. While it is famously consumed with pooris in both Maharashtra and Gujarat, I like to partake of it, in moderation, with fresh, soft chappatis or toasted white bread. You know what is even better? Pair it with a dark chocolate mousse as they do at the Dishoom chain of Indian restaurants in London. Oh my god—it is like a Bollywood item number in the mouth.

So there we are. A multi-course meal that is diverse, interesting and showcases the rich mix of cultures and influences and traditions that make India what it is today. Think what you want about Narendra Modi and his party, but there surely could have been no better, more auspicious start to his government.

Jai hind. Jai food.

India: The New Junk Food Frontier

TARA DESHPANDE TENNEBAUM

By 2050 India's biggest food war may not be how to feed 400 million more people but how to save them from becoming addicted to junk food.

In Govandi slum, one of Mumbai's largest, Shakeela wakes up at 3 a.m. to fill buckets of water. Water will be available at 4 a.m. and the line is already half-a-mile long. A widow, with seven children, she can only carry two buckets. Her eldest Fauziya, thirteen, could have helped, but must remain at home to watch over the others. On her way back, Shakeela stops at a local shop. These are two a penny in Govandi, row upon row of huts with windows showcasing tobacco, beedis, gutka and something else that's become equally ominous: neon-coloured, child-friendly, imported and local crisps, snacks and aerated drinks. Shakeela will purchase some of these. They are light to carry, stay fresh for days and they buy her some peace when her young children

246

cry. It also means she doesn't have to use water to boil eggs for breakfast or wash dishes.

Fauziya will place a packet in each of her sibling's hands and they will munch them all the way to school. Except her younger brother Raiz who is so malnourished he can't walk to school anymore. But despite his ill health he will continuously demand to eat packaged noodles. Two of Shakeela's boys are grossly overweight, but their vitamin profiles are morbidly poor.

It is estimated that more than 50 per cent of the children in Dharavi, another Mumbai slum, are moderately or severely malnourished. While malnutrition has always been associated with starvation, India is now developing the new trend, a malnutrition associated not with being poor, but with poor eating habits, similar to America's growing obesity from unsuitable diets.

According to the American Diabetes Association in 2012, 29.1 million Americans are afflicted by diabetes, often caused by unsuitable diets, with another 86 million diagnosed with pre-diabetes. Now compare this to Indian statistics: diabetes has increased from 1.2 per cent in 1971 to 12.1 per cent in 2013. The International Diabetes Federation estimates that India has 65 million diabetic adults which is projected to increase to 109 million by 2035. The problem is particularly acute in urban slums. But what's worse is Indian children develop it ten years earlier than their Western counterparts do. In 2012, it was estimated to have killed about one million Indians.

And all of it is linked directly to the consumption of foods that are high in fat and sugar. It is a well-known fact that Indians favour expensive, calorific food as a way of showing hospitality. Lavishing sweets on guests and relatives is a matter of pride for us, a sign of prosperity. Crisil rates that India's current fast food market is set to double to Rs 70 billion by 2016. In fact it is estimated that by 2015, India, Russia and Brazil will spend a larger percentage of their GDP on food than Japan, making India a major retail grocery market worldwide.

So the biggest fast-food companies have swooped down on India to feed the emerging needs of a burgeoning middle class with products that are under increased scrutiny by the Food and Drug Administration (FDA) in America. PepsiCo, Coca Cola, Dominos, Taco Bell, Kraft are now in India with myriad strategies to woo customers: low cost, speedy delivery and modified recipes that cater specially to India's palate—a spicy burger at McDonald's or masala-laced chips from Lays. Pizzas and burgers account for 80 per cent of the quick service food in India. Spending in Tier 2 and 3 cities is expected to increase by 150 per cent by 2016, faster than in big metros.

And in keeping with their historical, global marketing policies, children were fair game. It was only in 2010 that eleven companies in India, including PepsiCo and Kellogg's, agreed to consider not advertising to children under the age of twelve in India and avoid targeting primary schools unless their product met nutritional requirements.

But what is 'junk' food? Is it calorific food? If so, think again about your Naniji's oily theplas. Is it GMO or genetically modified food? In which case PepsiCo India's Uncle Chips is on Greenpeace's 'green list' while Nestle's Lactogen is not. Or is it food with enhancers and additives for that Umami taste you love so much? Is it hormones in your milk or pesticide-treated wheat? The bad news is there is no escape. The definition of junk food is expanding and it's either one of these or a combination of all.

While it is easy to blame multinationals for India's growing junk food addiction, a closer look at our desi diet also raises doubts. For instance, is a typical Indian breakfast healthier than a bowl of Honey Loops or a breakfast burrito? Aloo paranthas, poha, congee, medu vada, idlis—all carbohydrate and fat-rich, meant to kick-start the day, are not low-calorie meals. How many vitamins does a butter dosa have, how much fibre is there in a plate of Sheera? So can you blame golden cereal with skim milk for your diabetes? While homemade food may not contain as many preservatives, may have been cooked with cleaner oil and fresher produce, a Mysore bonda is still a fatty, salty snack. While 100 g of Cream and Onion Lays has approximately 544 calories, a similar-sized plate of deep-fried samosas[3] has about 508.

The average meal served at American chains like Wendy's or IHOP have ranged from 1200-1800 calories without dessert and sides. But how is this any different from our thalis which consist of repeated servings of rice and ghee-smeared rotis? As it turns out, not very different at all. The average Indian thali with dessert but, only one helping, ranges from 1600-2000 calories. A Haldiram's 10 g bag of aloo bhujia is 63 calories. This means it's more calorific than 10 g of Cheeto's Cheez Puffs at 51.3 calories. A vada pao is a cheap meal for someone on a budget, at Rs 15-20 for a roughly 300-calorie potato-fritter bun. But how many Indians will blame this snack for heart disease or sue any pao bhaji vendor outside Bandra Kurla Complex? And how different is a portion of Doritos from freshly-fried kachoris or Kailash Parbat's aloo chaat?

There are differences. Some real, some psychological, and many to do with product reach. Cheeto's Cheese Balls are described on the PepsiCo India website as 'Goodness of

---

3 Calorie counts for items like samosas and vada paos can vary based on content and size.

Wholegrain' and 'Made with Real Cheese'. When was the last time a Punjabi cheese parantha was described this way?

Packaged food provides a similar kind of comfort that your local halwai or artery-clogging mughlai tadka dal does, except it's cheaper, stays for days, you can buy it from any grocer, supermarket, movie theatre, mall, airport and you can take it with you anywhere. But are you less likely to contract dysentery from street side pani puri or from a carton of juice?

Large food companies market aggressively and as more young adults in India will have access to cell phones, it will be harder to resist advertising. These products are also a homogenizing factor in a country with class and caste differences. While brandishing an iPad in school may not be possible yet for a slum-dweller's child, there is pride in eating the same chocolate bar as the employer's son.

While portion sizes for food in India are smaller and the super-size concept is yet to take hold,[4] we have, like other countries in Asia and Africa, moved away from long-established diets to Western eating. There has been a drop in consumption of the common man's food: cassava, plantains, yams and millets in India's urban diets, and an increase in maida, polished rice and animal products.

[5]Fast food is optimized and engineered like pharmaceuticals and perfumes. Mouth-feel, crunch factor, suggestive colours, high salt and sugar content, MSG often described as flavour enhancer E621, these foods are meant to sell in volume and the only way to do that is to make them addictive. The creation of Prego Spaghetti sauce, Dr Pepper soda or Campbell's soups

4   Anne Gibbons, 'The Evolution of Diet', *National Geographic* magazine, September 2014.

5   Michael Moss, 'The Extraordinary Science of Addictive Junk Food', *The New York Times* magazine, 20 February 2013.

take millions of dollars of marketing. But are they more or less addictive than your favourite jalebi?

India is yet to be introduced in a big way to one of the commercial-food industries' most beloved and controversial ingredients: high fructose corn sugar (HFCS). From allegations of being a major cause of obesity and fatty liver in America, it has even been suggested that HFCS is a brain inhibitor. It doesn't let the brain tell your body that you've had enough and well, you keep eating.

So while we argue the demerits of HFCS, the question is: how can we not create a generation of sofa aloos (couch potatoes)? Do we need to go back to eating like our Stone-Age ancestors? Will that turn diabetics into Dronacharyas? Does India need a Juhu Beach version of the South Beach Diet to survive the onslaught of carbonated drinks and space age 'just-add-hot-water'[6] Taco Bell condensed-bean flakes? Should we give up vegetarianism, sharpen our spears and head to the few remaining acres of forest land we have in search of deer? Fortunately, no.

The belief that hunter-gatherer tribes ate mostly meat is untrue. While game was the most coveted meal, it had to be pursued and luck often did not favour the hunter.[7] Reports by National Geographic have argued that plant diet comprised 70 per cent of the intake of some prehistoric tribes and it came from foraging for roots and fruits. Demonstrably chasing pig-like tapirs (meat prized by the Tsimanes of Bolivia) required more energy than writing computer code. It's fair to hope that Alaskan seal, unlike factory meat, is not pumped with hormones, which remain even after cooking.

---

6   Eric Schlosser, *Fast Food Nation: The Dark Side of the All-American Meal Book.*

7   Anne Gibbons, 'The Evolution of Diet', *National Geographic* magazine, September 2014.

While 30 per cent of Indians are vegetarian by choice, many are vegetarians out of necessity. As environmentalists preach the urgent need to decrease meat consumption, India will not listen. Many Indians, given the opportunity, will eat meat and if provided with the right price point, will buy gigantic burgers and insulin defying Twinkies.

Take a look at the KFC menu and it's a finger-licking wasteland of chicken, salt and oil. Six pieces of KFC chicken cost Rs 399, with a 20 per cent discount for orders over Rs 1000, which is instantly available, while entire chicken can be purchased for Rs 180-250 at the local butcher, but has to be washed, refrigerated or cooked immediately. India has become the world's largest consumer of farmed poultry raised on a questionable diet, crammed into cages, strung up by their legs and slaughtered in unhygienic environments. But then goat meat is far more expensive.

How good can food like this be for us? While the Western world is reeling from its mechanized farming debacles, India seems determined to move in this direction by marginalizing small farmers, ignoring seasonal diets, adopting GMO foods, pumping money into milking machines and causing untold misery to animals.

Human diets evolve over time, but so do human bodies in their capacity to break down what they eat. Less Indians are lactose intolerant than their Chinese neighbours, whose traditional diet post breast-feeding doesn't contain much lactose while paneer and lassi are must-haves for us.[8] Studies suggest that the Mayans never had diabetes until the 1950s when they turned to North American diets. After the fall of the Soviet Union the

---

8 Ibid.

Yakut tribals who discovered market foods, developed weight problems.

Indians still consume more fresh vegetables and whole grains than their Western counterparts. This may be in part due to ancient eating habits, with a majority of our population living off the land, but also because we eat more home-cooked meals and the traditions of our elders still hold sway. I recall the discussions during my 2013 book tours with women both in India and the United States about the difficulties of keeping the home-cooked meal alive. India's disposable household income has trebled since 2004, and while statistics on the labour force are debatable, we do see more women at work in both formal and informal sectors. While there are more double income rural than urban families, the numbers will increase as India realizes enticing women into businesses will significantly boost growth rates.

So as more women go out to work, they will have less time to roll chapattis–some will even resent it. I recall my mother waking up early to cook breakfast before heading out to work, then returning home to make dinner. Priorities and needs have changed since then, albeit slowly. One newly-married Hyderabad techie told me her husband refuses to share the cooking. So she now purchases chapattis even though it costs four times as much as making them at home, but it buys her more time with her kids and two hours at the salon to keep her groomed for work. A fifty-year-old Chandigarh accountant and mother of three said she now cooks only thrice a week and orders takeout instead so she has more time to generate work online. In contrast, a Boston woman complained that taking 'home science' courses off the American curricula was a mistake, as young American women no longer know how to 'sew, cook or how to run a home'.

While these expectations may be sexist, there is little argument against sharing a freshly prepared meal with the family. But who is going to cook it?

British chef Jamie Oliver's mission to reduce children's exposure to processed foods led him to a high school in the United States, where an ice cream sundae contained the deliciousness of beaver anal glands and female lac bugs. Similarly, the Indian Mid-Day Meal Scheme for children at government schools, though far from being perfect, is at least a free meal of boiled rice and lentils, vastly different from my husband's Minnesotan school canteen lunches in the late eighties. His gourmet choices ranged from reheated pizzas, French fries, Otis Spunkmeyer cookies, nachos with synthetic cheese and vending machine vomited candy bars.

The cooking oil used at home contains some trans, saturated and poly unsaturated fats and while we will never know the exact pesticides used on our favourite mangoes, a decreased diet of prepared foods will reduce the intake of additives used to make commercial food tastier and longer-lasting.[9] At some point or another, food giants have introduced in their products, among dozens of other chemicals, glycerin; a shaving cream solvent, propylene glycol, found in antifreeze and sexual lubricants; dimethylpolysiloxane, a silicone used in plastic toys; calcium silicate, a sealant for roofs; and silicon dioxide found in quartz used as an anti-caking agent.

When the Maggi noodles lead scandal broke out in India, I wondered if Indians thought as much about the quantities of lead in our drinking water, wall paint, cigarettes and the effect of blitzing food in microwaves and the toxins in everyday plastic.

---

9   http://www.huffingtonpost.com/2013/11/20/fast-food-truths_n_4296243.html?ir=India&adsSiteOverride=in

Let's be fair, how can anyone expect a machine-made product in vacuum-sealed plastic which doesn't expire for months to be infallible? With fast-food the profits these companies make are for the convenience, novelty, ease, taste, prices, portion sizes and status they provide the public. Now we also want them to make it 100 per cent healthy. Open your fridge and kitchen cupboards and count the convenience products you have. Now imagine preparing these foods from scratch.

So what can India do to combat its potential junk food crisis without confining women to the kitchen, stifling food retail, chasing away foreign investment and potentially allowing Uncle Ram into the domain of personal menu planning? Will we someday have gastric bypass camps forced on us by zealous governments, or crunchy munchies seized from our pudgy paws by diet police?

To begin with, the debate for all commercial food should be unhealthy vs toxic, some days vs everyday, otherwise you will have to ban everything, even commodities, which can be GMO foods. While upper class Indian households can still employ cooks, the domestic help crisis will worsen as the workforce prefer to work in offices where they feel more respected.

Everyone cannot afford a farm where they grow their own 'pure' produce either. Joint families are losing favour and there are fewer people nurturing families. Homes for the elderly are scarce and geriatric care is still the responsibility of the bahu (daughter-in-law).

The bitter truth is that the desi wife is no longer willing to be sacrificed at the altar of curd rice. Gender roles will have to be modified. While going organic isn't a financially viable option in India yet, returning to some ancient foods like jowar, bajra, ragi, eating what is naturally in season, delving into India's treasure trove of Ayurvedic foods and relegating restaurant takeout to what they were twenty years ago, treats for special occasions and not everyday consumption, may be our only way out of this mess. We have long levied taxes on alcohol and tobacco. Will we consider a policy similar to the one adopted by the Navajo Indian tribes[10] who agreed to a two per cent tax increase on calorific food, to counter a high incidence of diabetes in their community? This law was preceded in 2014 by a decreased tax on fresh vegetables and fruits. The key in our daily diet will not just be the calorie count, but how many middle suppliers we manage to cut out by way of additives, preservatives and enhancers. 'Get Wealthy, Eat Healthy' may be the angioplasty that will save emerging India.

References

Diabetes Atlas, 6th Edition, International Diabetes Federation, 2013.

Anne Gibbons, 'The Evolution of Diet', *National Geographic* magazine, September 2014,

Ruth Graham, *Boston Globe*, 13 October 2013.

Tara Parker, 'Diabetes: Underrated, Insidious and Deadly', *The New York Times*, 1 July 2008.

Kasia Lipska, 'The Global Diabetes Epidemic', *The New York Times*, 25 April 2014.

Menaka Rao, 'How to Live and Die on the New Dharavi Diet', *Grist Media*.

www.crisil.com

www.arogyaworld.com

http://www.crisil.com/about-crisil/Fast-Food-in-Fast-Lane.html

---

10 http://www.tweentribune.com/article/tween56/navajonation-get-first-junk-food-tax-us/

http://www.pepsicoindia.co.in/Download/India%20Pledge.pdf
http://www.dsir.gov.in/reports/techreps/tsr150.pdf
http://vegetarianstar.com/2011/06/06/jamie-oliver-makesice-cream-sundae-with-bugs-human-hair-video/
http://www.diabetes.org/diabetes-basics/statistics/

The Theatre of the Table

ANITA NAIR

The phone rang just a bit before lunchtime. A neighbour's daughter had run away, the caller said, and proceeded to give my eighty-four-year-old father the details of the elopement. Later, as we sat for lunch, my father told my mother and me about what the girl had done. It wasn't as much as she had run away with an unsuitable boy as the fact that she had powdered sleeping pills and mixed it into the rasam which she knew her parents would eat with their rice for dinner.

'So all that talk about buying seer fish for Rs 600 a kilo when I was buying sardines for Rs 60 a kilo was just talk,' my mother said with a laugh. 'They eat just rasam and rice for dinner! Ha ...'

'So what do you think she would have eaten for dinner?' My father's face was a study in worry.

'Perhaps just curd and rice,' my mother said carefully as she nibbled on a piece of chicken. 'Or maybe she said she was unwell and skipped dinner.'

'Wouldn't she be hungry?' My father frowned. 'Don't you need energy to run away?'

'Do you think she actually physically ran away? The boy must have whisked her away in a car and I am sure they must have stopped for a snack once they were a little distance away.'

'What do you think she would have eaten?' my father asked, still concerned about the girl eloping on an empty stomach. 'What would you eat if you were running away?'

'I would have chapatti and mutton curry,' my mother said. 'One needs proteins and carbohydrates when one is setting out on a life-changing mission.'

There are times when I think the dining table conversation at my home would make even the Mad Hatter and the Queen of Hearts seem perfectly normal and functional.

My mother is seventy-two years old but she has not lost her enthusiasm for food and celebrates its ability to induce joy every day.

She had cooked a most delicious lunch: neychor (for the uninitiated into Kerala Moplah cuisine, this is rice cooked with ghee and a hint of spices, garnished with fried onions, cashews and raisins), chicken curry, cucumber and green chilli raita and puffy golden papadoms. For dessert we were going to have mangoes and custard. And now we had some juicy gossip to plump up the meal, I thought, unable to suppress a smile. But my parents were not inclined to gossip as much as speculate about the role of the rasam in the elopement. Elsewhere couples would have discussed the right and the wrong of what the girl had done, arrived at several conclusions on what would happen to the girl and the boy after they had been together for a week, and ranted about family honour and the shame. My parents were more concerned about why the girl's parents did not realize that the rasam had tasted different. Or what a girl must eat when she is planning to elope.

This is how it always is in my home. In a strange way, even though I have been married for twenty-eight years and have a house of my own, it's my parents' house I refer to as 'my home'. The rest are all houses and I think what makes it home is the presence of my parents. And the food.

Every few weeks I run away to Mundakotukkurussi to be with my parents. Apart from the peace and quiet and the supreme joy of being treated like I am stuck eternally at six years of age, my mother's food heals me. Our conversation there seldom veers beyond food. Our meals—breakfast, lunch, tea and dinner—punctuate our day. In my home in Bangalore, much as I appreciate good food, mealtimes are merely just that: meal times. Mostly I either prop up a book against a serving bowl and read as I eat, or I watch TV with a tray on my lap. Some days I even write as I eat.

In my parents' home though, mealtimes acquire the eloquence of a performance. It is the theatre of the table where food is the primary focus, a supremely important ritual where no compromises can be affected. Phone calls are frowned upon and texting on mobile phones even more so. The main door, which is otherwise open at all hours, is closed to discourage visitors who might pop in without advance notice. Even the postman, who comes by at quarter past one in the afternoon every day, knows enough to ring the bell and leave the mail on the swing seat in the porch.

Every morning my mother discusses in elaborate detail the planning of each meal with the cook, and then she informs my father about what will go into the making of every dish with the same relish with which she reads out tidbits from the newspaper to him. In a way, their only religion is food!

All over rural southern India, even to this day, when two people meet they don't say hello. Instead they greet one another with 'Have you eaten?' (All they do is change the name of the meal depending on the time of day.) To me this is a greeting that is born of a true interest in the other's well-being; it is also a coded way of asking, 'Is all well with you?' How meagre and superfluous the 'hello' seems in comparison!

For everyone everywhere, everything is about food. Births, deaths, engagements, marriages, birthdays, housewarmings, career advancements, triumphs—none of these occasions mean anything without an elaborate banquet accompanying them. When we feel our life has hit rock bottom or at our loneliest moments, food offers a solace nothing else does. Comfort eating isn't about bingeing because we are greedy. It is about using food as a cementing glue when we feel the circumstances of our life tearing us apart. Which is why I always wonder about the truly horrid manifestation of self-hate—anorexia—where even food that keeps us alive and going is shunned. How different is it from self-mutilation?

My mother has a theory: Human greed is never truly satiated. However, when you cook a meal and serve it to a person, watch how they start eating it with relish. But there soon comes a point when they are sated and it becomes impossible to swallow even a grain of rice. Hunger is the only appetite you can ever appease.

The wisdom in her words strikes me each time I sit down for a meal. When I was young, my parents fed me stories so I would eat. These days, they fill me with trivia because they think I spend too much time in the imaginary worlds I create so I need to be brought back to earth to engage with the real world.

Mealtimes with them are a joy. The food on the table is often simple but it is exquisite, each dish carefully planned so the mesh of tastes, flavours, colours and textures harmonize. There is a hushed reverence as we serve ourselves—the concentration of an archer with his eye on the target—as the first mouthful is eaten. Soon the conversation starts flowing. Good food encourages it. There is love at the table and a togetherness that we renew at each mealtime. At the end of the meal is a true sense of fulfilment: that all is well with the world despite everything that is dark and dreary.

I think of a Thanksgiving dinner in New York, of how the table groaned with food and the palpable air of expectation as the guests sat down to eat. The bounty at the table erased, for a time, everything else out of people's minds but a celebration of the now. At my parents' home, each meal is a thanksgiving to life and I think as long as one doesn't give up on food, one will not give up on life.

There are days when the world seems a bleak place. When life ceases to enthrall or excite. Then I go into the larder of my past and draw out one particular memory:

I am in the living room reading a book and can hear their conversation as my parents lie side by side in their bedroom, talking. Every night, without fail, just when they say goodnight to each other, I hear my father ask my mother: What's for breakfast? And my mother replies: What would you like, my darling?

I feel a great warmth envelop me. It is the promise two elderly people make to each other every night. Of waking up to a new day, of filling it with love and the joy they find in each other. And it occurs to me then that nothing says 'I love you' more than that: What's for breakfast? and What would you like, my darling?

Notes on Contributors

1. **Chitrita Banerji** grew up in Calcutta and received her master's degree in English from Harvard University. She is the author of several books on the food and culture of Bengal and India. She has written for *Granta*, *Gourmet*, *The New York Times* and *The Boston Globe*, and received awards at the Oxford Symposium of Food and Cookery. Her latest work is the novel, *Mirror City*, set in newly liberated Bangladesh. She is now working on another novel. She lives in Cambridge, Massachusetts.

2. **Floyd Cardoz** is a celebrated Indian-American chef in New York City, where he partnered with restaurateur Danny Meyer at the famed restaurants Tabla and North End Grill. Floyd started White Street Restaurant in New York and recently, The Bombay Canteen in Mumbai, India. He has also authored *One Spice*, *Two Spice*, which includes his favourite recipes while demystifying Indian flavours and is currently working on *Floyd Cardoz: Flavorwalla*, which will guide home cooks on cooking meals within their time capabilities and technical capacity.

3. **Manu Chandra** is the Chef Partner, responsible for the hugely fun and first of its kind Gastropub brand, Monkey Bar, in Mumbai, Bangalore and Delhi; the trendy Asian Gastro Bar, The Fatty Bao in Mumbai, Delhi and Bangalore. He is also the Executive Chef of the multi award winning and critically acclaimed Olive Beach in Bangalore. Manu graduated with top honours from the Culinary Institute of America and apprenticed in some of the top kitchens in New York. In 2004 Manu returned to India and since then he has received recognition and appreciation from around the world as one of the most talented chefs in the country.

4. **Mamang Dai** is a poet and novelist from Arunachal Pradesh writing in English. A long-time member of the North East Writers' Forum (NEWF), Dai's book, *Mountain Harvest- The food of Arunachal Pradesh* was the first of its kind offering a comprehensive introduction to Arunachal food with step by step recipes served up with a good dollop of the mythology, taboos and rituals associated with food. In 2011 Dai was awarded the Padma Shri (Literature and Education). She lives in Itanagar, Arunachal Pradesh, India.

5. **Kai Friese** is a freelance writer who lives in New Delhi.

6. **Bachi Karkaria** has created and edited some of the most distinctive sections of *The Times of India* (daily circulation is around 4 million) and was the first Indian board member of the World Editors Forum. She writes two popular columns: the satirical *Erratica* and *Giving Gyan*. She is a media trainer in India and abroad, specializing in local reporting. She is Festival Director of *The Times of India* Litfest, Mumbai.

She writes Op Ed pieces mainly on urban and gender issues for *The Times of India*, guardiancities.com, bbc.com and indiaink of nyt.com, and appears regularly on Indian TV news channels and BBC Radio. Her books include *Dare to Dream*, a best-selling biography of M.S. Oberoi, *Mills, Molls and Moolah*, tracing the metamorphosis of Mumbai, *Behind the Times*, stories from the trenches and war-rooms of the *ToI*. She received the US-based Mary Morgan-Hewitt Award for Lifetime Achievement and is a Jefferson Fellow of the East-West Centre, Honolulu.

7. **Saleem Kidwai** studied at Delhi and McGill University and taught history at the University of Delhi. He took early retirement to become an independent researcher/writer. He is the co-author of *Same-Sex Love in India: A Literary History*, and among other things has edited and translated the memoirs of Malka Pukhraj - *Song Sung True*, and a collection of animal stories by Rafiq Hussain called *Mirror of Wonders*. He lives in Lucknow.

8. **Niloufer Ichaporia King** is an anthropologist, food scholar, teacher and cook who studies tropical cuisines, plants for food and medicine and markets as an expression of cultural change and stability. Born in Mumbai, Niloufer King now lives in San Francisco with her husband and parrot. Her James Beard award-winning book, *My Bombay Kitchen: Traditional and modern Parsi home cooking* describes one family's version of the food of a fast-vanishing community. There isn't a market in the world she doesn't want to poke around, especially with Lyla.

9. **Jerome Marrel**, born in Lyon, the world's gastronomic capital in France, has travelled the world extensively visiting more than 135 countries. A graduate from the Catering

College in Toulouse, he has worked in the catering industry for over thirty years, worked in eight countries and in charge of twenty-five countries at the time of retiring. A senior contributor to *Trip Advisor*, cigar, wine and food afficiando, Jerome Marrel continues travelling the world and sampling all kinds of cuisines. An ardent believer in slow cooking, he cooks regularly at home and has been known to rustle up elaborate meals for over hundred guests in Goa with ease and panache. This is his first book contribution after a lifetime in the food business.

10. **Jhampan Mookerjee** developed an early interest in food and alcohol growing up in a family obsessed with cuisine. He has been researching production techniques, economics and cultural practices of drinking traditional Indian alcohol for over a decade now, travelling into the interiors of the country where his work takes him. His book on the subject, *Searching for Soma: A Quest for Indian Spirit*, is being published by Harper Collins.

11. **Anita Nair** is the author of the novels *The Better Man*, *Ladies Coupé*, *Mistress*, *Lessons in Forgetting* and *Idris*. She has also published a collection of poems titled *Malabar Mind*, a collection of essays titled *Goodnight & God Bless* and four books for children. Anita Nair has also written two plays and the screenplay for the movie adaptation of her novel *Lessons in Forgetting* which won the National Film Award in 2013. Among other awards, she was also given the Central Sahitya Akademi award. Her books have been translated into over thirty languages around the world. She is also the founder of the creative writing and mentorship programme *Anita's Attic*. Her new novella *Alphabet Soup for Lovers* will be published in late 2015.

12. Poet and dance producer/curator, **Karthika Naïr** is the author of *Bearings*, a poetry collection; *The Honey Hunter/Le Tigre de Miel*, a children's book illustrated by Joëlle Jolivet and *Until the Lions*, a revisiting of the Mahabharata in verse. She was also the principal scriptwriter of *Desh* (2011), choreographer Akram Khan's award-winning dance production.

13. **Naintara Maya Oberoi** a writer who lives in Paris and Delhi. She writes about food, literature, art and culture. She is currently a student at the École Normale Supérieure and at the École des Hautes Études en Sciences Sociales in Paris. Her work has appeared in *Time Out*'s India editions, where she was the Food and Drink Editor, and in *The Indian Express*, *Outlook Traveller*, *National Geographic Traveller India*, *Caravan*, *The Indian Quarterly*, *The Times of India (Crest)*, and *Biblio*. She writes a monthly column for *The Hindu Business Line Ink*.

14. **Janice Pariat** is the author of *Boats on Land: A Collection of Short Stories* and a novel *Seahorse*. She was awarded the Young Writer Award from the Sahitya Akademi and the Crossword Book Award for Fiction in 2013. She studied English Literature at St Stephen's College, Delhi, and History of Art at the School of Oriental and African Studies, London. Her work—including art reviews, cultural features, book reviews, fiction and poetry—has featured in a wide selection of national magazines and newspapers. She currently lives in New Delhi, India.

15. **Srinath Perur** writes on a variety of subjects, often to do with travel or science. He is the author of *If It's Monday It Must Be Madurai*, a book about travelling with groups. He lives in Bangalore.

16. **Bikramjit Ray** has made a career out of food, first as a restaurant reviewer for Delhi's *Today* newspaper and then as a host of CNN-IBN's highly successful *Secret Kitchen* TV series. He is also a creative and extravagant cook, but prefers eating simple and light.

    Sumana Mukherjee is a journalist whose work has covered the entire food spectrum, from farm to fork. She loves collecting recipe books and kitchen gadgets and will convince you that each, however esoteric, has a role to play in her kitchen.

    Jayaditya Gupta is a journalist whose other life revolves round food. He can't cook (yet) but can talk, shop, chop, cut, plan and dream about the next meal.

17. **Wendell Rodricks** is a fashion designer, writer and activist for Goa's environment. While his passion has always been fashion, the designer is trained in hotel management and worked in the industry for six years before going from dressing salads to dressing people. A self-confessed foodie-travelie, Wendell Rodricks has written two books, contributed to many more, writes for magazines and has completed his third book which has his favourite recipes as part of a Goan story. The designer lives in Goa with his partner, four dogs and three cats ... mainly in their kitchen.

18. **Nilanjana S. Roy** is the author of two novels, *The Wildings*, which won the Shakti Bhatt Prize in 2013, and *The Hundred Names of Darkness*. She has written on food for the *Business Standard*, *Outlook* and *Seminar* and is the editor of *Matter of Taste: The Penguin Book of Indian Writing on Food* (2004). *Eating Books*, a memoir of reading and book-love in India is out from HarperCollins in late 2015.

19. **Bulbul Sharma** is a painter and writer. She has published several books which include *My Sainted Aunts*, *The Perfect Woman*, *Anger of Aubergines*, *Banana Flower Dreams*, *Shaya Tales*, *Devi*, *Eating Women*; *Telling Tales*, *Now That I am Fifty Tailor of Giripul* and *Grey Hornbills at Dusk*. Her books have been translated into Italian, French, German, Chinese, Spanish and Finnish.

   Her books for children are *Fabled Book of Gods and Demons* and *The Children's Ramayana*. She conducts story-painting workshops for special needs children and is a founder-member of Sannidhi, an NGO that works in village schools.

20. **Rocky Singh and Mayur Sharma** have been sharing food and adventures since 1976. They believe food, fun, friendship and the joy of travel make life worth living. Their award-winning TV show, *Highway on My Plate*, one of their many shows on NDTV Good Times, The History Channel and Zee TV, is easily the most watched and loved food-and-travel show in India and abroad. Their books, *Highway on My Plate: The Indian Guide to Roadside Eating Vol 1* and *2*, were both awarded 'Best in the World' at the Gourmand World Cookbook awards in Paris (2012) and China (2015) respectively.

21. **Avtar Singh's** latest novel, *Necropolis*, is published by HarperCollins *Publishers* India. He is the managing editor of *The Indian Quarterly*. He has been a magazine editor in Mumbai and New Delhi and still visits Indonesia regularly. He lives in Delhi with his wife, son and singing dog.

22. A Mumbai native, actress **Tara Deshpande Tennebaum** (*Is Raat Ki Subah Nahin*, *Bombay Boys*, *Style*, *MTV Get a Voice*)

is the author of *Fifty and Done* and *A Sense for Spice: Recipes and Stories from a Konkan Kitchen*. She holds professional certificates from the French Culinary Institute and Le Cordon Bleu. Her cooking show, *Great Chocolate Cooking*, appeared on WGBH. Tara blogs about all things food at www.taradeshpande.in. She and her family divide their time between New York and Mumbai.

23. **Sidin Vadukut** is the author of *The Sceptical Patriot* and the *Dork* trilogy of office culture humour novels. He is an editor and columnist with the *Mint* newspaper.

Acknowledgements

I've been making a list—of all the people I want to thank, who made this book happen, who are in some way or the other connected with it—and it became way too long. I also kept agonizing over who might have been left out. Sorry to make it sound like a coping mechanism but this is a thank you to everyone: you know who you are, why I am grateful to you and exactly what all you have done for the book and for me. I wish I could do an exaggerated jig to show you how serious I am about expressing my gratitude, but I really am. Thank you for being you and thank you for being there.

Copyright Acknowledgements

'Memory's Savour' by Avtar Singh
This first appeared as 'Telor Balado' in *The Indian Quarterly*,
February 2015.